8/02

THE
HISTORIAN'S
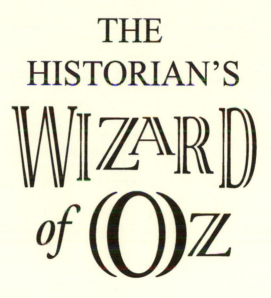

WIZARD
of OZ

"Ranjit Dighe's new book will be of immense interest to scholars seeking to understand Baum and his classic, and to teachers who wish to use Baum's story as a platform for discussing one of the crucial periods in American political and economic history. Although written in a straightforward and engaging style, the book is based on an impressive understanding of the primary and secondary sources. Professor Dighe has chosen judiciously among conflicting interpretations, developed new interpretations of his own, and dealt sensitively with the thorny issue of Baum's intentions. *The Historian's* Wizard of Oz will be the definitive work for a long time to come."

—Hugh Rockoff, Professor of Economics, Rutgers University

"With this book, Ranjit Dighe combines the economist's knowledge of monetary matters with the historian's sensibilities of the past to help us understand the context of America's classic children's story. His annotations are clear and concise, fair and balanced. Put simply, this is the best commentary we have on L. Frank Baum's *Wonderful Wizard of Oz*.

"Oz fans will discover more of American society than they could have possibly imagined in their favorite book. History buffs will enjoy seeing how the political, cultural, and economic issues of the late nineteenth century are reflected in the setting for Oz."

—David B. Parker, Professor of History, Kennesaw State University

"Readers will benefit mightily from the expertise this historical-minded economist brings to bear on the famous children's tale. It is with great pleasure and confidence therefore that I recommend *The Historian's* Wizard of Oz."

—Gene Clanton, author of *Congressional Populism and the Crisis of the 1890s*

"*The Historian's* Wizard of Oz is a comprehensive treatment of the relationship between *The Wonderful Wizard of Oz* and the political events in America just before the turn of the century. In a scholarly fashion, Dighe dispels many cherished myths about Baum's political beliefs and the intentions behind his writing. In one volume, Dighe assembles varied source material to help the reader see the real (and imagined) links between Oz and Populism. *The Historian's* Wizard of Oz is a welcome addition to the literature about Baum and politics."

—Michael Gessel, Editor-in-Chief, *The Baum Bugle* (1988–92)

"M.B.A. students are just like everybody else—they love a good story. Dighe tells the story behind the story. He tells it with verve and, in the process, teaches some good economics."

—Robert L. Greenfield, Professor of Economics,
Fairleigh Dickinson University

THE
HISTORIAN'S

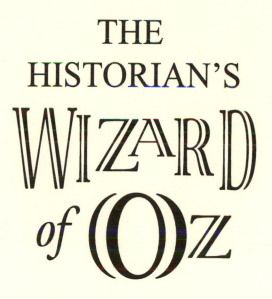

Reading L. Frank Baum's Classic as
a Political and Monetary Allegory

Edited by
RANJIT S. DIGHE

Westport, Connecticut
London

Library of Congress Cataloging-in-Publication Data

The historian's Wizard of Oz : reading L. Frank Baum's classic as a political and monetary allegory / edited by Ranjit S. Dighe.
      p.   cm.
    Includes bibliographical references and index.
    ISBN 0–275–97418–9 (alk. paper)—ISBN 0–275–97419–7 (pbk. : alk. paper)
    1. Baum, L. Frank (Lyman Frank), 1856–1919. Wizard of Oz.   2. Baum, L. Frank (Lyman Frank), 1856–1919—Political and social views.   3. Baum, L. Frank (Lyman Frank), 1856–1919—Knowledge—Economics.   4. Politics and literature—United States—History—20th century.   5. Children's stories, American—History and criticism.   6. Political fiction, American—History and criticism.   7. Fantasy fiction, American—History and criticism.   8. Economics in literature.   9. Money in literature.   10. Oz (Imaginary place)   11. Allegory.   I. Dighe, Ranjit S., 1965–
PS3503.A923 W6345 2002
813′.4—dc21   2001133084

British Library Cataloguing in Publication Data is available.

Copyright © 2002 by Ranjit S. Dighe

Library of Congress Catalog Card Number: 2001133084
ISBN: 0–275–97418–9
          0–275–97419–7 (pbk.)

First published in 2002

Praeger Publishers, 88 Post Road West, Westport, CT 06881
An imprint of Greenwood Publishing Group, Inc.
www.praeger.com

Printed in the United States of America

∞™

The paper used in this book complies with the
Permanent Paper Standard issued by the National
Information Standards Organization (Z39.48–1984).

10 9 8 7 6 5 4 3 2 1

Every reasonable effort has been made to trace the owners of copyright materials in this book, but in some instances this has proven impossible. The editor and publisher will be glad to receive information leading to more complete acknowledgments in subsequent printings of the book and in the meantime extend their apologies for any omissions.

To Julia

Contents

A photo essay follows p. 40.

Preface

Like millions of children around the world, I grew up watching MGM's splendid 1939 movie *The Wizard of Oz* every year on television. After watching it on the big screen years later as a college student, I came away with a new appreciation for the film, not only for its dazzling color cinematography and great performances, but also for the often wry and witty dialogue. Watching the movie on a campus thick with political activism, one easily heard political overtones in such lines as "I'm a very good man—I'm just a very bad wizard" and "Pay no attention to that man behind the curtain!" Years later, as a graduate student in economic history, I became fascinated by the late-nineteenth-century Populist movement and the 1896 presidential candidacy of William Jennings Bryan. When I pitched a Populism-related research idea to one of my advisers, David Weiman, he suggested I take a look at a journal article by Hugh Rockoff titled "The 'Wizard of Oz' as a Monetary Allegory," and showed me the syllabus for an undergraduate class he was teaching that actually used L. Frank Baum's original book version of the story as a required reading. Upon reading Rockoff's article, I was instantly hooked and decided to incorporate it into my own teaching of American economic history.

Rockoff's article was a hit with my students, and I decided the next semester to copy Professor Weiman's example and have the students read Baum's book, too. Most of the class, myself included, had never read the book before. While reading *The Wonderful Wizard of Oz* under the impression that it was a conscious monetary allegory (an impression that I now realize was inaccurate), I was continually struck by the parallels between Baum's book, written in the late 1890s, and the political economy of that time. My students loved the book, too, and were intrigued by the allegorical interpretation; but, without much prior exposure to 1890s economic history, most of them did not appear to draw many connections between the book and monetary populism. I drew two conclusions: first, that in using the *Oz* story to get Populism across, there was no substitute for reading the book, since it differed from the movie in several key respects and was a delightful read in its own right; and, second, that I needed to find a way to integrate more tightly Baum's story and 1890s economic history. *The Historian's* Wizard of Oz represents my attempt to do just that.

While political interpretations of Baum's book have taken on a life of their own, we must be careful to get the details right as regards not just 1890s political and economic history but also L. Frank Baum's politics and likely intentions. Baum left behind no concrete evidence that he wrote the book as a political allegory, and, as far as we can tell, virtually nobody read it as one until more than sixty years later, when Henry Littlefield's "The Wizard of Oz: Parable on Populism" was published in 1964. Chapter 1 of this book traces the development of the Oz-as-Populist-parable thesis, which by now has undergone many permutations, and examines it against the available evidence on Baum, most of which has been unearthed by current Baum scholars, notably Michael Patrick Hearn and Nancy Tystad Koupal. At the end of the day, Baum appears to be not a Populist but a progressive Republican, and most of all a man who did not take politics very seriously. Chapter 1 concludes that while we can no longer take the leading political interpretations of *Wizard* at face value, we can still get considerable mileage out of them as teaching tools for history and economics. As long as we are up-front about where Baum himself was (or was not) coming from, we can do justice both to 1890s monetary populism and to L. Frank Baum.

The heart of this book is the annotated version of Baum's *The Wonderful Wizard of Oz* that constitutes Chapter 4; the annotations point out the possible political and economic symbolism as the story unfolds, and in so doing they offer a roundabout lesson on the monetary populism of the 1890s. While there are numerous political interpretations of Baum's book, as will become obvious from reading the annotations, I have kept mum as far as advocating a particular interpretation. I think interpretation is something best left to the individual reader. For many readers, especially those with a strong background in monetary economics and Populist political history, the annotations in Chapter 4 can probably stand on their own. Since the gold standard and agrarian-based politics are slippery issues for many people, however, Chapter 2 offers an overview of the American monetary system and the roles that gold and silver once played in it, and Chapter 3 presents a short history of monetary populism. Chapters 2 and 3 are perhaps more for teachers than for students.

Appendix A is a very short excerpt from Baum's second Oz book (which actually appears to have been the most political of the Oz books, since much of it is an extended satire on the woman suffrage movement. Baum's mother-in-law, Matilda Joslyn Gage, was one of the most prominent and radical feminists of the late nineteenth and early twentieth centuries, and Baum was often outspoken in his support for women's rights). Like the Emerald City in the first book, the excerpt provides a tidy metaphor for the curative powers of fiat money (i.e., money that has value only because the government, by executive fiat, declares it to have value).

Bryan's "Cross of Gold" speech, like Baum's first Oz book, remains a somewhat overlooked gem, and thus I have included it as Appendix B. Bryan's rhetorical flair is evident even on paper; the text of the speech arguably does a better job of conveying the passion and excitement of the silver issue than anyone else has ever done in the space of so few pages. Since several of the references in Bryan's speech are now obscure, I have included a few annotations here as well.

The final appendix describes the *quantity theory of money*. While it is more technical than the book's other sections, the quantity theory played a vital role in the monetary debates of the late nineteenth century, as Bryan, William H. "Coin" Harvey, and other monetary populists explicitly and frequently invoked it in support of their cause.

Historiographically minded readers should note that all dates in the citations in this book refer to the original publication date of the work cited, rather than the (sometimes later) date of the particular edition used. Within the annotated *Wonderful Wizard of Oz*, I have tried to preserve the original 1900 edition of Baum's book to the greatest extent possible, including its sometimes unusual and inconsistent capitalization, punctuation, spacing, and spelling.

I am greatly indebted to many people, most especially my wife, Anne Pagano, whose helpful comments, enthusiasm, and meticulous reading of several drafts have been indispensable in improving the finished product. My daughter Julia, without whom I surely would never have read Baum's entire book aloud, has likewise been a tremendous source of inspiration. This book is also vastly improved thanks to those who read and offered comments on multiple chapters: Gene Clanton (whose disagreements with me on several particulars I duly note), Robert L. Greenfield, David B. Parker, Hugh Rockoff, and Sally Roesch Wagner. Michael Patrick Hearn (whose *Annotated Wizard of Oz* shall always remain the industry standard) and Nancy Tystad Koupal offered invaluable suggestions and insight, and conversations with Martin Gardner and Clara Houck were helpful as well. I also owe special thanks to Steve Abraham, Michael Gessel, Brad Hansen, David Hill, Richard Jensen, Gwen Kay, Tim Price, Tom Puchniak, Scott Redenius, Ken Reinert, Tom Rochon, Bob Salisbury, Liz Dunne Schmitt, Tim Thurber, David Weiman, and Judith Wellman. Final thanks go out to the Special Collections staff at Syracuse University's E.S. Bird Library, Linda Szcepanski at Cornell University's Olin Library, and to my economic history students.

THE
HISTORIAN'S

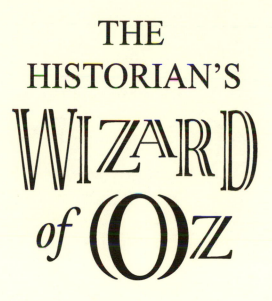

Chapter 1

Introduction: The Colors of Money

Each one of us is entitled to our own interpretation of *The Wizard*, but please remember: it is an individual interpretation, and not necessarily the author's intention.

—Ozma Baum Mantele,
first granddaughter of L. Frank Baum[1]

Few novels have ever permeated American popular culture as thoroughly as has L. Frank Baum's *The Wonderful Wizard of Oz*. Generations of American children have grown up reading the dozen-plus Oz books written by Baum, and millions more have been thrilled by yearly television broadcasts of the stunning 1939 film version starring Judy Garland. More than a century after the book's original publication in 1900, Baum's Oz imagery still seems to crop up everywhere, from countless political cartoons and magazine covers to popular songs (from bands as diverse as America, Basehead, and Minor Threat) to television shows (to the point where the satirical newspaper *The Onion* poked fun at *Wizard of Oz* takeoffs as a hackneyed plot device[2]). In 1964 a high school history teacher named Henry Littlefield extended the sweep of Oz imagery to embrace the economic and political events of the late nineteenth century.

Littlefield, in his article "The Wizard of Oz: Parable on Populism," published in the American studies journal *American Quarterly*, said Baum's story, on the

---

1. Mantele 2000, p. 12.
2. "Sitcom Resorts to *Wizard Of Oz*–Themed Fantasy Episode," *The Onion*, April 18, 2001.

surface just an imaginative fairy tale, contains "a symbolic allegory implicit within its story line and characterizations. . . . Baum delineated a Midwesterner's vibrant and ironic portrait of this country as it entered the twentieth century."[3] At the center of Baum's parable, according to Littlefield, were the struggles of the Western farmers of that time and the monetary remedy they sought from the government. Deflation (falling prices) had been the norm over the three decades after the Civil War, and the farmers believed that deflation was killing them economically, by raising the real (price-adjusted) interest rate and the real burden of their mortgage and other debts. Many farmers became political activists, urging the government to relieve their plight, and many of them thought a radical change in the U.S. monetary system offered the best hope of relief. The farmer-activists wanted the government to coin more silver, so as to expand the money supply, thereby enabling them to borrow more cheaply and pay off their debts more easily. "Prairie populism" generated a third-party political movement, assembled under the banner of the People's (or Populist) Party in 1892. By 1896, incumbent Grover Cleveland was out as the Democratic nominee for president, and William Jennings Bryan was in as the nominee of both the Democrats and the People's Party. Bryan is best remembered for his passionate advocacy of "free silver"—the insistence that the government stamp silver bullion into coins, upon demand, to increase the money supply and end the deflation—and for his stem-winder of a speech at the Democratic National Convention in 1896, in which he denounced the gold standard. In that speech Bryan proclaimed, "You shall not crucify mankind upon a cross of gold."

As reinterpreted by Littlefield, Baum's book works beautifully as an allegory about monetary populism. The book teems with references to the colors gold, silver, and green—the colors of money. Consider: the yellow (gold?) brick road, Dorothy's silver shoes (the 1939 movie version recast them as ruby slippers), the Emerald City. The story begins on a farm in Kansas, a state that was a hotbed of farm discontent and Populist politics. Dorothy lives on the farm with her aunt and uncle, whose lives seem bleak, because of the harshness of the weather and the hardscrabble nature of farming at the time. The cyclone that whisks Dorothy away recalls the free-silver movement, which at the time inspired comparisons to a cyclone. Once in Oz Dorothy, wanting only to get back to Kansas, is told that she should seek out the Great Wizard, who lives in the Emerald City, the political center of Oz. To get there she must follow the yellow brick road (gold standard), and her journey is made much easier by her new silver shoes (the Populist goal of replacing the gold standard with a "bimetallic" standard of gold and silver). Along the way she meets a scarecrow (farmer), an idle wood-chopper whose entire body has been replaced with tin (industrial workingman), and a cowardly lion (Bryan himself). Each of her new comrades badly wants something that, as we later learn, he had already had all along: brains (farmers were often derided as stupid and solely to blame for their economic woes), a heart (was industrialization alienating the worker from his own humanity?), and courage (Bryan's opposition to Amer-

---

3. Littlefield 1964, p. 50.

ica's war against Spain in 1898 was criticized as cowardly and unpatriotic). Having already killed the wicked Witch of the East (Wall Street and big business), Dorothy is told by the Wizard that he will return her to Kansas if she will slay the wicked Witch of the West (drought and other malign forces of nature). When Dorothy and her friends return to the Wizard, they discover that he is in fact a charlatan whose trickery has duped the citizens of Oz into believing that he is all-powerful. The Wizard offers to take Dorothy back to Kansas in his patchy hot-air balloon, but a rope snaps before Dorothy and her dog can get on board. The disappointed Dorothy ventures South, where Glinda the good Witch (symbolizing Bryan's natural allies in the Democratic-voting Solid South) informs her that she has had the power to return to Kansas all along. By clicking the silver shoes together three times and commanding them to carry her, they can take her to wherever she wants to go. So Dorothy is whirled back to Kansas, and along the way her silver shoes fall off her feet and are lost forever in the desert (just as the free-silver movement faded into oblivion after Bryan's defeat in 1896 and the prosperity and inflation that began in 1897).

Littlefield's article has had a lasting influence on many historians. Variations on Littlefield's interpretation of the *Wizard of Oz* as a political and monetary allegory have been offered by numerous historians and political scientists, notably Richard Jensen (1971), John G. Geer and Thomas R. Rochon (1993), and Gretchen Ritter (1997a, 1997b). By 1991, the thesis had come full circle, as historian Gene Clanton argued that the book was actually an *anti*-Populist parable, in which the wicked Witch of the West represents not malign nature nor President Grover Cleveland but rather the Populists themselves—"agrarian radicalism, socialism, or those on the left wing of the political spectrum generally." Clanton identified Democratic Senator "Pitchfork Ben" Tillman, a demagogic South Carolina free-silver supporter often lumped together with the Populists, as the Witch's most likely real-life counterpart. To Clanton, *The Wonderful Wizard of Oz* "was an apt metaphor or parable of Progressivism, not Populism. It mirrored perfectly the middle-ground ideology that was fundamental among those who favored reform yet opposed Populism." Clanton amplified that thesis in 1998, claiming that the book was actually a pro-gold-standard tract, in which the yellow brick road represents the true ticket to prosperity and silver is mostly a tool of the wicked Witches, as in the Eastern Witch's silver shoes and the Western Witch's silver whistle. Although the silver shoes do ultimately carry Dorothy back to where she wants to go, the book's happy ending also includes their being lost forever in the desert.[4]

Economic historian Hugh Rockoff introduced the Littlefield thesis to economists in 1990, with his *Journal of Political Economy* article "The 'Wizard of Oz' as a Monetary Allegory," perhaps the most comprehensive and complex interpretation to date. In Rockoff's retelling, the wicked Witches of the East and West are Presidents Grover Cleveland (of New York) and William McKinley (of Ohio), both of whom supported the gold standard. The Wizard is Mark Hanna, the Repub-

---

4. Clanton 1991, p. 150; Clanton 1998, pp. 183–86.

lican Committee chairman and businessman who was widely perceived as the man pulling the strings behind McKinley. Rockoff offers a symbolic interpretation of seemingly everything in Baum's book, including the harassing Kalidahs as newspaper reporters and the Deadly Poppy Field as the anti-imperialism movement of the late 1890s, which some free-silverites feared had captured the attention of Bryan to such an extent that he would neglect the silver issue. Rockoff's article has since become a staple of economic history courses and even rates a two-page sidebar in one of the leading introductory economics textbooks. Instructors in both history and economics have found the Oz imagery to be a delightful means of engendering student interest and understanding of the central economic issues of an era that might otherwise seem remote and irrelevant.

JUST BECAUSE THE BOOK CAN BE READ AS A POPULIST ALLEGORY DOES NOT MEAN THAT IT WAS WRITTEN AS ONE

The profusion of Oz-as-Populist-parable interpretations raises an obvious question: Did L. Frank Baum intend any of this? After all, the book became a bestseller and remained so for decades without, as far as we know, ever being identified as a political parable until Littlefield's article in 1964. As the Littlefield thesis gained currency among historians, especially in the late 1980s and early 1990s, it attracted a huge backlash among devotees of Baum's Oz books, who vehemently argued that *The Wonderful Wizard of Oz* is in no way, shape, or form a monetary or political allegory. Baum's great-grandson Roger went so far as to call the Populist-parable interpretation "insane."[5] Historians, on the other hand, have tended to stick with and extend the Littlefield thesis. Thanks to the research of Baum scholars Michael Patrick Hearn (currently writing a full-scale biography of Baum), Nancy Tystad Koupal, and others, a somewhat clearer view of Baum's intentions emerged in the 1990s. *The Wonderful Wizard of Oz* now appears to have been neither a piece of pure escapism written "solely to pleasure children of today," as Baum claimed in the book's preface, nor the highly symbolic rendering of economic and political issues that Littlefield and others described. From the assembled evidence it is clear that if Baum had any intentions of writing a Populist allegory, he kept them to himself.

For decades it was widely believed that Baum was a Democrat whose political participation reached its zenith in the presidential campaigns of William Jennings Bryan in 1896 and 1900. The basis for those beliefs is the recollections of Baum's eldest son, Frank Joslyn. A much-cited paragraph from the younger Baum's 1961 biography of his father gave the following account:

Not long after moving [to Chicago], Baum took a brief interest in politics. Stirred by William Jennings Bryan's "Cross of Gold" speech at the 1896 Democratic convention, he marched in torchlight parades in behalf of Bryan's candidacy. Again in 1900 he took part in Bryan's second campaign. But aside from these two campaigns and from voting regularly

---

5. Quoted in Moyer 1998, p. 46.

in elections, usually for Democratic candidates, he ignored the problems and personalities of public life. Other matters always seemed more important.[6]

A similar paragraph, based on interviews with Frank Joslyn Baum, had appeared in a biographical essay on Baum by Martin Gardner four years earlier. According to Gardner, Baum was generally inactive in politics but "consistently voted as a democrat" and marched "in a few torchlight parades" for Bryan.[7] While the younger Baum's assessment of his father as basically apolitical seems to have been correct—L. Frank Baum did not air his political views publicly (except in the early 1890s when he edited a newspaper in South Dakota), and his letters to family members and associates virtually never mention politics—the assertion that his father was a Democrat was likely mistaken. Baum scholars have turned up virtually nothing in the way of confirmation that Baum was ever a Democrat or a Bryan supporter, while finding numerous bits of evidence that suggest he was a Republican or at least leaned Republican. Moreover, Baum scholars have noticed numerous factual errors in Frank Joslyn Baum's biography and tend to regard that biography as unreliable.[8] Frank Joslyn Baum was only about 12 years old in 1896 and could easily have mis-remembered his father's comments about the political parties and candidates of the time. (Martin Gardner said recently that he thought that guess was "plausible.") In fact, in an early typescript of his biography of his father, Frank Joslyn Baum *did* get the Democratic and Republican parties mixed up, writing that Southerners bitterly resented "the Republican [*sic*] Administration of President Andrew Johnson." Hearn relates that in his exhaustive research on Baum's life and times he found some newspaper references to torchlight parades in Chicago for McKinley in 1896 but none to torchlight parades for Bryan; thus it is questionable whether Baum even could have marched in such parades while living in Chicago.[9]

The true nature of Baum's party affiliation, and even how he voted in 1896, remain unknown. We do know, however, that he wrote the following poem in support of William McKinley and the Republican economic platform in the summer of 1896:

---

6. Baum and MacFall 1961, p. 85.

7. Gardner and Nye 1994 [1957], p. 29.

8. Conversations with Michael Patrick Hearn, June 7, 1998 and August 29, 2000. Hearn said in another interview that Frank Joslyn Baum "knew little about his father, and what he didn't know he made up. The only trustworthy parts of [his biography] are his reminiscences of personal experiences with his father" (quoted in Koupal 2001, p. 156 n.9).

9. Conversation with Martin Gardner, October 5, 2000; second typescript of Frank J. Baum's biography, p. 90, L. Frank Baum papers, Box 6, Syracuse University, E.S. Bird Library, Special Collections. Mixing up the Democratic and Republican parties of the nineteenth century, as Frank J. Baum clearly did in the case of Andrew Johnson and possibly did in the case of his own father, would have been easy to do, since the two parties basically swapped ideologies between the nineteenth and twentieth centuries, as the Party of Lincoln became the more conservative party and the Democrats, once the party of Southern white supremacy, became the more liberal party.

When McKinley gets the chair, boys,
There'll be a jollification
Throughout our happy nation
And contentment everywhere!
Great will be our satisfaction
When the "honest money" faction
Seats McKinley in the chair

No more the ample crops of grain
That in our granaries have lain
Will seek a purchaser in vain
Or be at the mercy of the "bull" or "bear"
Our merchants won't be trembling
At the silverites' dissembling
When McKinley gets the chair!

When McKinley gets the chair, boys,
The magic word "protection"
Will banish all dejection
And free the workingman from every care;
We will gain the world's respect
When it knows our coin's "correct"
And McKinley's in the chair![10]

At a minimum, Baum's authorship of that poem indicates that Baum was something other than a Populist true believer. On the other hand, taking that poem at face value may be unwarranted. *Times-Herald* publisher Herman Kohlsaat was an ardent Republican (and was even lampooned in the pro-silver manifesto *Coin's Financial School* [1894]), and Baum may have written that poem for the money, knowing that Kohlsaat would happily pay him for it. The poem's teasing tone strikes me as somewhat sardonic. The quotation marks around "honest money" and "correct," for example, seem to mock the rhetoric of gold standard supporters. The poem's hyperbole on behalf of protective tariffs—"The magic word 'protection' / Will banish all dejection / And free the workingman from every care"—verges on parody. In sum, the poem can be read either as a straightforward salute to McKinley or as satire. Hearn, who unearthed the poem in 1992, also cautions against treating it as conclusive proof of Baum's standpoint.

Most of the other available strands of evidence regarding Baum's politics are thinner but also indicate that Baum was probably a Republican and not especially sympathetic to the Populists. As the editor of a weekly newspaper, the *Aberdeen Saturday Pioneer*, in South Dakota in 1890–91, Baum strongly supported the state's Republican Party.[11] Baum initially spoke kindly of South Dakota's early

---

10. Originally published in the *Chicago Times-Herald*, July 12, 1896. Reprinted in Hearn 1992.

11. Then again, considering that the *Pioneer* was a Republican newspaper before Baum took it over and that Baum made no secret that he was seeking political patronage for his newspaper, we should perhaps take that support with a grain of salt. Moreover, Baum's editorial stances, including vigorous support for woman suffrage and a questioning attitude

Populist party (the Independents), but in the 1890 election campaign he served as secretary of Aberdeen's Fourth Ward Republican caucus. After the election he denounced the Independents in no uncertain terms: "Judging from an unbiased standpoint, they are seeking to rectify some evils which have never existed, and to counterbalance others . . . with those no less to be condemned and avoided. They lack the experience and ability to reconstruct the debased politics of this country."[12] Likewise, Baum editorialized in favor of the Silver Purchase Act (which, in any event, was a halfway measure partly designed to head off free-silver agitation) but qualified his support in another editorial, saying that many of the bill's backers had drastically oversold it. In his dialogue and lyrics for the 1902 stage musical of *The Wizard of Oz*, Baum poked fun at a wide range of political targets, including large-P Populists like the famous ones from Kansas (where "our cranks are snubbed in vain," sang Dorothy) and the small-p populist rhetoric of President Theodore Roosevelt.[13] Baum's most overtly political novel, *Aunt Jane's Nieces at Work*, published under the pseudonym Edith Van Dyne in 1909, took a generally progressive stance, while casting most of the villains as Democrats.[14] Finally, Baum took a broad swipe at Bryan in his script for the 1915 musical *The Uplift of Lucifer*. When a character suggests Lucifer turn over his job as Satanic Majesty to William Jennings Bryan, Lucifer replies, "Are not my people tortured enough?"[15]

Arguably, however, the most telling statement about Baum's politics is the following anecdote, relayed by Hearn:

During the 1896 campaign, Baum was on the road in Illinois, selling crockery, when a friend asked him to speak before a Republican Party rally. He agreed and that night delivered a tirade against the opposition. Then he was asked by the Democrats to speak at their rally and delivered the same speech, this time directed against the Republicans.

Hearn adds, "Baum had little faith in politicians, considering most of them to be,

---

toward organized religion, hardly followed a party line.

12. *Aberdeen Daily News*, July 13 and 16, 1890; *Aberdeen Saturday Pioneer*, November 8, 1890. Cited by Koupal 2001, p. 159.

13. The distinction between "large-P" Populism and "small-p" populism is as follows: *Populism* refers to the People's Party and more generally to the farm-based protest movement of the late nineteenth century, whereas *populism* refers to any political rhetoric or movement that targets rank-and-file voters and denounces powerful elites. For more on this distinction, see the opening pages of Chapter 3.

14. Erisman 1968, p. 617 n. 3. Baum's dislike of Democrats, which may have been a function of his having grown up in traditionally Republican central New York, was also evident in one of his early works of fiction (a short story titled "Our Landlady," part of a regular, dialect-heavy column of the same name that ran regularly in the *Pioneer*). A character declares, "a feller as'll take a poor kid's last dollar is mean enough to join the demicrats" (August 2, 1890; reprinted by Koupal 1996, p. 94).

15. Baum 1963 [1915], pp. 39–40.

like the Wizard of Oz, humbugs."[16] Baum was, at heart, a skeptic.[17] Rather than trying to pigeonhole him as a loyal Republican or Populist, we are better advised to think of him as something of a court jester. A friendly acquaintance of Baum's once noted, "Everything he said had to be taken with at least a half-pound of salt." Likewise, Baum's nephew stated, "Mr. Baum always liked to tell wild tales, with a perfectly straight face, and earnestly, as though he really believed them himself."[18] I think it is safe to conclude that Baum did not take politics or politicians very seriously and would have enjoyed the subsequent confusion about his true political leanings.

Rockoff suggests that Baum may have subconsciously, rather than deliberately, incorporated political and monetary symbolism into his story. The book does contain some likely references to current events, as even as thorough-going a skeptic as *Baum Bugle* editor Michael Gessel has acknowledged, and Baum "probably considered his references to current events to be a series of sly jokes, like the puns that dot the text, rather than something to be worried about by future generations." Littlefield said in 1991 that he "almost [didn't] care" if the book was written as a Populist parable. His objective, he said, was just to "invest turn-of-the-century America with the imagery and wonder I have always found in [Baum's] stories."[19]

My own research leads me to a similar middle ground. *The Wonderful Wizard of Oz* is almost certainly not a conscious Populist allegory, and to say that it unambiguously is one is to traffic in misinformation. But the parallels between characters, incidents, and settings in the book and real-life issues in late-nineteenth-century America are striking, whether intended or not; the book *works* as a Populist allegory. As historian David B. Parker writes, "Recent scholarship might have taken away Baum's intent, but the images are still there, vivid as ever."[20] Once one is even vaguely aware of the concept of the book as a Populist parable, reading the book becomes a matter of "seek and ye shall find." Perhaps instead of viewing *The Wonderful Wizard of Oz* as an allegory of 1890s political economy, we should view 1890s political economy as an allegory of *The Wonderful Wizard of Oz*. I say this only half-facetiously; good history is good storytelling. So I submit *The Historian's*

---

16. Hearn 1992. For further evidence of Baum's basic cynicism about politics and politicians, see Baum's lyrics and script for the *Wizard of Oz* musical (notably the Wizard's song "When You Want to Fool the Public"), which unlike the novel was clearly aimed at adults. In *Aunt Jane's Nieces at Work* (1909), which is about a political campaign in rural New York, even the good campaigners engage in vote-buying. The book's apparent voice of wisdom, a lawyer named Watson, says, "There is no difference of importance" between the two major parties, but, when pressed for his preference, says, "I've always been a Republican, whenever I dabbled in politics, which hasn't been often" (p. 50). One of the nieces says managing a winning campaign is "child's play," which seems an apt description of how Baum felt about politics in general.

17. Hearn 1991.

18. Gardner and Nye 1994 [1957], pp. 28, 43.

19. Rockoff 1990, p. 756; Gessel 1992, p. 23; Littlefield 1992a.

20. Parker 1997, p. 4.

Wizard of Oz as a teaching tool, an enjoyable way for teachers and students of history and monetary economics to explore the issues of a century ago.

Chapter 2

"If I Only Had a Brain": A Primer on Gold, Silver, and the American Monetary System

The Populists quite properly belong to, in the words of Lord Keynes, "the brave army of heretics . . . who, following their intuitions, have preferred to see the truth obscurely and imperfectly rather than to maintain error, reached indeed with clearness and consistency and by easy logic, but on hypotheses inappropriate to the facts."

—economist William P. Yohe,
on the Populists' original monetary platform

Bryan went the way of the pterodactyl—the clumsy version of an idea which later succeeded.

—Saul Bellow[1]

INTRODUCTION

Over the course of the past century, the role of gold in the American economy has shrunk dramatically and the role of silver has been virtually nonexistent. As a result, for many students and teachers today, the centrality of gold and silver in the monetary and political debates of the 1890s is perhaps the biggest obstacle to understanding what the Populists and William Jennings Bryan were trying to

---

1. Yohe: from Goodwyn 1976, p. 581; Bellow: from *Ravelstein* 2000, p. 2.

accomplish.[2] Moreover, both the gold standard and the *bimetallic* (gold-and-silver) standard that preceded it were highly complex monetary and financial systems, the details of whose operations are still subject to debate and disagreement among economic historians. The purpose of this chapter is to provide the reader with a basic understanding of the American monetary system, both then and now, as well as a condensed history of the changing roles of gold and silver in that system.

Before proceeding any further, we need to get past a couple of common misconceptions about money and the economy. Because the term *money* is so often used to refer to income (as in "She makes a lot of money") or wealth (as in "He has a lot of money"), people tend to confuse the money supply with measures of national income or output, such as gross domestic product (GDP) or gross national product (GNP), or measures of national wealth, such as the total stock of people's savings. In fact, the term *money supply* refers generally to the total amount of currency in circulation (paper money and coins) plus the total amount of bank account deposits.[3] The money supply is much smaller than and conceptually different from, say, GDP, which is the total value of goods and services produced within a year. Another common misconception about money is that the U.S. dollar is supported by the government's store of gold in Fort Knox and thus has real value because it is redeemable for gold. That statement was true only when the United States was on a metallic standard, which has not been the case since 1933, when President Franklin D. Roosevelt took the country off the gold standard.[4] The current monetary system in the United States, and in most countries today, is a *fiat-money system*, in which our dollars have value because the government declares them to be legal tender for all payments of debts, public or private, and because people believe these dollars to have value. If people suddenly lost their faith in our

---

2. To be precise, the People's (or Populist) Party and William Jennings Bryan had somewhat different approaches to the silver question, and to monetary issues in general. Bryan's presidential campaigns focused on restoring government coinage of silver at the old exchange ratio that valued sixteen ounces of silver the same as one ounce of gold. The Populists shared Bryan's goals of increasing the money supply and ending the deflation of the late nineteenth century, but they favored increasing the money supply by a variety of means, including the issuance of paper money not redeemable for gold or silver. In 1896 Populist Senator William A. Peffer of Kansas explained his party's position as follows: "The money that the People's party demands is gold, silver, and paper. Populists believe in the unlimited and free coinage of both the metals, and if there is not enough of coin money in the country, supplement it with paper money" (quoted by Clanton 1991, p. 125).

3. Currently the Federal Reserve keeps track of three different measures of the money supply. The two simplest are M1 or "transactions money," equal to currency in circulation plus checking account deposits plus traveler's checks and money orders; and M2, equal to M1 plus savings account deposits plus small certificates of deposit (CDs) plus money-market deposit accounts plus individuals' holdings of money-market funds.

4. Alternatively, one might say that 1971 was the last year in which the U.S. gold reserve had practical significance. The Bretton Woods system of fixed international exchange rates, in effect from 1945 to 1971, allowed foreign central banks (though not foreign or American individuals) to exchange dollars for gold, so the dollar still maintained some linkage with gold.

currency, it would quickly lose its value, becoming nothing more than pieces of paper with intricate green-ink designs.

Another key distinction is between the money supply and the *monetary base*. Roughly speaking, the money supply is the total amount of cash in circulation plus bank account deposits, whereas the monetary base is the total amount of cash in circulation plus bank reserves. Modern banking, including banking in the late nineteenth century, is a system of *fractional reserve banking*, in which banks accept deposits and loan most of them out, keeping only a small fraction of the cash deposited with them as reserves to meet demands for withdrawals (and to comply with whatever reserve levels are mandated by law). Currently bank reserves include all cash held by the bank (e.g., in its vault, at its tellers' windows, in its automatic-teller machines) and the bank's reserve account with the U.S. central bank, the Federal Reserve System, also known as "the Fed." Thus the monetary base is the total amount of cash plus any additional reserves created by the Federal Reserve (which is empowered to create reserves as it sees fit, in order to meet the needs of the banks and the economy). By controlling the monetary base, the Fed effectively controls the money supply, which is a multiple of the monetary base, and is able to affect interest rates. Under a gold standard, in which paper money is redeemable for gold at a fixed exchange rate, the monetary base is the total amount of gold *specie* (i.e., gold coins). Under a bimetallic standard, in which paper money is redeemable for gold and silver at fixed exchange rates (with, say, sixteen ounces of silver equal in value to one ounce of gold), the monetary base is the total amount of gold and silver specie. Under a metallic standard, then, the monetary base and the money supply are determined by the domestic supply of one or two precious metals, and government and Fed policymakers exert little influence over them.

For most of the past 2,000 years, the world's monetary economies, such as they were, used one metal-based monetary system or another; the regular use of a pure fiat-money system, with no official role for gold or silver, was by and large a twentieth-century innovation. In fact, the terms *money* and *mint* date back to 390 B.C., when the Romans stored their gold and silver coins in a temple and gave thanks to Moneta, the Roman goddess of warning, for foiling a surprise attack on that temple by the Gauls. Paper-money transactions, in the form of *bills of exchange* (promises to pay a debt in a particular nation's currency), had become common by the end of the sixteenth century, but with few exceptions such paper money was backed by—that is, redeemable on demand for a specific amount of —gold or silver specie. For centuries the British pound sterling, by far the longest-lived currency in the world, was defined as literally a pound weight of sterling silver.[5] The United States put itself on a bimetallic standard with the Mint Act of 1792, which provided for gold and silver coins and no paper money. Following the recommendations of Treasury Secretary Alexander Hamilton, the basic monetary

---

5. The association of the word *pound* with metallic currency dates back to the late eighth century A.D., when Charlemagne, king of the Franks and eventual emperor of the Holy Roman Empire, established a gold coin weighing one pound and set it equal in value to 240 silver pennies.

unit would be the dollar, and people could bring silver or gold to the U.S. mint and get it stamped into coins, according to federal weight and purity standards. The initial standards established a silver dollar as containing 371.25 grains of pure silver and a gold dollar as containing 24.75 grains of pure gold (480 grains = 1 troy ounce). The ratio of those two numbers is 15-to-1, chosen so as to reflect the relative market prices of silver and gold at the time. In 1834 the official silver-to-gold exchange ratio was raised to 16-to-1, a relation that William Jennings Bryan would turn into perhaps the most famous ratio in American political history.

Although the United States was officially on a bimetallic standard from 1792 to 1900, the nation was on a *de facto* gold standard for nearly a century after 1834. Gold's price on the world's market in 1834 was somewhat lower than the official price set by the government and also less than 16 times the market price of silver; that is to say, gold fetched a higher price at the U.S. mint than on the free market. As a result, people with gold bullion took it to the mint to get it stamped into coins, and silver coins—which under the new ratio were worth more as metal than as coins—gradually dropped out of circulation. Gold became still more plentiful after the California gold rush of 1848–49, causing gold's market price to fall even further relative to silver's, which in turn caused silver to disappear almost entirely from circulation. The United States temporarily abandoned the bimetallic standard during the Civil War, when the Union government issued a fiat-money paper currency called greenbacks as an emergency war-finance measure, but took steps a decade later to return to a metallic standard. In 1875 Congress passed the Specie Resumption Act, pledging the Treasury to redeem greenbacks for their face-value equivalent in gold coin beginning in 1879. The resumption was ultimately successful, but in the meantime Congress had effectively put the United States on a gold-only standard (or a *monometallic gold standard*) by passing the Coinage Act of 1873, which dropped the silver dollar from the list of coins that the U.S. government would mint and put an end to the official exchange ratio (i.e., 16-to-1) of silver for gold. The Gold Standard Act of 1900 officially placed the United States on a gold standard, and the country would remain so until 1933.

HOW MONEY AFFECTS THE ECONOMY

In a modern economy, money's most basic function is as a *medium of exchange*: people use it to buy goods and services and receive money for whatever goods and services they themselves provide. In this context "transactions money" refers to cash and checking account deposits (and, secondarily, traveler's checks and money orders).[6] Since the size of an economy is measured not by its stock of money but by its total production of goods and services, the effects of money, and changes in the money supply, on the economy are not self-evident. While it is

---

6. Credit is also a common means of finance, but credit-based transactions are simply an advanced form of money-based transactions. When you pay for something with a credit card, the bank that issued the card is effectively loaning you the money for the purchase, and you repay the bank by writing a check.

widely accepted that money "greases the wheels of commerce" by eliminating the need for barter and thus allowing for much greater specialization by people according to what they do best, economists' disagreements about how money otherwise affects the economy are legion. Does an increase in the money supply raise real (inflation-adjusted) output and people's real incomes, or does it merely lead to higher prices (i.e., inflation)? Most, though certainly not all, economists would probably answer that question as follows: in the long run, the level of real output depends not on the supply of money but on an economy's endowments of labor, capital (tools, machinery, and other equipment used in production), technology, and related factors. In the short run, however, changes in the supply of money will cause changes in interest rates, which will affect real output by raising or lowering the real cost of borrowing, thus affecting the volume of consumption spending by households and capital-goods spending by firms. Currently the Federal Reserve regularly increases the money supply so that it will keep pace with people's demand for transactions money, which naturally increases most every year as real incomes and prices increase. The Fed also regularly adjusts the level of bank reserves and the money supply so as to affect interest rates. Other things being equal, increases in the supply of money will cause interest rates to fall, lowering the cost of borrowing and hence encouraging consumption and capital-goods spending, which raises real output and the price level. Decreases in the supply of money will have the reverse effects.[7]

The relationship between the money supply, the price level, and real output is embodied in a standard equation of economics, called the *quantity equation of money* (see Appendix C for details). As regards cause and effect, the usual interpretation of that equation is that an increase in the money supply will typically cause an increase in real output, the price level, or both. Likewise, a decrease in the money supply will tend to cause a decrease in real output (recession), a fall in prices (deflation), or both. A variant of the quantity equation of money, developed in the nineteenth century and espoused by William Jennings Bryan and William H. Harvey (author of *Coin's Financial School* and touted as "the Tom Paine of the free-silver movement"), is the *quantity theory of money*, which holds that an increase in the supply of money will cause a *proportional* increase in prices and real output. Bryan and many Populists believed that the price deflation of the late nineteenth century was caused by an insufficient amount of money in circulation, and that a substantial increase in the supply of money would end the deflation, which they viewed as economically devastating to the farmers. They were certainly correct in their general prescription for ending the deflation: The consensus view among economists is that an increase in the supply of money will generate an

---

7. Alternatively, one could describe the effects of money-supply increases on real output according to the following sequence: the Fed increases the supply of bank reserves, giving banks more available money to loan out, which causes an increase in loans to consumers and businesses, who use those loans to purchase consumer goods and capital goods. Note that this explanation does not necessarily depend on a reduction in interest rates to stimulate spending.

increase in prices. Deflation, however, had many proponents in the late nineteenth century, as will become clearer in the next section.

GREENBACKS, RESUMPTION, AND THE "CRIME OF 1873"

The Civil War caused a massive disruption to America's monetary system. The Union and Confederate governments both suspended allegiance to the gold standard and, in order to finance their war efforts, issued paper-money currencies that were not redeemable for specie, at least not until some unspecified time in the future. (The Union's fiat-money currency, officially called the U.S. note, earned the nickname *greenback*, because, figuratively speaking, it had only its green coloring to back it up.) The Confederacy experienced a hyperinflation, and, obviously, Confederate dollars were worthless after the war. The Union experienced a rapid inflation of its own, as the wholesale price level more than doubled from 1861 to 1865. At war's end, the dominant political leaders believed that a return to the gold standard was necessary to reestablish America's credibility abroad and to reassure current and prospective holders of Treasury bonds. But American prices had become so high relative to world prices that American goods were uncompetitive internationally, and the greenback dollar had lost so much of its value relative to gold that if *resumption* (redemption of greenbacks for specie at the official exchange ratio of one greenback dollar for one gold dollar) had commenced at that time, the U.S. government's gold reserve would soon have run out. The government therefore faced a choice of devaluation—i.e., decreasing the gold content of the dollar, by minting a smaller gold dollar and declaring the old gold dollars to be worth, say, $2—or deflation. The presidential administrations of Andrew Johnson and Ulysses S. Grant, as well as the Republican-controlled Congress of 1866, chose deflation. In the first three years after the Civil War, the government retired a substantial amount of greenbacks, the money supply fell, and deflation set in. By the start of 1879, when resumption officially began (as provided for by the Specie Resumption Act of 1875), wholesale prices had fallen all the way to their prewar level.

The Specie Resumption Act prompted the formation of a new political party, the Greenback Party, dedicated to repealing resumption and keeping the greenback as the dominant U.S. currency. Members of the new party opposed the government's pro-deflation policies and urged the issuance of more greenbacks. Public support for deflationary policies had already begun to ebb during the post-Civil War recessions of the late 1860s, and ebbed further after a banking panic in September 1873 kicked off a six-year economic contraction. Congress had suspended the retirement of greenbacks in 1868 and passed a bill to expand the supply of greenbacks, known as the Inflation Bill and ultimately vetoed by President Grant, in 1874. The Specie Resumption Act of 1875 was actually passed in January by a lame-duck Republican Congress that had lost its majority in the House of Representatives for the first time since 1860. "Greenbackism" gained support during the deflationary economic contraction of 1873–79: a bill to repeal the Specie Resumption Act passed the House and almost passed the Senate in late 1877, a bill forbidding any further retirement of greenbacks (though not affecting resumption) passed Congress in May 1878, and the Greenback Party won 10 percent of the vote and 14 seats in Congress in the Congressional midterm elections of 1878. About $300 million worth of those greenbacks would continue to circulate, though as an increasingly trivial proportion of the total U.S. money supply.[8]

Still more controversial was the Coinage Act of 1873, which omitted the silver dollar from the list of coins to be minted by the Treasury and ended the government's official valuation of silver at one-sixteenth its weight in gold. The act's stated aim was merely to simplify the coinage system, but it unofficially put the United States on a gold standard. Since silver was still worth more on the market ($1.298 an ounce) than at the traditional mint price ($1.292 an ounce, or one-sixteenth the official price of $20.67 for an ounce of gold), no one wanted to bring silver bullion to the mint to be stamped into coins anyway, so the act created little stir at the time. Within a few years, however, monetary populists would view it as one of the all-time betrayals, calling it the "Crime of '73." What had changed in the meantime? The biggest change was that the market price of silver plummeted, to a price much lower than the traditional mint price. Had the government continued its commitment to silver coinage, holders of silver bullion everywhere would have rushed to the mint to get their silver stamped into coins, and the monetary base and money supply would have soared, bringing a likely end to the deflation.[9] Monetary populists, as well as silver miners in the West, would spend much of the next quarter-century demanding that the government return to bimetallism, at the old 16-to-1 exchange ratio.

The Coinage Act's architects, most notably Senator John Sherman, had foreseen that silver's market price was about to fall sharply, on account of new discoveries of silver in the West and the ongoing abandonment of bimetallism in favor of a gold standard among the major economies of Europe, notably Germany in the early 1870s.[10] Coinage of new silver dollars under the old weight standards would have been inflationary, since the intrinsic value of the silver in those dollars would have been much less than a dollar. Monetary populists downplayed the danger of inflation, arguing instead that *reflation*—a return of prices to their previous, higher levels, perhaps those of the 1860s—would have provided relief to farmers. After all, the deflation of that time was severe—in all, from 1865 to 1879 wholesale prices fell more than 50 percent and consumer prices fell by about 40 percent—and farmers believed they bore the brunt of it. They charged that crop prices fell even faster than other prices did, causing the farmers' terms of trade to

---

8. This account of the politics of resumption draws heavily on Friedman and Schwartz 1963, pp. 44–49. Statistics on greenback circulation are from U.S. Department of Commerce 1975, Series X 433.

9. Friedman (1994) quantitatively estimates the yearly price levels that, hypothetically speaking, would have prevailed if the government had *not* ended its silver coinage policy in 1873, and finds that the policy would indeed have stemmed the deflation and brought about a mild inflation after 1887. Notes Friedman: "If my estimates are anywhere near correct, a bimetallic standard—really a silver standard—would have produced a considerably steadier price level than did the gold standard that was adopted" (p. 76).

10. Nugent 1967, pp. 85–92.

worsen.[11] Deflation offered no relief from mortgage and other debts; on the contrary, since those obligations were in fixed-dollar terms, as falling prices reduced the farmers' income those debts became more burdensome. Was resumption of specie payments and commitment to a gold standard really so important, the Greenbackers asked, as to be worth the costs that such a substantial deflation imposed? Thus monetary populists considered the Coinage Act a crime because it disallowed people from doing the natural thing that would have countered the deflation—namely, bringing silver bullion to the mint to be stamped into coins.

THE GOLD STANDARD AND MONETARY POPULISM, 1880–1900

On the surface, the gold standard would appear to have been a very simple system. People could bring gold bullion to the U.S. mint, and the government would stamp that gold into coins according to fixed weight standards. Paper-money dollars, called "gold certificates" (which at the time were issued by private banks, not by the federal government or a central bank), were redeemable for gold at an official exchange rate of $20.67 for one ounce of gold, or one paper dollar for one gold dollar containing 23.22 grains of gold. Internationally speaking, since the world's major currencies had fixed prices in terms of gold, it followed that each of those currencies had a fixed price in terms of every other major currency. If a country experienced higher inflation than other countries, the relative prices of its goods went up both in that country and everywhere else around the world, by the same amount. That country's exports would be uncompetitive on world markets, and gold would flow out of that country and into other countries, creating a *balance-of-payments deficit*. The resulting gold outflow would reduce that country's monetary base and money supply, causing prices to fall until they were competitive with world prices again. Conversely, a country whose products were relatively cheap and thus in high demand internationally would experience a gold inflow, causing its monetary base and money supply to increase, which in turn would inflate its prices back to world levels. (This automatic adjustment process was known as the *price-specie-flow mechanism* and was developed by the economist David Hume in the mid-eighteenth century.) By fixing the dollar's value in terms of an intrinsically valuable metal, the gold standard was thought to promote price stability. Likewise, as more and more countries adopted it, the gold standard was believed to promote international trade by providing a stable system of fixed exchange rates.

---

11. The data on wholesale and consumer prices are from U.S. Department of Commerce 1975, Series E 52 and E 135. The point about the farmers' worsening terms of trade appears in Rockoff 1990, pp. 741–42, and Walton and Rockoff 1998, p. 337, and is based on price data in U.S. Department of Commerce 1975 and Friedman and Schwartz 1982. We should note, however, that some earlier studies concluded that the farmers' terms of trade *improved* during the late nineteenth century (see, for example, Lee and Passell 1979 or North, Anderson, and Hill 1966). The answer to the question of whether farm prices fell farther than other prices appears to be highly sensitive to one's choice of price series.

In practice, the gold standard was far more complex and problematic. Price deflation was hardly a painless process, as the preceding section indicates, and by the 1890s monetary populists had raised awareness that the ongoing deflation was somehow attributable to the gold standard. To the extent that the gold standard worked, in the sense of maintaining stable exchange rates and avoiding balance-of-payments crises (which would have depleted countries' gold reserves), it worked not automatically but because governments and central banks went to great lengths to avoid balance-of-payments crises. Gold standard countries were still vulnerable to bank panics, since most of them practiced fractional reserve banking, meaning that the gold reserves held by banks were much smaller than the total volume of bank deposits and paper currency (e.g., gold certificates) in circulation.[12] A general "run on the banks" would have quickly exhausted the banks' holdings of gold, and bank panics (which were fairly common at the time) caused many banks to suspend specie payments. Finally, since currencies were tied to a commodity, whose production and market price were naturally subject to random fluctuations, sudden discoveries of gold could create a general inflation and shortfalls in gold production could create a general deflation. A survey published in 1995 indicates that the vast majority of economic historians hold the gold standard in low regard. Nearly two-thirds of respondents disagreed with the statement, "During the late nineteenth and early twentieth centuries, the Gold Standard was effective in stabilizing prices and moderating business-cycle fluctuations," and only 12 percent accepted it without provisos.[13]

Resumption began on the first day of 1879 and, together with a strong upturn in the economy that was accompanied by a brief burst of inflation, including a whopping 38 percent increase in wholesale farm prices in 1879–82, caused the Greenback Party's agenda to lose its urgency. The party platform of 1880, in a sign of things to come, shifted its focus from stopping resumption to replacing private bank notes with government-printed paper currency and allowing free and unlimited coinage of silver at the old 16-to-1 ratio (a.k.a. "free silver"). When prices quickly fell back to earth in the next economic contraction (1882–85) and continued to trend downward (which they would do through 1897), pressure built up once again for monetary remedies.[14] Although the Greenback Party was basically defunct after 1884, Greenback ideas about fiat-money currency took hold among many farmers' organizations, as described in Chapter 3. But such ideas were slow to take hold among the general public, who did not appear ready for a permanent

---

12. Robert Triffin, in a 1968 essay reprinted in Eichengreen and Flandreau, noted that gold accounted for barely one-tenth of the world's money supply, with paper currency and bank deposits accounting for the rest, in 1913, the last year of the "classical gold standard" (1997, p. 152).

13. The survey results are from Robert Whaples (1995). For a pithy critique of the late-nineteenth-century gold standard, see Eichengreen's essay in McCloskey 1993.

14. Farm price data are from U.S. Department of Commerce 1975, Series E 42. On the Greenbacks' 1880 platform, see Friedman and Schwartz 1963, p. 48. For basic economic data for 1879–1906, see Friedman and Schwartz 1963, pp. 94–95, and Rockoff 1990, p. 742.

fiat-money currency at that time. Even William Jennings Bryan's free-silver platform of 1896 was comparatively conservative, in that it still anchored the dollar to silver and gold.

Pro-silver agitation had begun in the mid-to-late 1870s, well before resumption. Initially the most active free-silver advocates were Western silver-mining interests, not farmers. Previously minted silver coins returned to circulation in the 1870s when, as predicted, silver prices fell below their traditional exchange price of one-sixteenth the price of gold. But Western miners who brought silver to the federal mint for coinage were incredulous when the government turned most of it away (all but what was needed for small subsidiary coins, as the Coinage Act of 1873 had provided). Silver interests were well organized in such states as Idaho and Nevada, and the senators from silver-producing states clamored for a return to unlimited coinage of silver at the old 16-to-1 ratio. The best they could manage was a compromise, the Bland-Allison Act of 1878, which provided for limited coinage of silver to be purchased by the government at market prices. Despite those purchases, silver prices continued to fall through the end of the century, as the supply of silver increased much faster than the demand. In response to continued pro-silver agitation, Congress passed the Sherman Silver Purchase Act of 1890, directing the Treasury to buy still more silver (in all, 4.5 million ounces per month) at market prices. Both of those silver purchase acts were half-measures and did little to stop the continued slide of silver prices. Even with the increased purchases, the nominal value of the silver purchased was no higher in the early 1890s than in the 1880s. Not surprisingly, then, the silver purchases were not nearly large enough to stem the tide of general price deflation.

Farm populists, including those belonging to the newly formed Populist (or People's) Party, were naturally sympathetic to the cause of free silver, since additional silver coinage would help to counter the deflation, but intellectually their monetary prescriptions were much closer to those of the Greenbackers. Populist leader William A. Peffer of Kansas, elected to the U.S. Senate in 1890, was among the most outspoken advocates of a fiat-money system. While the Populists' visionary "Omaha platform" in the 1892 election called for free coinage of silver at the 16-to-1 ratio, free silver was in fact a small part of the platform's monetary plank, which called for a paper-money "national currency, safe, sound and flexible, issued by the General Government only, a full legal tender for all debts public and private" and embraced the Greenbackist "subtreasury plan" proposed by the Southern Farmers' Alliance in 1889 (see Chapter 3). The Omaha platform also demanded that "the amount of circulating medium be speedily increased to not less than $50 per capita," a goal that further implied that free coinage would need to be supplemented with paper-money issues.[15] What finally pushed free silver to the forefront, causing it to be forever associated with Populism, was President Grover Cleveland's 1893 repeal of the Silver Purchase Act.

Cleveland's action came in response to fears among investors that the Silver Purchase Act meant that the United States was on the verge of abandoning the gold

---

15. Reprinted in Boorstin 1985 [1966], p. 538.

standard. The act's passage in July 1890 had prompted some international investors to convert their dollars into gold, causing gold to flow out of the United States and a brief economic contraction to begin. Gold flowed back into the United States in 1891 and 1892, thanks to a surge in European demand for American food crops, but thereafter the exchange of dollars for gold continued. News of numerous business failures in early 1893 and a stock market crash in May touched off a run on the banks, particularly in the West and South. The Cleveland administration, blaming the banking panic on uncertainty over the gold standard, announced in June that it would seek repeal of the Silver Purchase Act. Repeal was achieved four months later, but the run on the banks continued and the economic contraction turned into a depression. The 1890s depression would last four years and would be the worst economic slump the country had yet experienced.

That the slump got worse instead of better after the Silver Purchase Act's repeal seemed to strengthen the free-silver position. William H. Harvey's illustrated pamphlet *Coin's Financial School* (1894) articulated that position in a witty, accessible manner and became a manifesto for the free-silver movement. The "school" was an imaginary series of lessons given by the young and precocious Coin at the Art Institute of Chicago, extolling the virtues of 16-to-1 bimetallism and denouncing the "crime of 1873," the rapacious "financial trust," and the financial orthodoxy that continued to defend silver's demonetization, decades of deflation, and gold "monometallism." Among the pamphlet's highlights were Coin's devastating retorts to questions from real-life gold advocates like University of Chicago economics professor J. Laurence Laughlin and Chicago banker Lyman J. Gage (a distant relative of L. Frank Baum's wife, Maud Gage, and later the secretary of the Treasury in the McKinley administration). While those exchanges were, of course, fictional, many readers regarded them as real and even sent querying letters to Laughlin, Gage, and other "students" of Coin. The book sold an estimated one million copies and prompted a backlash of pro-gold rebuttals— pamphlets with titles like *Coin's Financial Fool: or, the Artful Dodger Exposed*; *The Mistakes of Coin;* and *A Freak in Finance.*[16] Perhaps the strongest counterpoint to Coin was the continued slide of silver's price relative to gold's: the market price ratio of gold to silver was upwards of 30-to-1 from 1894 on, lending credence to the charge that free coinage of silver at the 16-to-1 ratio would be wildly inflationary. Coin's answer to the charge was that the relative prices of the two metals had been very stable at about 15- or 16-to-1 for almost two centuries, until silver's demonetization in the 1870s, and that a return to 16-to-1 bimetallism by the United States would tend to stabilize the market price of silver at that ratio, thus avoiding a major inflation. But not many people outside the silver movement bought that argument, and at points in the book's final chapter Coin seemed to contradict himself, saying that 16-to-1 bimetallism "would double the value of all property" and cause "higher prices—*bimetallic prices*" to prevail.[17] When the Democrats and Populists nominated William Jennings Bryan for president on a free-silver platform

---

16. Hofstadter 1963, pp. 5–7.
17. Harvey 1894, pp. 133, 141 (emphasis in the original).

in 1896, Republicans seized on the runaway-inflation argument. A Republican campaign poster proclaimed, "16-to-1 Free Silver Means that a Silver Dollar is worth only 53 Cents." Economist Milton Friedman, in a series of essays about late-nineteenth-century monetary political economy that are generally sympathetic to Bryan, concludes that maintaining the 16-to-1 bimetallic standard would have been a wise course in 1873 but that, by 1896, the damage had been done and Bryan's 16-to-1 free-silver plan would indeed have been overly inflationary. Bryan, he says, was trying to close the barn door after the horse had already been stolen.[18]

The "battle of the standards" that pitted Bryan against William McKinley in the presidential contest of 1896 is described in the next chapter. The Republican platform on which McKinley ran, and won, called for America to hew to the gold standard until an international agreement on a bimetallic standard could be nego-tiated. While such an agreement was a long shot at best—the international gold standard itself was the product not of any international agreement but of individual countries' decisions to adopt a gold standard—the platform plank allowed McKinley to have it both ways in a sense, by supporting silver coinage *and* price stability. As president, McKinley continued the "sound-money," pro-gold policies of Grover Cleveland, securing passage of a Gold Standard Act in 1900; but economic circumstances dealt McKinley a much better hand. In particular, dis-coveries of new gold supplies in South Africa, the Yukon, Alaska, and elsewhere, together with the invention of the cyanide process for extracting gold more efficiently from its ore, produced a rapid expansion of the money supply. The big deflation of the late nineteenth century was over, and prosperity returned. Bryan continued to back free silver, believing that the increased supplies of gold could not be counted on to last. He said, with some justification, that the gold inflation actually vindicated his position; he had been arguing all along that an expansion of the money supply would bring recovery, and that was exactly what happened. The only difference was that he had had a different metal in mind. In his memoirs, he illustrated that point with a parable:

Suppose the citizens of a town were divided, nearly equally, on the question of water supply, one faction contending that the amount should be increased, and suggesting that the increase be piped from Silver Lake, the other faction insisting no more water was needed; suppose that at the election the opponents of an increase won (no matter by what means); and suppose, soon after the election, a spring which may be described as Gold Spring, broke forth in the very center of the city, with a flow of half as much water as the city had before used; and suppose the new supply was turned into the city reservoir to the joy and benefit of all the people of the town. Which faction would, in such a case, have been vindicated?

Just such a result has followed a similar increase in the nation's supply of money to the joy of all—thus proving the contentions of the bimetallists.[19]

---

18. Friedman 1994, p. 118.
19. Bryan and Bryan 1925, p. 471; quoted by Rockoff 1990, p. 759.

GOLD IN THE TWENTIETH CENTURY

The "classical gold standard" era of 1880–1913 came to an abrupt end with the outbreak of World War I in the summer of 1914. The exigencies of war finance during the four years of war caused the European belligerents to abandon the gold standard, just as the United States had left the gold standard during the Civil War. The United States, which did not enter the war until 1917, remained on the gold standard throughout but imposed some restrictions, both formal and informal, on the convertibility of dollars into gold. But with most European countries at war and suspending convertibility of their currencies into gold, the international gold standard was effectively dead. Many officials sought to return to the gold standard after the war, a quest that in hindsight was a grave mistake, at least as carried out. The principal problem was that the market-determined currency exchange rates after the war were vastly different from the prewar parities (i.e., the exchange rates that had prevailed under the prewar gold standard). The dollar's foreign-exchange value had increased, and the pound's and the franc's had decreased. Yet in 1925 Britain opted to return to the gold standard at the prewar parity, and other countries did the same.[20] The result was a system of exchange rates that were fixed but severely misaligned. For example, the pound's exchange price in terms of dollars had fallen well below its prewar price of $4.86, but the return to prewar parities returned the pound's dollar price to $4.86. The combination of the old exchange rates and changed economic circumstances made British goods uncompetitive on world markets, causing Britain to have chronic gold losses, and U.S. goods artificially cheap to foreign customers, causing massive gold inflows. Under the "rules of the game" of the classical gold standard, Britain needed to pursue deflationary policies (such as wage reductions or increases in interest rates) and the United States needed to pursue inflationary policies, so as not to continually drain gold away from other countries. Yet that kind of symmetrical response rarely occurred. Instead, in the late 1920s countries jealously guarded their gold reserves: Countries experiencing gold inflows often took steps to counter the inflation that the gold inflow was supposed to bring. Thus, gold standard countries at that time were more likely to pursue deflationary policies than inflationary ones, and to focus on maintaining their gold reserves to the exclusion of all other concerns. Economic historians have increasingly come to regard the deflationary bias of the interwar

---

20. To be precise, the 1925–31 system was not so much a gold standard, with gold coins circulating freely, as a *gold-exchange standard*, a fixed-exchange-rate system in which every currency was worth a specified weight of gold. The system was a strange one, in that the official gold content of each currency was unchanged from 1913 even though virtually every country had experienced substantial inflation since then. Governments, reluctant to devalue their currencies by lowering their gold content and fearful of general gold shortages, discouraged the use of gold coins for private payments and sought to concentrate gold holdings in central banks (Mayer, Duesenberry, and Aliber 1984, p. 491). But, since the face value of gold coins was much less than their value as metal on the open market, few people would have wanted to use those coins for payment anyway.

gold standard as one of the key factors behind the Great Depression of the 1930s; one calls it "the principal threat to financial stability and economic prosperity between the wars."[21]

As the Great Depression deepened, bringing with it a worldwide deflation, countries began to reassess their commitments to the gold standard. Now-standard policies to stimulate an economy by increasing the money supply and lowering interest rates (expansionary monetary policy), or through increased government spending and lower taxes (expansionary fiscal policy), were not well articulated or understood at the time, but governments did recognize that exiting the gold standard would allow them to devalue their currencies, thus making their exports cheaper and improving their trade balances. Britain was the first major economy to abandon the gold standard and devalue its currency, which it did in September 1931. In consequence Britain experienced one of the earliest and quickest recoveries from the Great Contraction of the early 1930s. "There are few Englishmen who do not rejoice at the breaking of our gold fetters," exulted the British economist John Maynard Keynes. Just as Britain's return to gold in 1925 inaugurated the interwar gold standard, so did British devaluation in 1931 mark the beginning of the end of the gold standard. Other countries were quick to follow Britain's lead, including the United States in April 1933: The number of gold standard nations fell from 45 in 1931 to 22 in 1932 to 14 in 1933. By 1937, nobody remained on the gold standard.[22]

The U.S. departure from the gold standard could hardly have been more dramatic. On March 9, 1933, literally one day after declaring at a press conference that the gold standard was safe, newly elected President Franklin D. Roosevelt pushed emergency legislation through Congress authorizing him to prohibit the export or hoarding of gold and authorizing the secretary of the Treasury to require surrender of all gold coin, bullion, and certificates held by the public. In April, by executive order, Roosevelt exercised both of those powers. Private export of gold was prohibited, and people were required to deliver all of their gold in exchange for paper currency or deposits at banks, which in turn were required to deliver their gold to the Federal Reserve. (Ironically, part of the rationale for the Fed's creation in 1913 had been to help manage the American gold standard.) Also that month, Congress passed legislation giving the president the power to reduce the gold content of the dollar. Now allowed to float on international currency markets, the dollar depreciated by about 30 percent against the pound from April to July. Roosevelt went so far as to say, in his written "bombshell" statement of July 3, that rigid gold exchange standards were "old fetishes of so-called international bankers" and that it was "a specious fallacy" to assume that exchange-rate stability was

---

21. Eichengreen 1992, p. 4. See also Temin 1990 and Sumner 1997.
22. Eichengreen 1992, pp. 21, 188–91.

necessary for economic recovery. Surging industrial production, business investment, and stock prices in the second quarter of 1933 seemed to vindicate the new policy.[23]

Another executive order, in January 1934, fixed the official price of gold at $35.00 an ounce (up 69 percent from its old price of $20.67). The Gold Reserve Act, passed the same day, announced that the United States stood ready to buy gold at that price in unlimited quantities (although the United States would still not give people gold in exchange for dollars). Gold flowed into the United States faster than ever before, and by World War II the United States held 60 percent of the world's monetary gold. The country's swelling gold reserve became the bulwark of the Bretton Woods System of fixed exchange rates that prevailed from 1945 to 1971. As escalating U.S. inflation rates during the Vietnam War led some foreign central banks to convert their dollar holdings into gold, generating fears that the U.S. gold reserve would eventually run out, President Richard Nixon announced in 1971 that the United States would no longer redeem dollars for gold, thus effectively ending the Bretton Woods system and severing the dollar's last official link to gold. Soon thereafter, now that the dollar's official convertibility into gold was a relic of the past, the government lifted the ban on private gold ownership. As if to underscore the declining importance of the U.S. gold reserve, the Treasury auctioned off a total of about 6 percent of its stock of gold in 1975, 1978, and 1979.

With virtually no remaining role in governmental or monetary affairs, gold reverted to its original status as a commodity. Far from fading into obscurity, however, the gold market went on a wild ride during the next three decades. Assets with intrinsic value, like gold and real estate, are useful hedges against inflation, so when inflation is rampant, as in the 1970s, their prices tend to rise much faster than the general price level. The price of gold shot up from $35 an ounce in 1968 to a peak of $850 in January 1980; as restrictive Federal Reserve policies tamed that inflation in the early 1980s, gold fell to just over $300 an ounce. As is true of any commodity, gold's price continues to exhibit great fluctuations, but continued low inflation rates have caused that price to trend downward: gold fell below $300 an ounce in 1997 and has mostly remained there through 2001.

The closest that the United States has since come to returning to the gold standard was in the early 1980s, and we didn't come all that close. Donald Regan, secretary of the Treasury in the Reagan administration, appointed a Gold Commission in 1981 in accordance with a bill sponsored by Senator Jesse Helms and passed in 1980. The commission's members were drawn from Congress, the presidential administration, the Federal Reserve, and the public. By that time economic orthodoxy on monetary issues had changed 180 degrees from the sentiments of half a century earlier, when 30 prominent economists told President-Elect Roosevelt that the gold standard "should be unflinchingly maintained." The commission had its share of "gold bugs," but they were outnumbered by more conventionally-

---

23. For accounts of the dramatic events of 1933–34, see Temin 1990, pp. 96–100, Eichengreen 1992, pp. 329–33, and Bernstein 2000, pp. 320–25. The bit about the Fed and the gold standard in 1913 is from Eichengreen 1993, p. 86.

minded economists and policymakers. The commission's report, issued in 1982, made no sweeping recommendations and even suggested that the Treasury retain the right to auction off some of its gold. That report was arguably the final nail in the coffin of the gold standard.[24]

CONCLUSION

Few economists today would regard the Gold Commission as a missed opportunity. The mainstream view among contemporary economists is that a return to a gold standard would be a mistake, bordering on insanity, since it would deprive the Federal Reserve of its power to regulate the economy and would anchor the U.S. money supply and price level to a commodity whose production is subject to random shocks and whose price fluctuations are so extreme that most investors avoid it. After two decades of low inflation and near-continuous economic expansion, President Herbert Hoover's admonition, "We have gold because we cannot trust governments," has given way to the Age of Greenspan, an era of unprecedented public confidence in the Federal Reserve. While gold's mystique will never disappear, the exile of gold money to museums and coin collections seems destined to be a permanent one.

---

24. See Stein 1994, pp. 300–302, and Bernstein 2000, pp. 318, 360–62.

Chapter 3

"Populism Will Put Them to Sleep": A Short History of the Populist Movement of the 1890s

Populism is sure to retain its fascination for students of history as long as people remain sensitive to questions of democracy and human rights in a world increasingly driven by the consequences of an ongoing technological-corporate revolution.

—Gene Clanton[1]

INTRODUCTION

The word *populism* appears frequently in political discourse. In the 2000 presidential campaign, for example, pundits commented endlessly on the "populist" tone of Al Gore's acceptance speech at the Democratic Convention, in which he promised to fight for ordinary Americans against "the powerful interests." A *New York Times* editorial noted "Warring Populisms" on the part of the two major parties: Democrats tend to stress an economic populism, in which they claim to be the defenders of working-class Americans against the excesses of big business, while Republicans tend to stress a cultural populism, in which they claim to be the defenders of traditional values against intellectual elites, and an economic populism of their own, aimed at big government and "tax-and-spend liberals."

Populist appeals of those kinds date back a long way in American politics, at least as far back as the "Jacksonian Democracy" of the 1820s and the early days of the Republican Party as the party of "Free Soil, Free Labor, and Free Men" in the 1850s. Such appeals to "the common man" reached their fullest expression in

---

1. Clanton 1991, p. 168.

the turbulent decade of the 1890s, with the formation of a third party that grew out of farmers' protest movements and sought to ally itself with blue-collar workers and opponents of monopolies. The term *Populist* was coined in 1891 to denote members of the incipient party, which was officially known as the People's Party.[2] The Populist Party convention in Omaha in 1892 issued a visionary platform and nominated James B. Weaver for president. Weaver finished a distant third behind Grover Cleveland and Benjamin Harrison but won over a million votes and became the first third-party candidate since the Civil War to carry any states.

The Populist movement came to a crescendo of sorts in the presidential campaign of 1896. The Populists and Democrats both nominated William Jennings Bryan, a Nebraska Democrat known for zealous advocacy of increasing the money supply by restoring silver coinage, after his stirring "Cross of Gold" speech at the Democratic Convention.[3] The 1896 campaign between Bryan and Republican William McKinley was perhaps the most exciting ever, combining old-time political theater such as rallies and torchlight parades and (in McKinley's case) the last-ever "front-porch campaign" with innovations such as mass marketing, celluloid campaign buttons, and (in Bryan's case) all-out personal campaigning marked by stump speeches and whistle-stop train tours. Voter turnout was a record high, surpassing that of the previous election by two million. Bryan lost, but he captured nearly 48 percent of the popular vote despite being vastly outspent and opposed by the press and the business community. While Bryan, who was also the Democratic nominee in 1900 and 1908, would never become president, his 1896 candidacy clearly did have a lasting legacy. It resurfaced in the burst of progressive legislation in the first decade and a half of the twentieth century and in Franklin D. Roosevelt's New Deal programs.

---

2. For the sake of clarity, we should explicitly distinguish between "large-P" Populism, referring to the agrarian and working-class movement of the late nineteenth century (and to the People's Party in particular), and "small-p" populism, which refers more generally to any mass political movement that aims its appeals to rank-and-file voters and disdains economic or intellectual elites. The chapter's opening quote refers to large-P Populism.

3. Not all historians agree that the 1896 campaign was the climax of Populism. At the time, radical Populist Henry Demarest Lloyd chided his fellow Populists for embracing Bryan and his "free-silver" agenda, which was much narrower and more conservative than the original Populist program, as articulated in the Omaha platform of 1892. Numerous historians have followed Lloyd's lead in championing the 1892 vintage of Populism over the 1896 vintage (see Durden 1965, p. 2 n. 3). A notable recent example is Clanton 1991.

In a sense, both sides are right. In terms of idealism, intellectual clarity, and breadth of vision, the 1892 Populist platform eclipsed the 1896 Democratic platform on which Bryan ran. But Bryan's 1896 campaign generated far more attention and excitement, not to mention votes, than any earlier Populist effort. Clearly Bryan's 1896 campaign was the climax of something; perhaps we should call it the climax of "small-p" populism. Never before, and never since, had the battle between "hard-money" and "easy-money" (or "soft-money") interests been so central to a presidential election campaign.

BACKGROUND AND ORIGINS

The decades after the Civil War marked America's passage from a rural-agrarian society to an urban-industrial one. Consider a few aspects of the transformation from 1870 to 1920. Farming was far and away the top industry in America in 1870 (and remained number one in 1880), accounting for a larger share of the economy than any other sector. The population in 1870 was overwhelming rural, with people in rural areas outnumbering urban dwellers by nearly three to one. Nearly half of all American workers were farmers, and farmers outnumbered factory workers by more than five to one. The first transcontinental railroad had been in operation for just a year, and fewer than a million people lived in the Western states. But by 1890, the rapidly growing manufacturing sector had surpassed agriculture in terms of the value of its products. By 1900, factories produced *double* the value of output of the farms. By 1910, nearly as many people lived in urban areas as in rural areas; by 1920, the nation would be majority-urban and factory workers would outnumber farm workers.

While farming shrank in relation to the size of the economy in the late nineteenth century, farm settlement and production swelled rapidly. The number of farms tripled from two million in 1860 to six million in 1900, and new farm machinery produced ever-greater grain yields per acre. Those developments were mixed blessings for farmers, however. The Homestead Act of 1862, which opened up vast tracts of the West at bargain-basement prices, led to unprecedented Westward migration, aided by the expansion of the railroads, to the point where the Census Bureau officially noted the disappearance of the American frontier in 1890. Many of the new settlements were on arid lands not well suited for farming, yet the huge increase in the amount of farm acreage led to overproduction of many crops, which caused their prices to fall, both in absolute terms and (it appears) relative to the general price level.[4] The combination of frequent droughts and falling prices

---

4. Rockoff 1990, pp. 741–42; Walton and Rockoff 1998, p. 337 (based on price data in U.S. Department of Commerce 1975 and Friedman and Schwartz 1982). As noted in the previous chapter, it is not absolutely certain that farm prices fell further than other prices did, because conclusions about whether the farmers' terms of trade worsened or improved during the late nineteenth century appear sensitive to one's choice of price series, and those series themselves may be subject to substantial errors.

In fact, there is considerable disagreement among economic historians about the sources of Midwestern farm discontent in the later decades of the nineteenth century, and even about whether the farmers' economic status really did worsen during that span. A mid-1990s poll of economic historians found the field widely divided on three basic propositions about the causes of the farm protest movement. While majorities of the economists and historians surveyed agreed, with or without qualifications, that the farm protest movement was a reaction to the commercialization of agriculture and to movements in prices, and a majority of the historians also agreed that it was a reaction to the deteriorating economic status of farmers, sizable minorities of those surveyed disagreed with each of the propositions. Moreover, the economists surveyed were almost evenly split on whether the farmers' lot worsened during that time; 46 percent gave qualified or unqualified agreement to that proposition, while 54 percent disagreed (Whaples 1995, p. 142).

naturally put many Western farmers under great economic strain. Overproduction also became a major problem in the Cotton South, as many small farmers moved from self-sufficiency to producing cash crops for the market; cotton prices fell steeply, on account of expanded supplies both in the American South and elsewhere in the world. Farm tenancy rates grew substantially in the 1880s and 1890s, especially in the South, and by 1900 more than one in three farmers nationwide was either a sharecropper or a tenant farmer.[5]

Farmers had numerous other complaints as well. They alleged that "monopolists" in the railroad, finance, and grain-storage industries were gouging them with excessive freight charges, interest rates, and storage costs. Farmers had borrowed heavily to pay their mortgages buy new equipment, and many fell deeply into debt—the Western and Midwestern farmers typically to banks and the Southern farmers typically to country-store merchants, who often put liens (claims) on their next crops. The prevailing deflation (decline in the general price level) made those debts more burdensome, since the falling prices meant that the dollars the farmers paid back were worth more than the dollars they had borrowed. In many farmers' eyes, big business and Wall Street were their greatest enemies, and the government was a pawn of Eastern financial interests because it went along with the deflationary policies that those interests wanted. (The flip side of deflation's being bad for debtors—by raising their real, or inflation-adjusted, interest payments and the real value of their debts—is that deflation is good for creditors, because it raises their real interest income and the real value of their wealth.) Indeed, the long-term deflation of 1865–97 was in large part a matter of deliberate governmental policy, as explained in Chapter 2.

Many farmers looked for political and economic solutions to their plight. Among the first political organizations of farmers was the National Grange of the Patrons of Husbandry, a Great Lakes-based group formed in 1867. Originally founded as an educational society for farmers, the Grange soon developed into a militant crusade against railroads and middlemen, both of whom the farmers blamed for excessive spreads between the crop prices paid by consumers and what was actually received by the farmers. The Grange's membership swelled to 850,000 by 1875, as the 1870s depression induced many farmers to look for panaceas. The Grangers succeeded in getting several Midwestern states to regulate railroad rates, but an ill-fated attempt at cooperative manufacture of farm machinery saddled the Grange with such debts as to force its breakup soon thereafter.[6]

Several other farm orders sprang up in the late 1870s and 1880s, most notably the Farmers' Alliances. The Alliances emphasized cooperative buying and selling among farmers. Like the Grangers, their agenda became increasingly political: the Southern Alliance attacked the crop-lien system and the "money trusts," while the Northern Alliance echoed the Grangers' attacks on the railroads. Both the Northern and Southern Alliances pressed for sweeping changes to the monetary system, so as to make credit cheaper and more available. Naturally distrustful of banks, Alli-

---

5. Shannon 1945, p. 418, from Census data.
6. Shannon 1945, p. 331.

ance members believed that the then-current system under which banks could issue their own currency (state or national "banknotes") worked against them. Many of them advocated a more "elastic" currency similar to the greenbacks issued by the Union government during the Civil War—that is, a paper-money currency, not tied to gold or silver supplies, whose issue would be controlled by the government and which would be increased to accommodate the needs of farmers, small business-men, and other borrowers, and also as a growing economy created greater demand for cash. As mentioned in Chapter 2, such a system would be very similar to the fiat-money system we have today under the Federal Reserve, but in the nineteenth century it was a truly radical idea, much more so than William Jennings Bryan's "bimetallism" in 1896. Within the Alliances, fiat-money ideas crystallized in the "subtreasury plan" proposed by the Southern Alliance's C.W. Macune in 1889. The subtreasury plan called for a national governmental network of warehouses in every agricultural county, where farmers could store their crops at a nominal fee and borrow legal-tender paper money at low rates, using their stored crops as collateral. The plan became a rallying point for farm populists, who repeatedly claimed it would "emancipate productive labor from the power of money to op-press." It drew fire from conservative "sound-money" interests, who denounced it as inflationary and "hayseed socialism." By 1890, members in the Alliances and other farm orders numbered well over a million.

The subtreasury plan owed much to the Greenback Party, a third party that had already come and gone. Formed during the 1870s depression, the Greenback Party focused on permanently changing the monetary system, by replacing the gold-and-silver standard with a paper-money, or fiat-money, standard and letting the money supply expand with production. The Greenback Party elected some congressmen in 1876 and 1878 and ran candidates for president in 1880 and 1884, neither of whom was able to attract more than 5 percent of the popular vote, let alone any electoral votes. The party had already lost much of its steam when prices went up in the late 1870s and when "resumption" (the federal government's preannounced policy of redeeming greenbacks for gold and silver coins at face value) began in 1879. The party was effectively gone after 1884, though some Greenbackers remained through the end of the nineteenth century.

Many ex-Greenbackers would become Populists in the 1890s. The Populist, or People's, Party sprang from the successes of local third parties in a few states (Kansas, Nebraska, South Dakota) and from attempts to organize the Alliances and other discontented farmers into a political party. A convention of agrarian and working-class reformers in Cincinnati in May 1891 attracted over 1,400 partic-ipants from the Alliances and other associations, including some third parties. The outcome of the conference was the creation of the People's Party, with plans to nominate a candidate in the presidential election of 1892, and a party platform similar to earlier manifestoes issued by the Alliances. Southern farm populists had been reluctant to leave the Democratic Party and were noticeably underrepresented at the Cincinnati convention, but at key meetings of the Southern-based National Farmers' Alliance and Industrial Union (NFA&IU) in November 1891 and Feb-ruary 1892, the last hurdle was finally cleared for the People's Party to become a national party. To loud cheers, NFA&IU President Leonidas L. Polk declared:

"The time has arrived for the great West, the great South, and the great Northwest to link their hands and hearts together and march to the ballot box and take possession of the government, restore it to the principles of our fathers, and run it in the interest of the people."[7] A joint meeting-merger of representatives from the People's Party and the NFA&IU set the stage for the first-ever presidential nominating convention of the People's Party, to be held on July 4, 1892 in Omaha, Nebraska.

THE TUMULTUOUS DECADE OF THE 1890s

Even without the Populist movement, the 1890s would have gone down as a decade of drama and ferment: the much-noted "closing of the frontier"; the final military aggression against American Indians at Wounded Knee; a great wave of immigration, marked by the opening of Ellis Island in 1892; America's entry into the quest for overseas empire, culminating in the Spanish-American War of 1898 and the occupation of the Philippines; the 1893–97 depression, at the time the most severe economic contraction in American history; violent showdowns between capital and labor in the Pullman and Homestead strikes; the continued rise of big business; the 1893 World's Fair in Chicago, whose total attendance equaled half of the U.S. population and which seemed to symbolize America's passing from an agricultural to an industrial nation. In 1892, however, populism, of both the small-p and large-P forms, was the biggest story.

Although the nonfarm economy was in generally good shape (the depression of the 1890s would not begin until 1893), the discontent of working-class "tillers and toilers" was obvious and had already begun to influence national policy. Republican Senator John Sherman had prevailed on his colleagues to pass the Sherman Antitrust Act and the Sherman Silver Purchase Act of 1890, in order to head off more radical changes. Sherman told his fellow Senators that they must acknowledge popular demands for change "or be ready for the socialist, the communist, the nihilist. Society is now disturbed by forces never felt before."[8] A plant-wide strike at Carnegie Steel Works in Pittsburgh, perhaps deliberately provoked by management in order to crush union organizing efforts, had escalated into violence that resulted in the deaths of twenty strikers, the maiming of several Pinkerton guards, and the calling in of 7,000 state militiamen to protect the strike-breakers. Democrat and former President Grover Cleveland, in his rematch against Benjamin Harrison, condemned the "selfish and sordid" actions of Carnegie management and linked them to "unjust governmental favoritism" that the Republican tariff had provided to steel and other industries, at the expense of working

---

7. Quoted by Clanton 1991, p. 78.

8. Quoted by Zinn 1995, p. 254. Despite his association with the Silver Purchase Act, of which he denied authorship, Sherman was actually a staunch gold-bug and hard-money man. He was also commonly known as "Mr. Republican." He had been a force behind the Coinage Act of 1873, known to Populists as the "Crime of '73," and supported repeal of the Silver Purchase Act in 1893. See Stern 1964 for further details.

people who bore the cost of the tariff in the form of higher prices. Cleveland, himself a conservative, took a further populist tack by choosing Illinois silverite Adlai Stevenson as his running mate. The People's Party ran the most energetic campaign of all, denouncing government "of Wall Street, by Wall Street, and for Wall Street" and charging that "the corporation has been placed above the individual."

The Populists ran a ticket of James B. Weaver of Iowa, a former Union general who had been the Greenback-Labor Party nominee in 1880, and James G. Field of Virginia, a former Confederate general. Despite the vigor of their campaign, the People's Party of 1892 is best remembered for its convention platform, a revolutionary document that some Populists called a "second Declaration of Independence." The preamble served notice that this was no ordinary campaign platform: it declared that "the very existence of free institutions" was at stake, threatened by plutocrats who "despise the republic and endanger liberty."[9] The Omaha platform, as it was known, called for monetary reform, most notably the adoption of C.W. Macune's subtreasury plan (discussed in the previous section), which sought to establish a new fiat-money paper currency and provide farmers with a source of cheaper credit than they could have gotten from banks. The platform's monetary plank also called for the free and unlimited coinage of silver, at the fixed ratio of 16-to-1 (fixing the mint price of silver at one-sixteenth the price of gold, instead of its price being dictated by supply and demand). Thus the original Populist platform viewed fiat-money currency and free coinage of silver as natural complements, not substitutes; four years later, when Bryan ran for president on a free-silver platform, many Populist true believers would regard Bryan's vision of monetary reform as overly narrow and beholden to conventional wisdom that the U.S. monetary system had to have a gold or silver anchor. Elsewhere in the Omaha platform the Populists advocated land reform and governmental ownership of the railroads (and telegraphs), so as to protect farmers from exploitative rate charges. Additional resolutions, separate from the official platform, called for an end to corporate subsidies, a graduated income tax, an eight-hour day for governmental workers, immigration restriction, and an end to the Pinkerton system of corporate militias.

Weaver campaigned extensively, drawing large and enthusiastic crowds in the West and Midwest, but ultimately failed to shake the grip of the two-party system. The million-plus votes he drew were impressive by third-party standards, but amounted to less than 9 percent of total votes cast. He carried four states—the Populist stronghold of Kansas, plus the silver-mining states of Colorado, Idaho, and Nevada. His showing in the South was disappointing, although in hindsight the obstacles of Weaver's having been a Union general and the traditional attachment of white Southerners to the Democrats were perhaps too much to overcome. The Populists' main impact was probably to deliver the election to Grover Cleveland, by siphoning off votes in the Republican West and by stoking voter discontent with the Harrison administration. Of the Populist policy prescriptions, free coinage of

---

9. Reprinted in Boorstin 1985 [1966], pp. 535–37.

silver seemed to have the strongest appeal, and that appeal broke wide open the following year when President Cleveland got Congress to repeal the Sherman Silver Purchase Act and came out foursquare for the gold standard.

Cleveland's actions occurred largely in response to the Panic of 1893, a financial panic that struck the country soon after his inauguration and which he and many businessmen believed was brought on by apprehension over the Silver Purchase Act. But basic macroeconomic theory suggests that a contractionary monetary policy action like the act's repeal would tend to worsen a recession, and a major depression, lasting from 1893–97, did indeed accompany the act's repeal. Whether the depression owed more to the Silver Purchase Act or to its repeal is an open question, but to monetary populists there was no question at all: They were certain that the money supply needed more silver, not less. The deepening of the depression won numerous converts to the free-silver cause. The pro-silver American Bimetallic League, established in 1889, grew in membership and prominence, and silver clubs mushroomed around the country. An illustrated pamphlet titled *Coin's Financial School*, by William H. Harvey, made its debut in 1894 and quickly became the bible of the free-coinage movement. Seemingly ubiquitous, and available for sale in such venues as railroad trains and cigar stores, the short book sold anywhere from 650,000 to 1.5 million copies.[10]

The Democratic Party effectively split into pro- and anti-silver factions, with many Southern and Western Democrats leading the pro-silver charge and harshly criticizing Cleveland. On account of the depression, congressional Democrats lost big in the 1894 midterm elections, which also observed some fusion of Populists with both Democratic and Republican candidates and major Populist victories in North Carolina and Nebraska. The depression also prompted several marches on Washington by "industrial armies" of unemployed workers in 1894, most notably Coxey's Army, a group of about 500 men led by "General" Jacob S. Coxey, an Ohio businessman and Greenbacker. Coxey and his followers urged the government to spend money on public works projects and finance them with fiat money or interest-free bonds. Cleveland's refusal to meet with a delegation from Coxey's Army seemed to signify a president who was out of touch with working-class voters, a perception that was kindled by Cleveland's refusal to provide relief for the unemployed and his heavy-handed attempts to quash the Pullman Strike (by having his attorney general get an injunction and swear in 3,600 emergency deputies, then by sending in 2,000 federal troops) that same year.

As Cleveland's star fell, William Jennings Bryan's rose. In 1896 the 36-year-old Bryan was a former two-term U.S. congressman from Nebraska. He had been one of the key figures in the silver movement ever since his delivery of an eloquent and impassioned speech on the House floor in the summer of 1893, opposing repeal of the Silver Purchase Act. The speech earned Bryan such nicknames as Nebraska Cyclone, Knight of the West, and the Silver-Tongued Orator. After a failed Senate bid in 1894, he accepted the largely ceremonial job as editor of the pro-silver *Omaha World Herald*, for whom he wrote several editorials each week,

---

10. Hofstadter 1963, pp. 4–5.

usually about silver, and worked tirelessly to promote the free-silver cause and bring its adherents together. Still, Bryan was a relatively new figure in the Democratic Party, and prior to 1896 most people expected the Democrats to renominate Cleveland or some other senior party figure, very likely another gold-bug conservative, for president that year. With that in mind, leaders of the People's Party, including Weaver and U.S. Senators Marion Butler and William V. Allen, expected to have the increasingly popular free-silver issue all to themselves in 1896. They seized on free silver as the "common denominator" issue that could unite farmers, workers, and reformers and elect a Populist president.[11] In January 1896 a silver conference in Washington, D.C., led to the unification of the old silver associations under a new banner (the American Bimetallic Union) and to the formation of a political party, the American Silver Organization, which would hold its own presidential nominating convention that summer at the same time as the Populists. Few could have anticipated the extent to which the free-silver movement would take over the Democratic Party at the Democrats' nominating convention in Chicago in July.

By the late spring of 1896, however, it was evident from the results of state nominating conventions that the silverites had gained the upper hand in the Democratic Party and would select one of their own when the national convention met in July. The front-runner was Congressman Richard Parks Bland of Missouri, the author of the Bland-Allison Act of 1878 (see Chapter 2) and a towering figure in the free-silver movement. Bryan was ambitious but recognized that several other silver Democrats were ahead of him in the party hierarchy and that overt attempts at self-promotion might backfire. Instead, Bryan ran a stealth campaign for the Democratic nomination, quietly working on delegates to support his unannounced candidacy. Even on the eve of the convention, speculation centered on Bland or another senior silverite—perhaps even Colorado Republican Henry M. Teller, who had led a dramatic walkout of 22 pro-silver delegates from the previous month's Republican Convention, which adopted a platform plank backing the gold standard. What secured the nomination for Bryan was his electrifying speech on July 9, one of the most memorable political addresses of all time. (The speech appears in full in Appendix B.) In it, Bryan eloquently argued for free silver and, as the Populists had hoped to do themselves, turned it into (in Marion Butler's words) "the one overshadowing issue in the next great struggle between the classes and the masses." Bryan thundered:

---

11. Durden 1965, pp. 12–14. Populist and socialist Henry Demarest Lloyd's disparaging line about this strategy is often quoted: "Free silver is the cow-bird of the Reform movement." Lloyd charged that free silver had come to crowd out more fundamental issues, and that the free-coinage advocates had followed an opportunistic strategy similar to that of the predatory cow-bird: "It waited until the nest had been built by the sacrifices and labor of others, and then it laid its eggs in it, pushing out the others which lie smashed on the ground." Durden argues, by contrast, that "events rather than planning by any person or group forced the silver issue irresistibly to the front in the mid-1890s" (p. 6).

Having behind us the producing masses of this nation and the world, supported by the commercial interests and the toilers everywhere, we will answer their demand for a gold standard by saying to them: You shall not press down upon the brow of labor this crown of thorns. You shall not crucify mankind upon a cross of gold.

Bryan's "Cross of Gold" speech articulated an issue that has since become one of the great divides in American politics, and perhaps the greatest economic division between Republicans and Democrats today. Namely, should government policies toward the economy focus on encouraging the economic endeavors of the rich, the providers of much of the country's employment and savings, or on advancing the condition of the poor and working class, the people most in need of help? Bryan said:

There are two ideas of government. There are those who believe that, if you will only legislate to make the well-to-do prosperous, their prosperity will leak through on those below. The Democratic idea, however, has been that if you legislate to make the masses prosperous, their prosperity will find its way up through every class which rests upon them.

Succeeding generations of progressives have labeled these contrasting paths to prosperity "trickle-down" and "percolate-up" economics.[12]

Bryan's speech received a thunderous fifteen-minute ovation. Delegates stood on their chairs and waved hats, canes, umbrellas, or whatever they could find. Some took off their coats and threw them in the air. Even as steadfast a Republican as William Allen White, author of the scathing anti-Populist manifesto "What's the Matter with Kansas?", conceded decades later that the speech was moving and powerful: "It was the first time in my life and in the life of a generation in which any man large enough to lead a national party had boldly and unashamedly made his cause that of the poor and oppressed."[13] The Democrats went on to nominate Bryan on the fifth ballot and to choose as his running mate Arthur Sewall, a Maine shipbuilder and free-silver supporter. The "battle of the standards" was under way.

Bryan's nomination took the political world by storm. The People's Party and American Silver Organization held their conventions later that same month and quickly fell into line behind Bryan, believing that "fusion" with the pro-silver Democrats and their charismatic nominee offered their best chance for victory. A few discontented "middle-of-the-road" Populists (so named because of their commitment to Populism as a third-party movement that would take the most direct route possible to securing their goals) argued against fusion, but had to settle for replacing Sewall with Populist icon Thomas E. Watson, a former congressman from Georgia. Gold-bug Democrats had held their tongues during the convention, but a small group of them formed their own splinter party, the National Democratic Party, and nominated 79-year-old John M. Palmer, a conservative U.S. senator from Illinois.

The general-election campaign was a corker. Breaking with the tradition in

---

12. Clanton 1991, p. 158.
13. Glad 1964, pp. 136–37.

which candidates did little campaigning on their own behalf, Bryan crisscrossed the country, setting records for speeches given (including 36 in one day), miles traveled (18,000 by train), and people seen in a campaign (about five million). The less dynamic McKinley countered with a "front-porch campaign," which, with the aid of cut-rate railroad excursion fares, drew 750,000 visitors to his Ohio home. The McKinley campaign deployed almost 1,500 speakers around the country and flooded the country with some 275 million leaflets, pamphlets, and other pieces of literature, more than half again as many as the Republican National Committee had distributed in all previous elections.[14] Celluloid campaign buttons made a splashy debut, with over a thousand different designs. The myriad other campaign paraphernalia included "gold-bug" and "silver-bug" figurines, some with mechanical moving parts. McKinley supporters wore gold neckties and gold hatbands and rode on gold-trimmed bicycles. Editorial cartoons, which had been around for decades, truly came of age in the 1896 campaign, becoming a daily feature of many newspapers. Bryan, his Populist allies, and McKinley campaign manager Mark Hanna became regular fodder for newspaper cartoonists.

Few candidates in presidential history have ever stirred as much enthusiasm among their supporters as Bryan did in 1896, but ultimately Bryan could not overcome the many obstacles in his way. First, although Bryan's monetary stance represented a complete break from President Cleveland's, Bryan was still the candidate of the incumbent Democratic Party, and voters tend to punish the incumbent party for economic depressions. Also, the Republicans outspent the Democrats by almost 30-to-1, convincing swing voters (with the aid of the generally conservative press) that Bryan's free-coinage plan would cause a ruinous price inflation. Even blue-collar industrial workers gave most of their votes to McKinley, swayed by the plausible argument that their wages would not keep up with that inflation. Finally, many Democrats were themselves "sound-money men" and never even considered supporting Bryan. Although the gold-bug Democratic ticket headed by Palmer got less than 1 percent of the vote, its main purpose all along was to stop Bryan by helping to swing key Midwestern and border states to McKinley and conducting an "educational campaign" on the money issue.[15]

Republicans had touted McKinley as "the advance agent of prosperity," and the economic events of McKinley's inaugural year seemed to bear that out. New gold discoveries and the advent of the cyanide process of gold extraction brought about an end to monetary contraction, deflation, and depression. On the farms a decade-long drought finally came to an end, and a crop shortfall in Europe pumped up demand and prices for American produce. The free-silver cause lost its urgency, though Bryan and other hard-core silverites kept up the battle cry. McKinley's popularity got a further boost from the Spanish-American War of 1898, a "splendid little war" over the Spanish colony of Cuba, in which the United States emerged victorious after just four months. In the treaty that followed, Cuba gained its independence (albeit with American military occupation) and Spain ceded Puerto

14. Glad 1964, p. 170.
15. Jones 1964, p. 275.

Rico and Guam to the United States and allowed the United States to purchase the Philippines for $20 million. The war was wildly popular among the American public but it sparked an anti-imperialist movement that would provide Bryan with another issue for his anticipated rematch with McKinley in 1900. Anti-imperialist criticism of McKinley became more pointed as the administration moved to suppress an independence movement in the Philippines, a bloody counterrevolution that began in 1899 and would last three years, involving 70,000 American troops and taking thousands of American lives. In the 1900 election, Bryan ran a spirited but doomed campaign; the Democrats' favorite campaign icon was a three-leaf clover symbolizing the issues of antitrust, anti-gold, and anti-imperialism.

THE LEGACY OF POPULISM

Bryan's 1896 campaign did not win the election, but it did achieve two important and lasting goals: It pushed the Democratic Party sharply to the left on economic issues, and it co-opted most of the Populists within the reformed Democratic Party. Moreover, the Bryan campaigns of 1896 and 1900 were parts of a growing clamor for reform, and in the next decade and a half the two major parties began to listen. Although the visionary ideals of the Populists' 1892 Omaha platform were never put into practice, the political pendulum swung in a decidedly more liberal direction after the turn of the century. McKinley was assassinated by an anarchist six months after his inauguration, and Vice President Theodore Roosevelt became president. The 42-year-old Roosevelt became one of the country's most dynamic presidents and came to personify the Progressive Era, a burst of governmental activism that lasted through mid-decade after 1910. Borrowing much of the Populists' rhetoric, Roosevelt denounced the corporate "malefactors of great wealth," called John D. Rockefeller and his contemporaries "the biggest criminals in the country," and allied himself with the "little man."[16] Unlike Cleve-

---

16. Roosevelt's Populist-influenced rhetoric and reforms, however, are but one side of the man, who was surely one of America's most complex presidents. Roosevelt was emphatically not a Populist sympathizer, as he employed similarly inflated rhetoric *against* the Populists and their program. When President Cleveland sought repeal of the Sherman Silver Purchase Act in 1892, Roosevelt lauded him as "a bulwark against all financial heresies!"— a most unusual move for a politician of the opposing party. A few years later, at the height of the free-silver agitation, then-New York police commissioner Roosevelt said the Populist leaders were "plotting a social revolution and the subversion of the American Republic" and that he wished the government could "stand up the leaders of the silver movement against a brick wall and shoot them to death" (quoted in Clanton 1998, pp. 69, 204 n.22). Finally, President Roosevelt's military interventions in Latin America could hardly have been more at odds with the anti-imperialism of Bryan and the Populists. Small wonder, then, that Clanton calls Roosevelt "the most prominent anti-Populist of them all" (p. 15).

Historian Gabriel Kolko, in a classic revisionist account of the Progressive Era, has written that its reforms (and Roosevelt's in particular) were fundamentally conservative, "a means of preventing radical social change" (1963, p. 76). We should not rule out the possibility, however, that Roosevelt may have undergone a genuine conversion on the domestic

land and McKinley, he actively enforced the Sherman Antitrust Act, declaring himself a "trust buster" and launching numerous antitrust suits, including a successful one against Rockefeller's Standard Oil. Roosevelt's intervention in the anthracite coal strike of 1902 marked the first time that a president had taken labor's side in a major industrial dispute. The Populist goal of meaningful railroad rate regulation was finally achieved with congressional passage of the Elkins Act of 1903, the Hepburn Act of 1906, and the Mann-Elkins Act of 1910. The Progressive Era continued through the administrations of William Howard Taft and (the first term of) Woodrow Wilson, as others of the original Populist demands became law: a progressive income tax, an eight-hour day for governmental contractors, direct election of U.S. senators. Provisions for workers' compensation, child-labor regulations, and tougher antitrust protection (the Clayton Antitrust Act and the Federal Trade Commission Act in 1914) also became part of the legal landscape. The next economic crisis, the Panic of 1907, prompted Congress to create a National Monetary Commission and then the Federal Reserve System in 1913, providing a centralized monetary authority that could regulate the supply of money and credit and provide some measure of financial relief in hard times.

World War I effectively ended the Progressive Era, and the War's economically chaotic and diplomatically disappointing aftermath ushered in a decade of conservative Republican dominance. President Warren G. Harding proclaimed a return to "normalcy" in 1921, putting further progressive reforms on hold. Bryan spent his last decade in the political wilderness: he had resigned as Wilson's first secretary of state in 1915, in protest of Wilson's apparent willingness to let the United States become entangled in World War I (the United States would formally enter the war in 1917); and thereafter he became increasingly identified with Christian fundamentalism. Bryan tried unsuccessfully to get the Democrats to add a Prohibition plank to their 1920 platform and urged state legislatures to prohibit the teaching of evolution in public schools. Bryan's last appearance on the public stage was in the infamous Scopes trial, where he testified for the prosecution in a Tennessee case against a public school teacher who had violated a state ban on the teaching of evolution. The prosecution won its case, but Bryan exposed himself to ridicule, especially under cross-examination from defense lawyer Clarence Darrow, Bryan's onetime Populist ally. (Their exchange has been immortalized in the play *Inherit the Wind*.) Bryan died in his sleep five days after the trial.

Two more Populist prescriptions were finally adopted amid the crisis of the Great Depression of the 1930s. President Franklin D. Roosevelt, shortly after taking office in 1933, signed an executive order taking the United States off the gold standard, thereby ending the severe deflation that had accompanied the first four years of the Depression and removing the single biggest obstacle to a more activist monetary policy. After the 1930s the United States would never again experience

---

policy front, in the manner of anti-Populist writer William Allen White, who, like Roosevelt, became one of America's most prominent Progressives. Years later White said, "All we Progressives did was catch the Populists in swimming and steal all their clothing except the frayed underdrawers of Free Silver" (quoted by Johnson in Boorstin 1985 [1966], p. 610).

a major deflation. The two Agricultural Adjustment Acts of that decade, especially the second one, committed the government to maintaining "fair" prices for crops and alleviating farm distress. Like the Progressive Era reforms, Roosevelt's New Deal programs fell far short of the economic revolution that the original Populists had in mind, but they did serve to smooth many of the harsh edges of American capitalism, and they did borrow liberally from the Populist agenda.

In the century since the Populist movement faded away, the United States has become more democratic in the sense that women and African-Americans have won full voting rights, U.S. senators are now directly elected by the public, and the franchise has been extended to younger voters. On the surface, it would seem that government must have become more responsive to the people, since so many more people are eligible to vote. Yet voter turnout has fallen precipitously from its rate in 1896, and turnout rates are especially low among poor people. The complaints of numerous Americans today seem to echo those of the 1890s, as people say that politics has no connection with their lives because government is out of touch with the needs of ordinary people and is beholden to corporate lobbyists and other special interests. Likewise, many Americans criticize institutions such as the Federal Reserve, the International Monetary Fund, and the World Trade Organization as antidemocratic and overly oriented toward corporate and financial constituencies. A decreasing percentage of voters are registered as either Democrats or Republicans, third-party presidential candidates such as Ross Perot and Ralph Nader have been able to appeal to millions of voters' sense of disaffection, and third-party candidates won the governorships of Maine and Minnesota in 1998. Although the American system, with its winner-take-all presidential contests, seems to point inevitably to an arrangement in which two parties race each other to the political center, one cannot rule out the possibility that a third party might soon emerge to tap that vein of public discontent more successfully than Perot or Nader was able to manage, and direct mainstream American politics toward a new course.

L. Frank Baum in 1899, around the time he wrote *The Wonderful Wizard of Oz*. (Courtesy of Syracuse University Library, Department of Special Collections)

Tenth Lesson.

The popular free-silver pamphlet *Coin's Financial School* likened the 1890s depression to a cyclone (much like the cyclone that carried away Dorothy's house, perhaps). *Coin's* "lessons" feature several illustrations like this one.

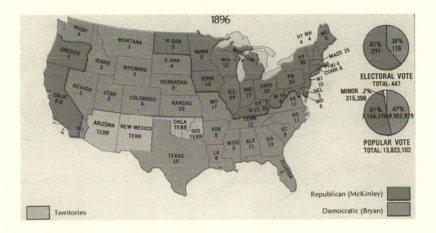

In Oz the wicked Witches are from the East and West, whereas the good Witches are from the North and South. Populists and Democrats may have held a similar view of U.S. geography after the 1896 election, since Republican William McKinley (bottom left) trounced William Jennings Bryan (bottom right) in the East and the coastal West, while Bryan carried the South and much of the North. (Photograph of Bryan courtesy of Illinois State Historical Library)

From bleeding Kansas's wind-swept plains,
Where whiskers take the place of brains,
You come with all your verbose strength
Of speeches of unending length.
Here, take the hint PUCK gives — resign !
Let Mary be your Valentine.

Just as the brainless Scarecrow turns out to be the cleverest member of Dorothy's party, Populists like Senator William Peffer of Kansas were often unfairly ridiculed as dumb-farmer types. The other figure in this 1896 cartoon from *Puck* is Kansas Populist Mary Elizabeth Lease ("Raise less corn and more hell"), who some have suggested was a real-life counterpart to Dorothy. (Courtesy of The Kansas State Historical Society, Topeka, Kansas)

VOL. 31 NO. 778   SEPTEMBER 12 1896   PRICE 10 CENTS

Judge

ENTERED AT THE POST OFFICE AT NEW YORK AS SECOND CLASS MATTER. COPYRIGHT 1896 BY THE JUDGE PUBLISHING CO. TITLE REGISTERED AS A TRADE MARK.

MAKING A MONKEY OF BRYAN.

Bryan and his free-silver platform had a disappointing showing among urban workingmen in 1896. Thus in Henry Littlefield's Populist interpretation of *Oz*, it is appropriate that the Lion (Bryan) "could make no impression" on the Tin Woodman (industrial laborer); as the Lion says, "he nearly blunted my claws." In the cartoon at left, Bryan begs for the vote of a skeptical laborer.

The People's, or Populist, Party was sometimes likened to a lion, as in this cartoon from the 1892 campaign in which the Populists nominated General James B. Weaver. In later campaigns Bryan and his roaring oratory drew comparisons to a lion, and his anti-imperialism was criticized by opponents as cowardly, making Bryan a logical counterpart to the Cowardly Lion. The scene in *Oz* in which the field mice pull the Lion out of the Deadly Poppy Field could symbolize the "little people" carrying Bryan to victory. (The image of General Weaver and the Lion is from an 1890s periodical and recently appeared in Scott G. McNall's *The Road to Rebellion* [Chicago: University of Chicago Press, 1998]. The "Free Silver" image is from an 1896 newspaper and recently appeared in *The Baum Bugle* [1992].)

of each mouse and the other end to the truck. Of course the truck was a thousand times bigger than any of the mice who were to draw it; but when all the mice had been harnessed they were able to pull it quite easily. Even the Scarecrow and the Tin Woodman could sit on it, and were drawn swiftly by their queer little horses to the place where the Lion lay asleep.

After a great deal of hard work, for the Lion was heavy, they managed to get him up on the truck. Then

the Queen hurriedly gave her people the order to start, for she feared if the mice stayed among the poppies too long they also would fall asleep.

At first the little creatures, many though they were, could hardly stir the heavily loaded truck; but the Woodman and the Scarecrow both pushed from behind, and they got along better. Soon they rolled the Lion out of the poppy bed to the green fields, where he could breathe the sweet, fresh air again, instead of the poisonous scent of the flowers.

The long beard of this soldier at the Palace of Oz, as originally drawn by W. W. Denslow, is reminiscent of the long beards that were customary of many Populists. William Peffer of Kansas was surely the best known in this regard. Another was Henry L. Loucks of South Dakota (below), of whom Baum wrote critically in his days as a newspaper editor in that state. In his lyrics and dialogue for the 1902 musical version of *Oz*, Baum endows the Guardian of the Gates of the Emerald City with a similar beard. Dorothy tells the Guardian that he should move to Kansas, where he would be elected governor within a year. (Photo of Henry L. Loucks Courtesy of South Dakota State Historical Society—State Archives)

The one-eyed wicked Witch of the West recalls the above cartoon from *Coin's Financial School*, deriding a "monometallic" (gold-only) monetary standard as clearly inferior to a gold-and-silver standard. One of the myriad interpretations of the Western Witch is as Republican kingmaker and industrialist Mark Hanna, who was McKinley's campaign manager in 1896.

Bryan and the Populists were sometimes lampooned as witches as well; historian Gene Clanton has suggested that the Western Witch actually represents the Populists. The figures in the first cartoon, originally captioned "Hell Broth," are South Carolina's "Pitchfork Ben" Tillman, Bryan (apparently), and Illinois's John Altgeld.

In political interpretations of *Oz*, the Winged Monkeys typically symbolize the Plains Indians on the basis of the monkey leader's line, "Once we were a free people, living happily in the great forest." Denslow's drawings of the Winged Monkeys also recall the racist depictions of Irish immigrants as monkeys in cartoons by *Puck's* Frederick Burr Opper and others in the nineteenth century.

PUCK'S GALLERY OF CELEBRITIES.

THE KING OF A-SHANTEE.

As the "humbug" politician who rules over Oz, the Wizard fittingly arrives and departs from Oz in a balloon powered by hot air. Bryan's florid oratory provoked his detractors to call him a windbag, as implied by the above cartoon. (Notably, the Wizard and Bryan hailed from the same state, Nebraska.) (The image of the Wizard in a hot-air balloon is from the Print Collection, Miriam and Ira D. Wallach Division of Art, Prints & Photographs, The New York Public Library, Astor, Lenox and Tilden Foundations.)

A PARTY OF PATCHES.
Grand Balloon Ascension—Cincinnati, May 20th, 1891.

Hot-air-balloon metaphors were common in 1890s political cartoons, as in this one of William Peffer, Jerry Simpson, and other Populists. The patchy balloon they ride recalls the "big bag of green silk" strips in which the Wizard makes his flawed farewell from Oz. (Courtesy of The Kansas State Historical Society, Topeka, Kansas)

Chapter 4

L. Frank Baum's
The Wonderful Wizard of Oz,
with Annotations

INTRODUCTION.

Folk lore, legends, myths and fairy tales have followed childhood through the ages, for every healthy youngster has a wholesome and instinctive love for stories fantastic, marvelous and manifestly unreal. The winged fairies of Grimm and Andersen have brought more happiness to childish hearts than all other human creations.

Yet the old-time fairy tale, having served for generations, may now be classed as "historical" in the children's library; for the time has come for a series of newer "wonder tales" in which the stereotyped genie, dwarf and fairy are eliminated, together with all the horrible and blood-curdling incident devised by their authors to point a fearsome moral to each tale. Modern education includes morality; therefore the modern child seeks only entertainment in its wonder-tales and gladly dispenses with all disagreeable incident.

Having this thought in mind, the story of "The Wonderful Wizard of Oz" was written solely to pleasure children of today. It aspires to being a modernized fairy tale, in which the wonderment and joy are retained and the heart-aches and nightmares are left out.

L. FRANK BAUM.

CHICAGO, APRIL, 1900 .[1]

---

1. L. Frank Baum's statement that the book "was written solely to pleasure children of today" seems almost to anticipate the barrage of Populist and other interpretations of *The Wonderful Wizard of Oz*. Indeed, this statement is often quoted by critics of allegorical interpretations of the book.

By providing such an odd disclaimer, Baum just might have been slyly dropping a hint that he was going to *disguise* any message or symbolism, rather than overtly imparting a "fearsome moral" in his story, since "the modern child seeks only entertainment in its wonder tales and gladly dispenses with all disagreeable incident." In the foreword to *American Fairy Tales* (1901) Baum seems to have been more candid: The stories, he said, "are not serious in purpose, but aim to amuse and entertain, yet I trust the more thoughtful readers will find a wholesome lesson hidden beneath such extravagant notion and humorous incident." Michael Patrick Hearn (1973, p. 39) observes, "He could have been thinking of *The Wizard of Oz* as well." Russel Nye concurs: "Whatever Baum's original disclaimer, the strain of moralism is strong in the Oz books. They are not simply pure entertainment, devoid of any lesson, for as Baum once admitted, he tried to hide 'a wholesome lesson' behind the doings of his characters . . . You have within you, Baum seems to say, the things you seek." Nye also points out that Baum once said he wanted his stories to "bear the stamp of our times and depict the progressive fairies of today" (in Gardner and Nye 1957, pp. 1, 5).

LIST OF CHAPTERS.

———

Chapter I.
The Cyclone.

Dorothy lived in the midst of the great Kansas prairies, with Uncle Henry, who was a farmer, and Aunt Em, who was the farmer's wife.[2] Their house was small, for the lumber to build it had to be carried by wagon many miles. There were four walls, a floor and a roof, which made one room; and this room contained a rusty looking cookstove, a cupboard for the dishes, a table, three or four chairs, and the beds. Uncle Henry and Aunt Em had a big bed in one corner, and Dorothy a little bed in another corner. There was no garret at all, and no cellar—except a small hole dug in the ground, called a cyclone cellar, where the family could go in case one of those great whirlwinds arose, mighty enough to crush any building in its path. It was reached by a trap-door in the middle of the floor, from which a ladder led down into the small, dark hole.

When Dorothy stood in the doorway and looked around, she could see nothing but the great gray prairie on every side. Not a tree nor a house broke the broad sweep of flat country that reached to the edge of the sky in all directions. The sun had baked the plowed land into a gray mass, with little cracks running through it. Even the grass was not green, for the sun had burned the tops of the long blades until they were the same gray color to be seen everywhere. Once the house had been painted, but the sun blistered the paint and the rains washed it away, and now the house was as dull and gray as everything else.

When Aunt Em came there to live she was a young, pretty wife. The sun and wind had changed her, too. They had taken the sparkle from her eyes and left them a sober gray; they had taken the red from her cheeks and lips, and they were gray also. She was thin and gaunt, and never smiled now. When Dorothy, who was an orphan, first came to her, Aunt Em had been so startled by the child's laughter that she would scream and press her hand upon her heart whenever Dorothy's merry voice reached her ears; and she still looked at the little girl with wonder that she could find anything to laugh at.

Uncle Henry never laughed. He worked hard from morning till night and did not know what joy was. He was gray also, from his long beard to his rough boots, and he looked stern and solemn, and rarely spoke.[3]

---

2. Dorothy, in most allegorical readings of the story, symbolizes the American people at their best—"honest, kindhearted, and plucky" (Rockoff 1990, p. 745). To Henry Littlefield, "Dorothy is Baum's Miss Everyman. She is one of us, levelheaded and human" (1964, p. 52).

3. The unrelentingly grim description of Dorothy's Kansas surroundings and her Aunt Em and Uncle Henry, sad people who have been beaten down by the hard life of farming on the drought-stricken prairie, contrasts sharply with the idyllic depiction of farm life at the beginning of the 1939 movie version. The description likely draws on Baum's own unsuccessful experience as a newspaper editor and merchant in Aberdeen, South Dakota, in 1888–91. In fact, during that time Baum wrote editorials lamenting the plight of the Midwestern farmer (though he was often critical of South Dakota's emerging farm-populist political party). Baum's sympathy for the struggling farmers is also evident in one of the

It was Toto that made Dorothy laugh, and saved her from growing as gray as her other surroundings. Toto was not gray; he was a little black dog, with long, silky hair and small black eyes that twinkled merrily on either side of his funny, wee nose. Toto played all day long, and Dorothy played with him, and loved him dearly.[4]

To-day, however, they were not playing. Uncle Henry sat upon the door-step and looked anxiously at the sky, which was even grayer than usual. Dorothy stood in the door with Toto in her arms, and looked at the sky too. Aunt Em was washing the dishes.

From the far north they heard a low wail of the wind, and Uncle Henry and Dorothy could see where the long grass bowed in waves before the coming storm. There now came a sharp whistling in the air from the south, and as they turned their

---

later Oz books, *The Emerald City of Oz* (1910), in which Uncle Henry loses his farm.

Why Kansas? Baum's niece Matilda told a biographer that in the 1890s Kansas was simply known "as the place where cyclones came from" (Hearn 1989). But Kansas was known for more than just cyclones. It was also the quintessential struggling farm state at the time. In Kansas, the factors in the Populist revolt "were always the most extreme" (Hicks 1931, p. 24). The agricultural slump that began in 1887 was so severe in that state that fully half the people of Western Kansas moved out between 1888 and 1892, many of them in covered wagons bearing legends like "In God we trusted, in Kansas we busted" (Hicks, p. 32). Kansas's Senator William A. Peffer and one of Kansas's Representatives, "Sockless" Jerry Simpson, were leaders in the Populist crusade, as were such Kansans as Mary Elizabeth Lease, Annie Diggs, and Sarah Emery. In addition, the farmers of Kansas were singled out for harsh criticism in an anti-Populist editorial by Kansas writer William Allen White in 1896, titled "What's the Matter with Kansas?", a piece that still stands as a remarkable example of blame-the-victim ideology. White's attack on the Populists was so cutting that Mark Hanna, the Republican National Committee Chairman and William McKinley's campaign manager, saw fit to circulate it across the nation in order to discredit Democrat-Populist nominee William Jennings Bryan (Johnson 1966, p. 610). Baum likely read it, as one of the newspapers that reprinted it was the *Chicago Evening Post*, for which he once worked as a reporter. (Baum may also have read White's more sympathetic, yet bleak, *The Real Issue: A Book of Kansas Stories*, also published in 1896.) In fact, Baum and White were apparently acquainted: The two shared the same publisher in Chicago (Way & Williams) and could have met at the home of Chauncey L. Williams or at the Chicago Press Club. White claimed in 1939 that he and Baum had talked about Kansas and that their discussions had inspired Baum's choice of Kansas as Dorothy's home state (Koupal 2001, p. 155 n.6).

Thus in any Populist interpretation of the book, Kansas is an appropriate starting point. Furthermore, Kansas City, Missouri, was to be the site of the 1900 Democratic National Convention, which renominated Bryan. "In 1900, going 'from Kansas to Fairyland' (an early title) meant following the campaign trail from Kansas City to Washington, D.C." (Rockoff 1990, p. 745).

4. The name "Toto" could be a play on "teetotalers," as the Prohibitionists were the Populists' longtime political allies (Jensen 1971, p. 283 n.22). One notable Populist-Prohibitionist was Annie Diggs, whom Brian Attebery saw as a possible inspiration for Dorothy (1980, p. 87). William Jennings Bryan was also a teetotaler (and would emerge as a staunch advocate of Prohibition in the decade after 1910).

eyes that way they saw ripples in the grass coming from that direction also.

Suddenly Uncle Henry stood up.

"There's a cyclone coming, Em," he called to his wife. "I'll go look after the stock." Then he ran toward the sheds where the cows and horses were kept.

Aunt Em dropped her work and came to the door. One glance told her of the danger close at hand.

"Quick, Dorothy!" she screamed. "Run for the cellar!"

Toto jumped out of Dorothy's arms and hid under the bed, and the girl started to get him. Aunt Em, badly frightened, threw open the trap-door in the floor and climbed down the ladder into the small, dark hole. Dorothy caught Toto at last and started to follow her aunt. When she was halfway across the room there came a great shriek from the wind, and the house shook so hard that she lost her footing and sat down suddenly upon the floor.

Then a strange thing happened.

The house whirled around two or three times and rose slowly through the air. Dorothy felt as if she were going up in a balloon.

The north and south winds met where the house stood, and made it the exact center of the cyclone.[5] In the middle of a cyclone the air is generally still, but the

---

5. The cyclone could represent the free-silver movement itself, which truly took the political world by storm in the 1890s (Rockoff 1990, p. 745). Indeed, the free-silver movement was often referred to as a political cyclone in the 1890s. The front-page headline in the New York *World* the day after McKinley's defeat of Bryan turned that metaphor on its head, proclaiming, "Sound-Money Cyclone Sweeps the Country" (November 4, 1896).

According to another abstract interpretation, the cyclone is the economic depression of 1893–97, which also shook the political world (Clanton 1998, p. 185 n.8). The popular pro-silver tract *Coin's Financial School* called the panic of the 1890s a "financial storm" and illustrated that point with several cartoons of cyclones upending people and houses (Harvey 1894, pp. 56–63). The depression toppled incumbent President Grover Cleveland (the Eastern Witch, in one version of the allegory) and split the Democratic Party into pro-silver and anti-silver factions.

The cyclone also recalls the great Populist orator Mary Elizabeth Lease, whom the press sometimes described as the "Kansas Cyclone." Lease is best known for saying that the farmers should "raise more hell and less corn." Brian Attebery (1980, pp. 86–87) identified the spirited Dorothy with Lease, as did Leslie J. Kelsay (1987). Beginning with the 1902 stage adaptation of *Wizard* and continuing through later Oz books and the 1939 movie version, Dorothy was given a last name, Gale, which also fits with the notion of Dorothy as the Kansas Cyclone. (The surname apparently alludes to the cyclone that whisks her into Oz and also to Dorothy Gage, Baum's niece, who died as an infant not long before the book's completion and who almost surely inspired the name of its heroine [Wagner 1984, p. 6].)

And yet, the fiery, often scabrous Lease bore little resemblance to the gentle Dorothy. Moreover, the racist, anti-immigrant views that Lease advanced in her infamous 1895 publication *The Problem of Civilization Solved* alienated numerous Populists and progressives. While Baum was apparently neither a Populist nor a racial progressive (as was evident from the anti-Indian editorials he wrote while in South Dakota), his stories generally do convey a "theme of tolerance" and contain "many episodes that poke fun and narrow nationalism and ethnocentrism" (Gardner and Nye 1957, p. 30). All things considered, if Lease has a fitting counterpart in the first Oz book, it is not Dorothy.

great pressure of the wind on every side of the house raised it up higher and higher, until it was at the very top of the cyclone; and there it remained and was carried miles and miles away as easily as you could carry a feather.

It was very dark, and the wind howled horribly around her, but Dorothy found she was riding quite easily. After the first few whirls around, and one other time when the house tipped badly, she felt as if she were being rocked gently, like a baby in a cradle.

Toto did not like it. He ran about the room, now here, now there, barking loudly; but Dorothy sat quite still on the floor and waited to see what would happen.

Once Toto got too near the open trap-door, and fell in; and at first the little girl thought she had lost him. But soon she saw one of his ears sticking up through the hole, for the strong pressure of the air was keeping him up so that he could not fall. She crept to the hole, caught Toto by the ear, and dragged him into the room again, afterward closing the trap-door so that no more accidents could happen.

Hour after hour passed away, and slowly Dorothy got over her fright; but she felt quite lonely, and the wind shrieked so loudly all about her that she nearly became deaf. At first she had wondered if she would be dashed to pieces when the house fell again; but as the hours passed and nothing terrible happened, she stopped worrying and resolved to wait calmly and see what the future would bring. At last she crawled over the swaying floor to her bed, and lay down upon it; and Toto followed and lay down beside her.

In spite of the swaying of the house and the wailing of the wind, Dorothy soon closed her eyes and fell fast asleep.

Chapter II.
The Council with The Munchkins.

She was awakened by a shock, so sudden and severe that if Dorothy had not been lying on the soft bed she might have been hurt. As it was, the jar made her catch her breath and wonder what had happened; and Toto put his cold little nose into her face and whined dismally. Dorothy sat up and noticed that the house was not moving; nor was it dark, for the bright sunshine came in at the window, flooding the little room. She sprang from her bed and with Toto at her heels ran and opened the door.

The little girl gave a cry of amazement and looked about her, her eyes growing bigger and bigger at the wonderful sights she saw.

The cyclone had set the house down, very gently—for a cyclone—in the midst of a country of marvelous beauty. There were lovely patches of green sward all about, with stately trees bearing rich and luscious fruits. Banks of gorgeous flowers were on every hand, and birds with rare and brilliant plumage sang and fluttered in the trees and bushes. A little way off was a small brook, rushing and sparkling along between green banks, and murmuring in a voice very grateful to a little girl who had lived so long on the dry, gray prairies.

While she stood looking eagerly at the strange and beautiful sights, she noticed coming toward her a group of the queerest people she had ever seen. They were not as big as the grown folk she had always been used to; but neither were they very small. In fact, they seemed about as tall as Dorothy, who was a well-grown child for her age, although they were, so far as looks go, many years older.

Three were men and one a woman, and all were oddly dressed. They wore round hats that rose to a small point a foot above their heads, with little bells around the brims that tinkled sweetly as they moved. The hats of the men were blue; the little woman's hat was white, and she wore a white gown that hung in pleats from her shoulders; over it were sprinkled little stars that glistened in the sun like diamonds. The men were dressed in blue, of the same shade as their hats, and wore well polished boots with a deep roll of blue at the tops. The men, Dorothy thought, were about as old as Uncle Henry, for two of them had beards. But the little woman was doubtless much older: her face was covered with wrinkles, her hair was nearly white, and she walked rather stiffly.

When these people drew near the house where Dorothy was standing in the doorway, they paused and whispered among themselves, as if afraid to come farther. But the little old woman walked up to Dorothy, made a low bow and said, in a sweet voice,

"You are welcome, most noble Sorceress, to the land of the Munchkins. We are so grateful to you for having killed the wicked Witch of the East, and for setting our people free from bondage."

Dorothy listened to this speech with wonder. What could the little woman possibly mean by calling her a sorceress, and saying she had killed the wicked Witch of the East? Dorothy was an innocent, harmless little girl, who had been carried by a cyclone many miles from home; and she had never killed anything in all her life.

But the little woman evidently expected her to answer; so Dorothy said, with hesitation,

"You are very kind; but there must be some mistake. I have not killed anything."

"Your house did, anyway," replied the little old woman, with a laugh; "and that is the same thing. See!" she continued, pointing to the corner of the house; "there are her two toes, still sticking out from under a block of wood."

Dorothy looked, and gave a little cry of fright. There, indeed, just under the corner of the great beam the house rested on, two feet were sticking out, shod in silver shoes with pointed toes.[6]

"Oh, dear! Oh, dear!" cried Dorothy, clasping her hands together in dismay; "the house must have fallen on her. What ever shall we do?"

"There is nothing to be done," said the little woman, calmly.

"But who was she?" asked Dorothy.

---

6. In any monetary-populist interpretation of this book, the silver shoes are key. The silver shoes give Dorothy her special powers in the Land of Oz, just as Bryan and the Populists believed silver had remarkable, almost magical, powers as part of a *bimetallic* monetary standard, in which both gold and silver would be the basis of the money supply.

"She was the wicked Witch of the East, as I said," answered the little woman.[7] "She has held all the Munchkins in bondage for many years, making them slave for her night and day. Now they are all set free, and are grateful to you for the favor."[8]

"Who are the Munchkins?" enquired Dorothy.

"They are the people who live in this land of the East, where the wicked Witch ruled."

"Are you a Munchkin?" asked Dorothy.

"No; but I am their friend, although I live in the land of the North. When they saw the Witch of the East was dead the Munchkins sent a swift messenger to me, and I came at once. I am the Witch of the North."

"Oh, gracious!" cried Dorothy; "are you a real witch?"

"Yes, indeed;" answered the little woman. "But I am a good witch, and the people love me. I am not as powerful as the wicked Witch was who ruled here, or I should have set the people free myself."

"But I thought all witches were wicked," said the girl, who was half frightened at facing a real witch.

"Oh, no, that is a great mistake. There were only four witches in all the Land of Oz, and two of them, those who live in the North and the South, are good witches. I know this is true, for I am one of them myself, and cannot be mistaken. Those who dwelt in the East and the West were, indeed, wicked witches; but now that you have killed one of them, there is but one wicked Witch in all the Land of Oz—the one who lives in the West."

"But," said Dorothy, after a moment's thought, "Aunt Em has told me that the witches were all dead—years and years ago."

"Who is Aunt Em?" inquired the little old woman.

"She is my aunt who lives in Kansas, where I came from."

---

7. The wicked Witch of the East could symbolize Eastern financial and industrial interests, most notably Wall Street (Littlefield 1964, p. 52). The Eastern banking establishment had long been a bogeyman of the farming and working classes, so this interpretation is straightforward enough.

Another interpretation of the wicked Witches is as the two pro-gold-standard presidents of the mid-1890s. The wicked Witch of the East is Grover Cleveland, of New York; the wicked Witch of the West is William McKinley, of Ohio. It is then appropriate that Dorothy acquires the silver shoes after her house lands on the wicked Witch of the East, since President Cleveland's political career was ended by the mid-1890s economic depression, which many Populists blamed on Cleveland's repeal of the Sherman Silver Purchase Act (1890) in 1893 (Rockoff 1990, pp. 746, 751). In 1896, the Democratic Party, split by the silver issue, declined to renominate Cleveland for president, instead nominating Bryan, the country's most prominent free-silver advocate.

8. "She has held all the Munchkins in bondage for many years, making them slave for her night and day": The enslavement of the Munchkins (the common people of the East) is of a piece with the Tin Woodman's mistreatment at the hands of the wicked Witch of the East, of which we learn in Chapter V and which could represent the exploitative, dehumanizing nature of urban industrial work in the Gilded Age (Littlefield 1964, pp. 51–52). The use of the word "slave" in this context recalls the phrase "wage slavery," a common radical-populist term for the industrial labor system at that time.

The Witch of the North seemed to think for a time, with her head bowed and her eyes upon the ground. Then she looked up and said,

"I do not know where Kansas is, for I have never heard that country mentioned before. But tell me, is it a civilized country?"

"Oh, yes," replied Dorothy.

"Then that accounts for it. In the civilized countries I believe there are no witches left; nor wizards, nor sorceresses, nor magicians. But, you see, the Land of Oz has never been civilized, for we are cut off from all the rest of the world. Therefore we still have witches and wizards amongst us."

"Who are the Wizards?" asked Dorothy.

"Oz himself is the Great Wizard," answered the Witch, sinking her voice to a whisper. "He is more powerful than all the rest of us together. He lives in the City of Emeralds."

Dorothy was going to ask another question, but just then the Munchkins, who had been standing silently by, gave a loud shout and pointed to the corner of the house where the Wicked Witch had been lying.

"What is it?" asked the little old woman; and looked, and began to laugh. The feet of the dead Witch had disappeared entirely, and nothing was left but the silver shoes.

"She was so old," explained the Witch of the North, "that she dried up quickly in the sun. That is the end of her. But the silver shoes are yours, and you shall have them to wear." She reached down and picked up the shoes, and after shaking the dust out of them handed them to Dorothy.

"The Witch of the East was proud of those silver shoes," said one of the Munchkins; "and there is some charm connected with them; but what it is we never knew."[9]

Dorothy carried the shoes into the house and placed them on the table. Then she came out again to the Munchkins and said,

"I am anxious to get back to my aunt and uncle, for I am sure they will worry about me. Can you help me find my way?"

The Munchkins and the Witch first looked at one another, and then at Dorothy, and then shook their heads.

"At the East, not far from here," said one, "there is a great desert, and none could live to cross it."

"It is the same at the South," said another, "for I have been there and seen it. The South is the country of the Quadlings."

---

9. The silver shoes have powers, which the Eastern Witch understood but which the Munchkins do not. In a Populist interpretation of the wicked Witch of the East, this distinction is important. Eastern financial and industrial interests gained from deflationary tight-money policies and hence had a vested interest, which they well understood, in suppressing inflationary free-silver legislation. Likewise, President Cleveland, whose political career was a casualty of the silver issue, would surely have understood its power as well. The signficance of the silver issue, however, eluded the citizens of the East (Munchkins), who voted overwhelmingly against Bryan in the 1896 election.

"I am told," said the third man, "that it is the same at the West. And that country, where the Winkies live, is ruled by the wicked Witch of the West, who would make you her slave if you passed her way."

"The North is my home," said the old lady, "and at its edge is the same great desert that surrounds this Land of Oz. I'm afraid, my dear, you will have to live with us."

Dorothy began to sob at this, for she felt lonely among all these strange people. Her tears seemed to grieve the kind-hearted Munchkins, for they immediately took out their handkerchiefs and began to weep also. As for the little old woman, she took off her cap and balanced the point on the end of her nose, while she counted "one, two, three" in a solemn voice. At once the cap changed to a slate, on which was written in big, white chalk marks:

"LET DOROTHY GO TO THE CITY OF EMERALDS."

The little old woman took the slate from her nose, and having read the words on it, asked,

"Is your name Dorothy, my dear?"

"Yes," answered the child, looking up and drying her tears.

"Then you must go to the City of Emeralds. Perhaps Oz will help you."

"Where is this city?" asked Dorothy.

"It is exactly in the center of the country, and is ruled by Oz, the Great Wizard I told you of."

"Is he a good man?" enquired the girl, anxiously.

"He is a good Wizard. Whether he is a man or not I cannot tell, for I have never seen him."

"How can I get there?" asked Dorothy.

"You must walk. It is a long journey, through a country that is sometimes pleasant and sometimes dark and terrible. However, I will use all the magic arts I know of to keep you from harm."

"Won't you go with me?" pleaded the girl, who had begun to look upon the little old woman as her only friend.

"No, I cannot do that," she replied; "but I will give you my kiss, and no one will dare injure a person who has been kissed by the Witch of the North."[10]

She came close to Dorothy and kissed her gently on the forehead. Where her

---

10. The good Witch of the North could represent the Northern electorate of middle America and the Witch's kiss their electoral support (Jensen 1971, p. 282). This geographical interpretation is appealing, since the electoral-vote breakdown of the 1896 presidential contest shows a stunning geographical split, with Bryan winning many of the Northern states (at least west of the Mississippi River) and nearly all of the Southern states but being virtually shut out in the East and on the West Coast. Hence the good Witches of the North and South and the wicked Witches of the East and West.

Attempts to identify the Northern Witch with any specific person are more elusive. As Sigmund Freud might have put it, sometimes a witch is just a witch. If one must find a real-life counterpart to the Northern Witch, a possibility is Arthur Sewall, the Maine businessman and banker who was Bryan's running mate in 1896 (Rockoff 1990, p. 746n).

lips touched the girl they left a round, shining mark, as Dorothy found out soon after.

"The road to the City of Emeralds is paved with yellow brick,"[11] said the Witch; "so you cannot miss it. When you get to Oz do not be afraid of him, but tell your story and ask him to help you. Good-bye, my dear."

The three Munchkins bowed low to her and wished her a pleasant journey, after which they walked away through the trees. The Witch gave Dorothy a friendly little nod, whirled around on her left heel three times, and straightway disappeared, much to the surprise of little Toto, who barked after her loudly enough when she had gone, because he had been afraid even to growl while she stood by.

But Dorothy, knowing her to be a witch, had expected her to disappear in just that way, and was not surprised in the least.

Chapter III.
How Dorothy Saved the Scarecrow.

When Dorothy was left alone she began to feel hungry. So she went to the cupboard and cut herself some bread, which she spread with butter. She gave some to Toto, and taking a pail from the shelf she carried it down to the little brook and filled it with clear, sparkling water. Toto ran over to the trees and began to bark at the birds sitting there. Dorothy went to get him, and saw such delicious fruit hanging from the branches that she gathered some of it, finding it just what she wanted to help out her breakfast.

Then she went back to the house, and having helped herself and Toto to a good drink of the cool, clear water, she set about making ready for the journey to the City of Emeralds.

Dorothy had only one other dress, but that happened to be clean and was hanging on a peg beside her bed. It was gingham, with checks of white and blue; and although the blue was somewhat faded with many washings, it was still a pretty frock. The girl washed herself carefully, dressed herself in the clean gingham, and tied her pink sunbonnet on her head. She took a little basket and filled it

---

11. The yellow brick road appears symbolic of the gold standard. It is therefore fitting that to get to the Emerald City, the political center of Oz, one must take the yellow brick road, just as the gold standard held political sway in Washington in the late nineteenth century. Most prominently, in the great "battle of the standards" in 1896, McKinley championed the gold standard and won a decisive victory over Bryan.

The duality of yellow bricks and yellow gold might well have crossed Baum's mind. In John Bunyan's *The Pilgrim's Progress*, which was a likely inspiration for the general plot and several specific aspects of *Wizard*, the streets of heaven are literally paved with gold. Moreover, the last story in Baum's earlier book, *Mother Goose in Prose* (1897)—the same story, incidentally, that introduces a gentle little farm girl named Dorothy—describes a castle made of gold and silver bricks (p. 261). Also, Baum's short story "The Wonderful Pump" (in *American Fairy Tales* 1901, p. 152) and the second Oz book (1904, p. 66) contain explicit references to yellow gold.

with bread from the cupboard, laying a white cloth over the top. Then she looked down at her feet and noticed how old and worn her shoes were.

"They surely will never do for a long journey, Toto," she said. And Toto looked up into her face with his little black eyes and wagged his tail to show he knew what she meant.

At that moment Dorothy saw lying on the table the silver shoes that had belonged to the Witch of the East.

"I wonder if they will fit me," she said to Toto. "They would be just the thing to take a long walk in, for they could not wear out."

She took off her old leather shoes and tried on the silver ones, which fitted her as well as if they had been made for her.

Finally she picked up her basket.

"Come along, Toto," she said. "We will go to the Emerald City and ask the great Oz how to get back to Kansas again."

She closed the door, locked it, and put the key carefully in the pocket of her dress. And so, with Toto trotting along soberly behind her, she started on her journey.[12]

There were several roads near by, but it did not take her long to find the one paved with yellow bricks. Within a short time she was walking briskly toward the Emerald City, her silver shoes tinkling merrily on the hard, yellow roadbed.[13] The sun shone bright and the birds sang sweet and Dorothy did not feel nearly as bad as you might think a little girl would who had been suddenly whisked away from her own country and set down in the midst of a strange land.

She was surprised, as she walked along, to see how pretty the country was about her. There were neat fences at the sides of the road, painted a dainty blue color, and beyond them were fields of grain and vegetables in abundance. Evidently the Munchkins were good farmers and able to raise large crops. Once in a while she would pass a house, and the people came out to look at her and bow low as she went by; for everyone knew she had been the means of destroying the wicked witch and setting them free from bondage. The houses of the Munchkins were odd looking dwellings, for each was round, with a big dome for a roof. All were painted blue, for in this country of the East blue was the favorite color.

Toward evening, when Dorothy was tired with her long walk and began to wonder where she should pass the night, she came to a house rather larger than the

---

12. If Toto is symbolic of the Prohibitionists, then his trotting "soberly" behind Dorothy is an appropriate pun.

13. Dorothy's brisk pace, with "her silver shoes tinkling merrily along on the hard, yellow [gold?] roadbed," evokes an idealized view of a bimetallic monetary standard. (See Littlefield 1964, p. 53, and Rockoff 1990, p. 746). The free-silver crusaders repeatedly emphasized that they wanted not merely to replace a gold standard with a silver standard, but to use both. They maintained that the money supply would be larger and more stable with a bimetallic standard than with either a gold standard or a silver standard (Rockoff 1990, p. 754). Earlier in the nineteenth century, for example, when the United States was on a bimetallic standard, a scarcity of silver did not cause a scarcity of money, because people simply used gold instead.

rest. On the green lawn before it many men and women were dancing. Five little fiddlers played as loudly as possible and the people were laughing and singing, while a big table near by was loaded with delicious fruits and nuts, pies and cakes, and many other good things to eat.

The people greeted Dorothy kindly, and invited her to supper and to pass the night with them; for this was the home of one of the richest Munchkins in the land, and his friends were gathered with him to celebrate their freedom from the bondage of the wicked witch.

Dorothy ate a hearty supper and was waited upon by the rich Munchkin himself, whose name was Boq. Then she sat upon a settee and watched the people dance.

When Boq saw her silver shoes he said,

"You must be a great sorceress."

"Why?" asked the girl.

"Because you wear silver shoes and have killed the wicked witch. Besides, you have white in your frock, and only witches and sorceresses wear white."

"My dress is blue and white checked," said Dorothy, smoothing out the wrinkles in it.

"It is kind of you to wear that," said Boq. "Blue is the color of the Munchkins, and white is the witch color; so we know you are a friendly witch."[14]

Dorothy did not know what to say to this, for all the people seemed to think her a witch, and she knew very well she was only an ordinary little girl who had come by the chance of a cyclone into a strange land.

When she had tired watching the dancing, Boq led her into the house, where he gave her a room with a pretty bed in it. The sheets were made of blue cloth, and Dorothy slept soundly in them till morning, with Toto curled up on the blue rug beside her.

She ate a hearty breakfast, and watched a wee Munchkin baby, who played with Toto and pulled his tail and crowed and laughed in a way that greatly amused Dorothy. Toto was a fine curiosity to all the people, for they had never seen a dog before.

"How far is it to the Emerald City?" the girl asked.

"I do not know," answered Boq gravely, "for I have never been there. It is better for people to keep away from Oz, unless they have business with him. But it is a long way to the Emerald City, and it will take you many days. The country here is rich and pleasant, but you must pass through rough and dangerous places before you reach the end of your journey."

This worried Dorothy a little, but she knew that only the Great Oz could help her get to Kansas again, so she bravely resolved not to turn back.

---

14. The identification of white as the witch color fits in with the colors-of-money symbolism, since silver is "the white metal." (In fact, the color of pure silver is closer to white than to silver.) The Witches in Oz understand the magical powers of silver—the Northern Witch to a lesser degree than the others, which is fitting because she seems to be the least powerful of the Witches.

She bade her friends good-bye, and again started along the road of yellow brick. When she had gone several miles she thought she would stop to rest, and so climbed to the top of the fence beside the road and sat down. There was a great cornfield beyond the fence, and not far away she saw a Scarecrow, placed high on a pole to keep the birds from the ripe corn.

Dorothy leaned her chin upon her hand and gazed thoughtfully at the Scarecrow. Its head was a small sack stuffed with straw, with eyes, nose, and mouth painted on it to represent a face. An old, pointed blue hat, that had belonged to some Munchkin, was perched on his head, and the rest of the figure was a blue suit of clothes, worn and faded, which had also been stuffed with straw. On the feet were some old boots with blue tops, such as every man wore in this country, and the figure was raised above the stalks of corn by means of the pole stuck up its back.

While Dorothy was looking earnestly into the queer, painted face of the Scarecrow, she was surprised to see one of the eyes slowly wink at her. She thought she must have been mistaken at first, for none of the scarecrows in Kansas ever wink; but presently the figure nodded its head to her in a friendly way. Then she climbed down from the fence and walked up to it, while Toto ran around the pole and barked.

"Good day," said the Scarecrow, in a rather husky voice.

"Did you speak?" asked the girl, in wonder.

"Certainly," answered the Scarecrow. "How do you do?"

"I'm pretty well, thank you," replied Dorothy politely; "how do you do?"

"I'm not feeling well," said the Scarecrow, with a smile, "for it is very tedious being perched up here night and day to scare away crows."

"Can't you get down?" asked Dorothy.

"No, for this pole is stuck up my back. If you will please take away the pole I shall be greatly obliged to you."

Dorothy reached up both arms and lifted the figure off the pole; for, being stuffed with straw, it was quite light.

"Thank you very much," said the Scarecrow, when he had been set down on the ground. "I feel like a new man."

Dorothy was puzzled at this, for it sounded queer to hear a stuffed man speak, and to see him bow and walk along beside her.

"Who are you?" asked the Scarecrow when he had stretched himself and yawned, "and where are you going?"

"My name is Dorothy," said the girl, "and I am going to the Emerald City, to ask the Great Oz to send me back to Kansas."

"Where is the Emerald City?" he enquired; "and who is Oz?"

"Why, don't you know?" she returned, in surprise.

"No, indeed; I don't know anything. You see, I am stuffed, so I have no brains at all," he answered, sadly.

"Oh," said Dorothy; "I'm awfully sorry for you."

"Do you think," he asked, "if I go to the Emerald City with you, that Oz would give me some brains?"

"I cannot tell," she returned; "but you may come with me, if you like. If Oz will not give you any brains you will be no worse off than you are now."

"That is true," said the Scarecrow. "You see," he continued, confidentially, "I don't mind my legs and arms and body being stuffed, because I cannot get hurt. If anyone treads on my toes or sticks a pin into me, it doesn't matter, for I can't feel it. But I do not want people to call me a fool, and if my head stays stuffed with straw instead of with brains, as yours is, how am I ever to know anything?"[15]

"I understand how you feel," said the little girl, who was truly sorry for him. "If you will come with me I'll ask Oz to do all he can for you."

"Thank you," he answered, gratefully.

They walked back to the road. Dorothy helped him over the fence, and they started along the path of yellow brick for the Emerald City.

Toto did not like this addition to the party at first.[16] He smelled around the stuffed man as if he suspected there might be a nest of rats in the straw, and he often growled in an unfriendly way at the Scarecrow.

"Don't mind Toto," said Dorothy to her new friend; "he never bites."

"Oh, I'm not afraid," replied the Scarecrow; "he can't hurt the straw. Do let me carry that basket for you. I shall not mind it, for I can't get tired. I'll tell you a secret," he continued, as he walked along; "there is only one thing in the world I am afraid of."

"What is that?" asked Dorothy; "the Munchkin farmer who made you?"

"No," answered the Scarecrow; "it's a lighted match."

---

15. The Scarecrow thinks he has no brains, but "soon emerges as a very shrewd and very capable individual" (Littlefield 1964, p. 53). In this regard, he seems almost surely to symbolize the American or Western farmer, whose economic troubles were attributed by many to a supposed lack of brains. The classic expression of that view is William Allen White's scabrous essay, "What's the Matter with Kansas?" (see note 3, Baum Chapter I). In his famous "Cross of Gold" speech at the 1896 Democratic Convention, Bryan turned that notion on its head, calling the farmer a businessman "who by the application of brain and muscle to the natural resources of the country creates wealth." Baum played on that notion in a later book, *Aunt Jane's Nieces at Work* (1909), in which one character tells another, "I know our country people, and they are more intelligent than you suppose" (pp. 68–69).

The Scarecrow "brings to life a major theme of the free-silver movement: that the people, the farmer in particular, were capable of understanding the complex theories that underlay the choice of a [monetary] standard" (Rockoff 1990, p. 746). Likewise, many congressional Populists, notably Kansans William Peffer and "Sockless" Jerry Simpson, were routinely, and unfairly, derided as dumb. Baum may have been playing on that notion in his original script for the stage musical *The Wizard of Oz* (1902), in the Scarecrow's line to Dorothy, "I might as well own up to it [having no brains], because people will get on to me sooner or later, and want me to go to Congress" (p. 353).

16. The word "party," which is used eight times in the book to refer to Dorothy and her traveling companions, can be read as an allusion to the Populist Party, which was also trying to get to the capital city. The repeated use of the word "comrade" reinforces that symbolism.

Chapter IV.
The Road through the Forest.

After a few hours the road began to be rough, and the walking grew so difficult that the Scarecrow often stumbled over the yellow brick, which were here very uneven. Sometimes, indeed, they were broken or missing altogether, leaving holes that Toto jumped across and Dorothy walked around. As for the Scarecrow, having no brains, he walked straight ahead, and so stepped into the holes and fell at full length on the hard bricks.[17] It never hurt him, however, and Dorothy would pick him up and set him upon his feet again, while he joined her in laughing merrily at his own mishap.

The farms were not nearly so well cared for here as they were farther back. There were fewer houses and fewer fruit trees, and the farther they went the more dismal and lonesome the country became.

At noon they sat down by the roadside, near a little brook, and Dorothy opened her basket and got out some bread. She offered a piece to the Scarecrow, but he refused.

"I am never hungry," he said; "and it is a lucky thing I am not, for my mouth is only painted, and if I should cut a hole in it so I could eat, the straw I am stuffed with would come out, and that would spoil the shape of my head."

Dorothy saw at once that this was true, so she only nodded and went on eating her bread.

"Tell me something about yourself and the country you came from," said the Scarecrow, when she had finished her dinner. So she told him all about Kansas, and how gray everything was there, and how the cyclone had carried her to this queer Land of Oz.[18] The Scarecrow listened carefully, and said,

---

17. Here the yellow brick road is patchy, causing the Scarecrow to fall on his face, just as a scarcity of gold caused deflation and damage for the farmer. (Then again, "[i]t never hurt him.") Notably, in this country where gold is scarce, "the farms were not nearly so well cared for as they were farther back," where gold was plentiful.

Note also that Dorothy "walked around" the patchy, yellow brick road in her silver shoes. Her walking around it evokes the way a bimetallic standard works—when one metal (say, gold) is scarcer than the other, causing the other metal (silver) to be relatively cheap, then people use silver for their purchases instead of using gold. (I am indebted to my former student Marc Weissberg for this last observation.)

18. The Land of Oz is a fantasy counterpart to America (Rockoff 1990, p. 745). Much of the recurring color imagery in Oz—the Emerald City, the yellow brick road, the numerous references to silver—corresponds to the colors of American money in the late nineteenth century—greenbacks and gold and silver coins.

"Oz" corresponds to the abbreviation "oz." for ounce, the unit in which gold and silver were measured (Jensen 1971, p. 283 n.22). Under the gold standard, "an ounce of gold has almost mystical significance" (Rockoff 1990, p. 745).

Baum's own, oft-repeated explanation of the name was that when casting about for a name for his imaginary new land, he gazed upon a file cabinet alphabetically labeled "O–Z." But Baum's story "is not entirely trustworthy" (Hearn 2000, p. 43). Baum's granddaughter Ozma Baum Mantele (2000) disputed the filing-cabinet story, saying that her grandmother

"I cannot understand why you should wish to leave this beautiful country and go back to the dry, gray place you call Kansas."

"That is because you have no brains" answered the girl. "No matter how dreary and gray our homes are, we people of flesh and blood would rather live there than in any other country, be it ever so beautiful. There is no place like home."

The Scarecrow sighed.

"Of course I cannot understand it," he said. "If your heads were stuffed with straw, like mine, you would probably all live in the beautiful places, and then Kansas would have no people at all. It is fortunate for Kansas that you have brains."

"Won't you tell me a story, while we are resting?" asked the child.

The Scarecrow looked at her reproachfully, and answered:

"My life has been so short that I really know nothing whatever. I was only made day before yesterday. What happened in the world before that time is all un-known to me. Luckily, when the farmer made my head, one of the first things he did was to paint my ears, so that I heard what was going on. There was another Munchkin with him, and the first thing I heard was the farmer saying,

" 'How do you like those ears?'

" 'They aren't straight,' " answered the other.

" 'Never mind,' said the farmer; 'they are ears just the same,' which was true enough.

" 'Now I'll make the eyes,' said the farmer. So he painted my right eye, and as soon as it was finished I found myself looking at him and at everything around me with a great deal of curiosity, for this was my first glimpse of the world.

" 'That's a rather pretty eye,' remarked the Munchkin who was watching the farmer; 'blue paint is just the color for eyes.'

" 'I think I'll make the other a little bigger,' said the farmer; and when the second eye was done I could see much better than before. Then he made my nose and my mouth. But I did not speak, because at that time I didn't know what a mouth was for. I had the fun of watching them make my body and my arms and legs; and when they fastened on my head, at last, I felt very proud, for I thought I was just as good a man as anyone.

" 'This fellow will scare the crows fast enough,' said the farmer; 'he looks just like a man.'

" 'Why, he is a man,' said the other, and I quite agreed with him. The farmer carried me under his arm to the cornfield, and set me up on a tall stick, where you found me. He and his friend soon after walked away and left me alone.

"I did not like to be deserted this way; so I tried to walk after them, but my feet would not touch the ground, and I was forced to stay on that pole. It was a lonely life to lead, for I had nothing to think of, having been made such a little while before. Many crows and other birds flew into the cornfield, but as soon as they saw

---

(and Baum's wife) wrote in her notes: "The word 'Oz' came out of Baum's mind just as did his queer characters. No one or anything suggested the word Oz. This is a fact."

me they flew away again, thinking I was a Munchkin; and this pleased me and made me feel that I was quite an important person. By and by an old crow flew near me, and after looking at me carefully he perched upon my shoulder and said,

" 'I wonder if that farmer thought to fool me in this clumsy manner. Any crow of sense could see that you are only stuffed with straw.' Then he hopped down at my feet and ate all the corn he wanted. The other birds, seeing he was not harmed by me, came to eat the corn too, so in a short time there was a great flock of them about me.

"I felt sad at this, for it showed I was not such a good Scarecrow after all; but the old crow comforted me, saying: 'If you only had brains in your head you would be as good a man as any of them, and a better man than some of them. Brains are the only things worth having in this world, no matter whether one is a crow or a man.'

"After the crows had gone I thought this over, and decided I would try hard to get some brains. By good luck you came along and pulled me off the stake, and from what you say I am sure the great Oz will give me brains as soon as we get to the Emerald City."

"I hope so," said Dorothy earnestly, "since you seem anxious to have them."

"Oh, yes; I am anxious," returned the Scarecrow. "It is such an uncomfortable feeling to know one is a fool."

"Well," said the girl, "let us go." And she handed the basket to the Scarecrow.

There were no fences at all by the roadside now, and the land was rough and untilled. Toward evening they came to a great forest, where the trees grew so big and close together that their branches met over the road of yellow brick. It was almost dark under the trees, for the branches shut out the daylight; but the travellers did not stop, and went on into the forest.

"If this road goes in, it must come out," said the Scarecrow, "and as the Emerald City is at the other end of the road, we must go wherever it leads us."

"Anyone would know that," said Dorothy.

"Certainly; that is why I know it," returned the Scarecrow. "If it required brains to figure it out, I never should have said it."

After an hour or so the light faded away, and they found themselves stumbling along in the darkness. Dorothy could not see at all, but Toto could, for some dogs see very well in the dark; and the Scarecrow declared he could see as well as by day. So she took hold of his arm and managed to get along fairly well.

"If you see any house, or any place where we can pass the night," she said, "you must tell me; for it is very uncomfortable walking in the dark."

Soon after the Scarecrow stopped.

"I see a little cottage at the right of us," he said, "built of logs and branches. Shall we go there?"

"Yes, indeed," answered the child. "I am all tired out."

So the Scarecrow led her through the trees until they reached the cottage, and Dorothy entered and found a bed of dried leaves in one corner. She lay down at once, and with Toto beside her soon fell into a sound sleep. The Scarecrow, who was never tired, stood up in another corner and waited patiently until morning came.

Chapter V.
The Rescue of the Tin Woodman.

When Dorothy awoke the sun was shining through the trees and Toto had long been out chasing birds and squirrels. She sat up and looked around her. There was the Scarecrow, still standing patiently in his corner, waiting for her.

"We must go and search for water," she said to him.

"Why do you want water?" he asked.

"To wash my face clean after the dust of the road, and to drink, so the dry bread will not stick in my throat."

"It must be inconvenient to be made of flesh," said the Scarecrow, thoughtfully; "for you must sleep, and eat and drink. However, you have brains, and it is worth a lot of bother to be able to think properly."

They left the cottage and walked through the trees until they found a little spring of clear water, where Dorothy drank and bathed and ate her breakfast. She saw there was not much bread left in the basket, and the girl was thankful the Scarecrow did not have to eat anything, for there was scarcely enough for herself and Toto for the day.

When she had finished her meal, and was about to go back to the road of yellow brick, she was startled to hear a deep groan near by.

"What was that?" she asked timidly.

"I cannot imagine," replied the Scarecrow; "but we can go and see."

Just then another groan reached their ears, and the sound seemed to come from behind them. They turned and walked through the forest a few steps, when Dorothy discovered something shining in a ray of sunshine that fell between the trees. She ran to the place, and then stopped short, with a little cry of surprise.

One of the big trees had been partly chopped through, and standing beside it, with an uplifted axe in his hands, was a man made entirely of tin. His head and arms and legs were jointed upon his body, but he stood perfectly motionless, as if he could not stir at all.

Dorothy looked at him in amazement, and so did the Scarecrow, while Toto barked sharply and made a snap at the tin legs, which hurt his teeth.

"Did you groan?" asked Dorothy.

"Yes," answered the tin man, "I did. I've been groaning for more than a year, and no one has ever heard me before or come to help me."[19]

---

19. The standard Populist-parable interpretation of the Tin Woodman is that he is a symbol of the urban workingman. (This symbolism will become clearer as the chapter unfolds.) As a wood-chopper, the tin man could more specifically symbolize a worker in the lumber industry, one of the largest manufacturing sectors at the time. Bryan's message resonated well among former Populists in lumber camps (Jensen 1971, p. 277).

As drawn by W.W. Denslow, the book's original illustrator, the Tin Woodman looks uncannily like a robot, furthering the idea of worker-as-machine. (Incidentally, the concept of a robot entered Baum's mind long before the term "robot" entered the language, in the early 1920s: In the third Oz book, *Ozma of Oz*, in 1907, Baum explicitly introduced a clockwork robot named Tik-Tok [Vidal 1977, p. 263].)

"What can I do for you?" she enquired, softly, for she was moved by the sad voice in which the man spoke.

"Get an oil-can and oil my joints," he answered. "They are rusted so badly that I cannot move them at all; if I am well oiled I shall soon be all right again. You will find an oil-can on a shelf in my cottage."[20]

Dorothy at once ran back to the cottage and found the oil-can, and then she returned and asked, anxiously, "Where are your joints?"

"Oil my neck, first," replied the Tin Woodman. So she oiled it, and as it was quite badly rusted the Scarecrow took hold of the tin head and moved it gently from side to side until it worked freely, and then the man could turn it himself.

"Now oil the joints in my arms," he said. And Dorothy oiled them and the

---

The tin man's enforced year of idleness due to rust recalls the unemployment of many industrial workers during the severe depression of 1893–97 (Littlefield 1964, p. 52). His lament that "I've been groaning for more than a year, and no one has ever heard me before or come to help me" recalls President Grover Cleveland's seemingly hard-hearted refusal to take active measures to promote economic recovery.

That the tin man has been idle for a year is in keeping with another idea advanced by Littlefield, that of Dorothy's party as Coxey's Army, a band of about five hundred unemployed men led by Ohio businessman and Greenback Party member Jacob Coxey, who trekked across the country to Washington, D.C., in 1894, one year into the 1890s depression. Several other industrial armies, including one from Chicago, trekked to Washington at the same time. Estimates of the total number of men involved ranged from three thousand to ten thousand (McMurry 1929, pp. 241–42). Coxey's Army hoped to meet with President Grover Cleveland and get him to take action to end the suffering wrought by the severe depression that had begun a year earlier. (They were successful on neither front.) Coxey's favored remedy was actually a public works program called the Good Roads Bill—a precursor, perhaps, of yellow brick road.

On a side note, Coxey's Army included an individual who called himself the Great Unknown. Like the Great Oz, the Unknown carefully cultivated an image of mystery. He began as a protégé of Carl Browne, co-leader of Coxey's march, and gained increasing influence within Coxey's Army. He dodged reporters' questions about his identity and background, insisting, "I am the Great Unknown, and the Great Unknown I must remain." Late in the march the Unknown staged a bloodless coup against Browne and was nearly successful, but Coxey himself intervened and expelled the Unknown from his Army. At a press conference at the end of that day, Browne told reporters that the Unknown "was in fact A.P.B. Bozarro, a patent medicine salesman, an occultist, and the '**Wizard**o Supreme' of an outfit calling itself the American Patriots" (Brands 1995, pp. 164–67; emphasis added). Whether Baum drew conscious or unconscious inspiration from this strange episode is an open question. But since the Unknown further identified himself as a blood-medicine manufacturer working out of 801 South Peoria Street, Chicago (McMurry 1929, p. 99), Baum could easily have read about him in the Chicago newspapers.

20. Oil rescues the tin man from his rust-enforced idleness, just as a monetary "lubricant" or "pump-priming" can help rescue a depressed economy with millions of idle workers. Such monetary pump-priming is a standard economic remedy and today is the typical first resort of public policy in combating recessions. Thus it is appropriate that the tin man says later, "if I should get caught in the rain, and rust again, I would need the oil-can badly."

Scarecrow bent them carefully until they were quite free from rust and as good as new.

The Tin Woodman gave a sigh of satisfaction and lowered his axe, which he leaned against the tree.

"This is a great comfort," he said. "I have been holding that axe in the air ever since I rusted, and I'm glad to be able to put it down at last. Now, if you will oil the joints of my legs, I shall be all right once more."

So they oiled his legs until he could move them freely; and he thanked them again and again for his release, for he seemed a very polite creature, and very grateful.

"I might have stood there always if you had not come along," he said; "so you have certainly saved my life. How did you happen to be here?"

"We are on our way to the Emerald City to see the great Oz," she answered, "and we stopped at your cottage to pass the night."

"Why do you wish to see Oz?" he asked.

"I want him to send me back to Kansas, and the Scarecrow wants him to put a few brains into his head," she replied.

The Tin Woodman appeared to think deeply for a moment. Then he said:

"Do you suppose Oz could give me a heart?"

"Why, I guess so," Dorothy answered; "it would be as easy as to give the Scarecrow brains."

"True," the Tin Woodman returned. "So, if you will allow me to join your party, I will also go to the Emerald City and ask Oz to help me."

"Come along," said the Scarecrow, heartily, and Dorothy added that she would be pleased to have his company. So the Tin Woodman shouldered his axe and they all passed through the forest until they came to the road that was paved with yellow brick.

The Tin Woodman had asked Dorothy to put the oil-can in her basket. "For," he said, "if I should get caught in the rain, and rust again, I would need the oil-can badly."

It was a bit of good luck to have their new comrade join the party, for soon after they had begun their journey again they came to a place where the trees and branches grew so thick over the road that the travellers could not pass. But the Tin Woodman set to work with his axe and chopped so well that soon he cleared a passage for the entire party.

Dorothy was thinking so earnestly as they walked along that she did not notice when the Scarecrow stumbled into a hole and rolled over to the side of the road. Indeed, he was obliged to call to her to help him up again.

"Why didn't you walk around the hole?" asked the Tin Woodman.

"I don't know enough," replied the Scarecrow, cheerfully. "My head is stuffed with straw, you know, and that is why I am going to Oz to ask him for some brains."

"Oh, I see," said the Tin Woodman. "But, after all, brains are not the best things in the world."

"Have you any?" enquired the Scarecrow.

"No, my head is quite empty," answered the Woodman; "but once I had brains, and a heart also; so, having tried them both, I should much rather have a heart."

"And why is that?" asked the Scarecrow.

"I will tell you my story, and then you will know."

So, while they were walking through the forest, the Tin Woodman told the following story:

"I was born the son of a woodman who chopped down trees in the forest and sold the wood for a living. When I grew up, I too became a wood-chopper, and after my father died I took care of my old mother as long as she lived. Then I made up my mind that instead of living alone I would marry, so that I might not become lonely.

"There was one of the Munchkin girls who was so beautiful that I soon grew to love her with all my heart. She, on her part, promised to marry me as soon as I could earn enough money to build a better house for her; so I set to work harder than ever. But the girl lived with an old woman who did not want her to marry anyone, for she was so lazy she wished the girl to remain with her and do the cooking and the housework. So the old woman went to the wicked Witch of the East, and promised her two sheep and a cow if she would prevent the marriage. Thereupon the wicked Witch enchanted my axe, and when I was chopping away at my best one day, for I was anxious to get the new house and my wife as soon as possible, the axe slipped all at once and cut off my left leg.

"This at first seemed a great misfortune, for I knew a one-legged man could not do very well as a wood-chopper. So I went to a tin-smith and had him make me a new leg out of tin. The leg worked very well, once I was used to it. But my action angered the wicked Witch of the East, for she had promised the old woman I should not marry the pretty Munchkin girl. When I began chopping again, my axe slipped and cut off my right leg. Again I went to the tinsmith, and again he made me a leg out of tin. After this the enchanted axe cut off my arms, one after the other; but, nothing daunted, I had them replaced with tin ones. The wicked Witch then made the axe slip and cut off my head, and at first I thought that was the end of me. But the tinner happened to come along, and he made me a new head out of tin.

"I thought I had beaten the wicked Witch then, and I worked harder than ever; but I little knew how cruel my enemy could be. She thought of a new way to kill my love for the beautiful Munchkin maiden, and made my axe slip again, so that it cut right through my body, splitting me into two halves. Once more the tinner came to my help and made me a body of tin, fastening my tin arms and legs and head to it, by means of joints, so that I could move around as well as ever. But, alas! I had now no heart, so that I lost all my love for the Munchkin girl, and did not care whether I married her or not.[21] I suppose she is still living with the old

---

21. The tin man's metamorphosis from an ordinary human wood-chopper into a man "made entirely of tin" seems to symbolize the alienation of industrial workers from human feelings and aspirations. Once the tinsmith's work was complete, the wood-chopper could work more efficiently than ever. "But, alas! I had now no heart, so that I lost all my love for the Munchkin girl." Littlefield wrote: "In this way Eastern witchcraft dehumanized a simple laborer, so that the faster and better he worked the more quickly he became a kind of ma-

woman, waiting for me to come after her.

"My body shone so brightly in the sun that I felt very proud of it and it did not matter now if my axe slipped, for it could not cut me. There was only one danger—that my joints would rust; but I kept an oil-can in my cottage and took care to oil myself whenever I needed it. However, there came a day when I forgot to do this, and, being caught in a rainstorm, before I thought of the danger my joints had rusted, and I was left to stand in the woods until you came to help me. It was a terrible thing to undergo, but during the year I stood there I had time to think that the greatest loss I had known was the loss of my heart. While I was in love I was the happiest man on earth; but no one can love who has not a heart, and so I am resolved to ask Oz to give me one. If he does, I will go back to the Munchkin maiden and marry her."

Both Dorothy and the Scarecrow had been greatly interested in the story of the Tin Woodman, and now they knew why he was so anxious to get a new heart.

"All the same," said the Scarecrow, "I shall ask for brains instead of a heart; for a fool would not know what to do with a heart if he had one."

"I shall take the heart," returned the Tin Woodman; "for brains do not make one happy, and happiness is the best thing in the world."

Dorothy did not say anything, for she was puzzled to know which of her two friends was right, and she decided if she could only get back to Kansas and Aunt Em, it did not matter so much whether the Woodman had no brains and the Scarecrow no heart, or each got what he wanted.

What worried her most was that the bread was nearly gone, and another meal for herself and Toto would empty the basket. To be sure neither the Woodman nor the Scarecrow ever ate anything, but she was not made of tin nor straw, and could not live unless she was fed.

Chapter VI.
The Cowardly Lion.

All this time Dorothy and her companions had been walking through the thick woods. The road was still paved with yellow brick, but these were much covered by dried branches and dead leaves from the trees, and the walking was not at all good.

There were few birds in this part of the forest, for birds love the open country where there is plenty of sunshine; but now and then there came a deep growl from some wild animal hidden among the trees. These sounds made the little girl's heart beat fast, for she did not know what made them; but Toto knew, and he walked close to Dorothy's side, and did not even bark in return.

---

chine. Here is a Populist view of evil Eastern [industrial] influences on honest labor which could hardly be more pointed" (1964, p. 52).

The tin man's mistreatment at the hands of the Eastern Witch parallels that of the Munchkins she had enslaved. (See note 8, Baum Chapter II.) Both cases are consistent with the notion of the Eastern Witch as Wall Street and other Eastern industrial capitalist bosses.

"How long will it be," the child asked of the Tin Woodman, "before we are out of the forest?"

"I cannot tell," was the answer, "for I have never been to the Emerald City. But my father went there once, when I was a boy, and he said it was a long journey through a dangerous country, although nearer to the city where Oz dwells the country is beautiful. But I am not afraid so long as I have my oil-can, and nothing can hurt the Scarecrow, while you bear upon your forehead the mark of the good Witch's kiss, and that will protect you from harm."

"But Toto!" said the girl anxiously; "what will protect him?"

"We must protect him ourselves if he is in danger," replied the Tin Woodman.

Just as he spoke there came from the forest a terrible roar, and the next moment a great Lion bounded into the road. With one blow of his paw he sent the Scarecrow spinning over and over to the edge of the road, and then he struck at the Tin Woodman with his sharp claws. But, to the Lion's surprise, he could make no impression on the tin, although the Woodman fell over in the road and lay still.

Little Toto, now that he had an enemy to face, ran barking toward the Lion, and the great beast had opened his mouth to bite the dog, when Dorothy, fearing Toto would be killed, and heedless of danger, rushed forward and slapped the Lion upon his nose as hard as she could, while she cried out:

"Don't you dare to bite Toto! You ought to be ashamed of yourself, a big beast like you, to bite a poor little dog!"

"I didn't bite him," said the Lion, as he rubbed his nose with his paw where Dorothy had hit it.

"No, but you tried to," she retorted. "You are nothing but a big coward."[22]

---

22. The usual Populist interpretation of the Lion is as William Jennings Bryan, the great "free-silver" advocate and Populist Party nominee in the climactic election of 1896. Bryan was a compelling and passionate speaker whose powerful oratory could easily be compared to a lion's roar. Bryan, six feet tall and muscularly built, fit the bill physically as well. Also, Bryan rhymes with lion (a rhyme immortalized some years later by poet Vachel Lindsay: "Prairie avenger, mountain lion/ Bryan, Bryan, Bryan, Bryan").

"Cowardly" could symbolize Bryan's pacifism and anti-imperialism in a jingoistic era (Littlefield 1992b, p. 24). The wildly popular Spanish-American War of 1898, in which the United States wrested control of Guam, Puerto Rico, and the Philippines from Spain, ushered in an age of U.S. expansionism. Bryan and other opponents of the war, such as the Anti-Imperialist League, were frequently derided as cowardly and unpatriotic. In this context, "cowardly" strikes me as an ironic term of endearment for Bryan. The Lion, after all, is not truly cowardly. Just as the Scarecrow shows great cunning and the Tin Woodman is compassionate, the Lion is courageous when it matters most, as we discover later.

An alternative explanation of Bryan's "cowardice" is that some Populists in the late 1890s, noting Bryan's growing preoccupation with anti-imperialism, feared that he would not fight for free silver as aggressively in the 1900 election as he had in 1896 (Rockoff 1990, p. 748). This interpretation strikes me as less compelling. Bryan never abandoned his free-silver quest, whereas his devotion to the anti-imperialist cause was hamstrung by his bizarre reversal in 1899, when he threw his support behind the treaty with Spain, which included U.S. acquisition of the Philippines. (Bryan said the reversal was a temporary tactical move.)

If the Lion is viewed as Bryan, it is fitting that the Lion is the last member to join Doro-

"I know it," said the Lion, hanging his head in shame. "I've always known it. But how can I help it?"

"I don't know, I'm sure. To think of your striking a stuffed man, like the poor Scarecrow!"

"Is he stuffed?" asked the Lion in surprise, as he watched her pick up the Scarecrow and set him upon his feet, while she patted him into shape again.

"Of course he's stuffed," replied Dorothy, who was still angry.

"That's why he went over so easily," remarked the Lion. "It astonished me to see him whirl around so. Is the other one stuffed also?"

"No," said Dorothy, "he's made of tin." And she helped the Woodman up again.

"That's why he nearly blunted my claws," said the Lion. "When they scratched against the tin it made a cold shiver run down my back.[23] What is that little animal you are so tender of?"

"He is my dog, Toto," answered Dorothy.

"Is he made of tin, or stuffed?" asked the Lion.

"Neither. He's a—a—a meat dog," said the girl.

"Oh! He's a curious animal and seems remarkably small, now that I look at him. No one would think of biting such a little thing, except a coward like me," continued the Lion, sadly.

"What makes you a coward?" asked Dorothy, looking at the great beast in wonder, for he was as big as a small horse.

---

thy's party. The Populist movement began with Western and Southern farmers, attracted the involvement of some blue-collar workers such as those in Coxey's Army, and was joined by Bryan only after it had already become well established (Rockoff 1990, p. 748).

One could instead view the Lion as symbolizing the People's Party or third parties in general (Kelsay 1987; Geer and Rochon 1993). Some 1890s cartoons actually represented the People's Party as a lion. While few would describe the Populists as cowardly, they did share Bryan's anti-imperialism (thus opening them up to jingoes' charges of cowardice); and a minority of Populists regarded as cowardly the Party's decision to fuse with the Democrats in support of Bryan in 1896, since Bryan's and the Democrats' vision was decidedly narrower than that of the landmark People's Party platform of 1892 (Geer and Rochon, p. 61).

23. It is appropriate that the Lion's claws "could make no impression" on the Tin Woodman, just as Bryan's and the Populists' efforts to appeal to urban industrial workers in 1896 were largely unsuccessful. One can make a reasonable case that Bryan's election would *not* have been in the workers' best interest (see Chapters 2 and 3), but campaign legend says otherwise. Bryan wrote in his memoir of that campaign that workers were coerced by their employers into voting for McKinley over Bryan. Historian Harold Faulkner found similar evidence (Littlefield 1964, pp. 53–54). A chronicle of the campaign (Shields-West 1992, p. 130) notes: "On the Saturday before the election, New York workingmen marched all day singing 'We'll hang Billy Bryan on a sour apple tree.' Under their breath, the song was something else:

'You ask me why 'tis thus
That I make this outward show
Because my millionaire employer
Says, Bryan must go.' "

"It's a mystery," replied the Lion. "I suppose I was born that way. All the other animals in the forest naturally expect me to be brave, for the Lion is everywhere thought to be the King of Beasts. I learned that if I roared very loudly every living thing was frightened and got out of my way. Whenever I've met a man I've been awfully scared; but I just roared at him, and he has always run away as fast as he could go. If the elephants and the tigers and the bears had ever tried to fight me, I should have run myself—I'm such a coward; but just as soon as they hear me roar they all try to get away from me, and of course I let them go."

"But that isn't right. The King of Beasts shouldn't be a coward," said the Scarecrow.

"I know it," returned the Lion, wiping a tear from his eye with the tip of his tail; "it is my great sorrow, and makes my life very unhappy. But whenever there is danger, my heart begins to beat fast."

"Perhaps you have heart disease," said the Tin Woodman.

"It may be," said the Lion.

"If you have," continued the Tin Woodman, "you ought to be glad, for it proves you have a heart. For my part, I have no heart; so I cannot have heart disease."

"Perhaps," said the Lion, thoughtfully, "if I had no heart I should not be a coward."

"Have you brains?" asked the Scarecrow.

"I suppose so. I've never looked to see," replied the Lion.

"I am going to the Great Oz to ask him to give me some," remarked the Scarecrow, "for my head is stuffed with straw."

"And I am going to ask him to give me a heart," said the Woodman.

"And I am going to ask him to send Toto and me back to Kansas," added Dorothy.

"Do you think Oz could give me courage?" asked the Cowardly Lion.

"Just as easily as he could give me brains," said the Scarecrow.

"Or give me a heart," said the Tin Woodman.

"Or send me back to Kansas," said Dorothy.

"Then, if you don't mind, I'll go with you," said the Lion, "for my life is simply unbearable without a bit of courage."

"You will be very welcome," answered Dorothy, "for you will help to keep away the other wild beasts. It seems to me they must be more cowardly than you are if they allow you to scare them so easily."

"They really are," said the Lion; "but that doesn't make me any braver, and as long as I know myself to be a coward I shall be unhappy."

So once more the little company set off upon the journey, the Lion walking with stately strides at Dorothy's side. Toto did not approve this new comrade at first, for he could not forget how nearly he had been crushed between the Lion's great jaws; but after a time he became more at ease, and presently Toto and the Cowardly Lion had grown to be good friends.

During the rest of that day there was no other adventure to mar the peace of their journey. Once, indeed, the Tin Woodman stepped upon a beetle that was crawling along the road, and killed the poor little thing. This made the Tin Woodman very unhappy, for he was always careful not to hurt any living creature; and as he walked along he wept several tears of sorrow and regret. These tears ran slowly down his face and over the hinges of his jaw, and there they rusted. When Dorothy presently asked him a question the Tin Woodman could not open his mouth, for his jaws were tightly rusted together. He became greatly frightened at this and made many motions to Dorothy to relieve him, but she could not understand. The Lion was also puzzled to know what was wrong. But the Scarecrow seized the oil-can from Dorothy's basket and oiled the Woodman's jaws, so that after a few moments he could talk as well as before.

"This will serve me a lesson," said he, "to look where I step. For if I should kill another bug or beetle I should surely cry again, and crying rusts my jaws so that I cannot speak."

Thereafter he walked very carefully, with his eyes on the road, and when he saw a tiny ant toiling by he would step over it, so as not to harm it. The Tin Woodman knew very well he had no heart, and therefore he took great care never to be cruel or unkind to anything.

"You people with hearts," he said, "have something to guide you, and need never do wrong; but I have no heart, and so I must be very careful. When Oz gives me a heart of course I needn't mind so much."

Chapter VII.
The Journey to The Great Oz.

They were obliged to camp out that night under a large tree in the forest, for there were no houses near. The tree made a good, thick covering to protect them from the dew, and the Tin Woodman chopped a great pile of wood with his axe and Dorothy built a splendid fire that warmed her and made her feel less lonely. She and Toto ate the last of their bread, and now she did not know what they would do for breakfast.

"If you wish," said the Lion, "I will go into the forest and kill a deer for you. You can roast it by the fire, since your tastes are so peculiar that you prefer cooked food, and then you will have a very good breakfast."

"Don't! Please don't," begged the Tin Woodman. "I should certainly weep if you killed a poor deer, and then my jaws would rust again."

But the Lion went away into the forest and found his own supper, and no one ever knew what it was, for he didn't mention it. And the Scarecrow found a tree full of nuts and filled Dorothy's basket with them, so that she would not be hungry for a long time. She thought this was very kind and thoughtful of the Scarecrow, but she laughed heartily at the awkward way in which the poor creature picked up the nuts. His padded hands were so clumsy and the nuts were so small that he dropped almost as many as he put in the basket. But the Scarecrow did not mind how long it took him to fill the basket, for it enabled him to keep away from the fire, as he feared a spark might get into his straw and burn him up. So he kept a good distance away from the flames, and only came near to cover Dorothy with dry leaves when she lay down to sleep. These kept her very snug and warm, and she slept soundly until morning.

When it was daylight the girl bathed her face in a little rippling brook and soon after they all started toward the Emerald City.

This was to be an eventful day for the travellers. They had hardly been walking an hour when they saw before them a great ditch that crossed the road and divided the forest as far as they could see on either side. It was a very wide ditch, and when they crept up to the edge and looked into it they could see it was also very deep, and there were many big, jagged rocks at the bottom. The sides were so steep that none of them could climb down, and for a moment it seemed that their journey must end.

"What shall we do?" asked Dorothy, despairingly.

"I haven't the faintest idea," said the Tin Woodman; and the Lion shook his shaggy mane and looked thoughtful. But the Scarecrow said:

"We cannot fly, that is certain. Neither can we climb down into this great ditch. Therefore, if we cannot jump over it, we must stop where we are."

"I think I could jump over it," said the Cowardly Lion, after measuring the distance carefully in his mind.

"Then we are all right," answered the Scarecrow, "for you can carry us all over on your back, one at a time."

"Well, I'll try it," said the Lion. "Who will go first?"

"I will," declared the Scarecrow; "for, if you found that you could not jump over the gulf, Dorothy would be killed, or the Tin Woodman badly dented on the rocks below. But if I am on your back it will not matter so much, for the fall would not hurt me at all."[24]

"I am terribly afraid of falling, myself," said the Cowardly Lion, "but I suppose there is nothing to do but try it. So get on my back and we will make the attempt."

The Scarecrow sat upon the Lion's back, and the big beast walked to the edge of the gulf and crouched down.

"Why don't you run and jump?" asked the Scarecrow.

"Because that isn't the way we Lions do these things," he replied.[25] Then giving a great spring, he shot through the air and landed safely on the other side. They were all greatly pleased to see how easily he did it, and after the Scarecrow had got down from his back the Lion sprang across the ditch again.

---

24. This passage also works as a political metaphor in which Bryan is supposed to carry the farmers and industrial workers to victory. The farmers have nothing to lose from backing Bryan, even if he fails to "jump over the gulf," since neither the gold Democrats nor the Republicans had been attentive to their interests anyway; but pro-Bryan workingmen might have faced severe reprisals from their employers (see previous note).

25. The Lion's exchange with the Scarecrow recalls one of the great myths of the 1896 campaign, that Bryan won the Democratic nomination without making any kind of a "run" for it. Although Bryan in fact had aspired all along to be that year's Democratic nominee, it is true that his campaign for the nomination was a discreet one. Bryan did not announce his candidacy until the Democratic National Convention was already under way and his "Cross of Gold" speech had already electrified the delegates.

Dorothy thought she would go next; so she took Toto in her arms and climbed on the Lion's back, holding tightly to his mane with one hand. The next moment it seemed as if she was flying through the air; and then, before she had time to think about it, she was safe on the other side. The Lion went back a third time and got the Tin Woodman, and then they all sat down for a few moments to give the beast a chance to rest, for his great leaps had made his breath short, and he panted like a big dog that has been running too long.

They found the forest very thick on this side, and it looked dark and gloomy. After the Lion had rested they started along the road of yellow brick, silently wondering, each in his own mind, if ever they would come to the end of the woods and reach the bright sunshine again. To add to their discomfort, they soon heard strange noises in the depths of the forest, and the Lion whispered to them that it was in this part of the country that the Kalidahs lived.

"What are the Kalidahs?" asked the girl.

"They are monstrous beasts with bodies like bears and heads like tigers," replied the Lion; "and with claws so long and sharp that they could tear me in two as easily as I could kill Toto. I'm terribly afraid of the Kalidahs."

"I'm not surprised that you are," returned Dorothy. "They must be dreadful beasts."

The Lion was about to reply when suddenly they came to another gulf across the road; but this one was so broad and deep that the Lion knew at once he could not leap across it.

So they sat down to consider what they should do, and after serious thought the Scarecrow said,

"Here is a great tree, standing close to the ditch. If the Tin Woodman can chop it down, so that it will fall to the other side, we can walk across it easily."

"That is a first rate idea," said the Lion. "One would almost suspect you had brains in your head, instead of straw."

The Woodman set to work at once, and so sharp was his axe that the tree was soon chopped nearly through. Then the Lion put his strong front legs against the tree and pushed with all his might, and slowly the big tree tipped and fell with a crash across the ditch, with its top branches on the other side.

They had just started to cross this queer bridge when a sharp growl made them all look up, and to their horror they saw running toward them two great beasts with bodies like bears and heads like tigers.

"They are the Kalidahs!" said the Cowardly Lion, beginning to tremble.[26]

"Quick!" cried the Scarecrow, "let us cross over."

So Dorothy went first, holding Toto in her arms; the Tin Woodman followed, and the Scarecrow came next. The Lion, although he was certainly afraid, turned to face the Kalidahs, and then he gave so loud and terrible a roar that Dorothy

---

26. The Kalidahs could symbolize hostile newspaper reporters. Metaphors of reporters as predatory animals (e.g., jackals) are by now commonplace. "Most of the papers were strongly opposed to Bryan and his cause, and they violently denounced the Populists" (Rockoff 1990, p. 749 n.12).

screamed and the Scarecrow fell over backward, while even the fierce beasts stopped short and looked at him in surprise.

But, seeing they were bigger than the Lion, and remembering that there were two of them and only one of him, the Kalidahs again rushed forward, and the Lion crossed over the tree and turned to see what they would do next. Without stopping an instant the fierce beasts also began to cross the tree. And the Lion said to Dorothy,

"We are lost, for they will surely tear us to pieces with their sharp claws. But stand close behind me, and I will fight them as long as I am alive."

"Wait a minute!" called the Scarecrow. He had been thinking what was best to be done, and now he asked the Woodman to chop away the end of the tree that rested on their side of the ditch. The Tin Woodman began to use his axe at once, and, just as the two Kalidahs were nearly across, the tree fell with a crash into the gulf, carrying the ugly, snarling brutes with it, and both were dashed to pieces on the sharp rocks at the bottom.

"Well," said the Cowardly Lion, drawing a long breath of relief, "I see we are going to live a little while longer, and I am glad of it, for it must be a very uncomfortable thing not to be alive. Those creatures frightened me so badly that my heart is beating yet."

"Ah," said the Tin Woodman sadly, "I wish I had a heart to beat."

This adventure made the travellers more anxious than ever to get out of the forest, and they walked so fast that Dorothy became tired, and had to ride on the Lion's back. To their great joy the trees became thinner the farther they advanced, and in the afternoon they suddenly came upon a broad river, flowing swiftly just before them. On the other side of the water they could see the road of yellow brick running through a beautiful country, with green meadows dotted with bright flowers and all the road bordered with trees hanging full of delicious fruits. They were greatly pleased to see this delightful country before them.

"How shall we cross the river?" asked Dorothy.[27]

"That is easily done," replied the Scarecrow. "The Tin Woodman must build us a raft, so we can float to the other side."

So the Woodman took his axe and began to chop down small trees to make a raft, and while he was busy at this the Scarecrow found on the riverbank a tree full of fine fruit. This pleased Dorothy, who had eaten nothing but nuts all day, and she made a hearty meal of the ripe fruit.

But it takes time to make a raft, even when one is as industrious and untiring as the Tin Woodman, and when night came the work was not done. So they found a cozy place under the trees where they slept well until the morning; and Dorothy

---

27. The foursome's odyssey through the forest and across the river is somewhat reminiscent not only of *The Pilgrim's Progress* but also of the biblical rhetoric employed by an Arkansas devotee of Bryan's, quoted in *The New York Tribune* on July 18, 1896:

He is undoubtedly the Moses to lead [us] out of this sin-cursed land of gold-bugs through the Red Sea of trouble, across the wilderness of trials, over the Jordan of depression and into the land of free silver, unlimited, unrestricted, 16 to 1. (quoted in Jensen 1971, p. 283)

dreamed of the Emerald City, and of the good Wizard Oz, who would soon send her back to her own home again.

Chapter VIII.
The Deadly Poppy Field.

Our little party of travellers awakened the next morning refreshed and full of hope, and Dorothy breakfasted like a princess off peaches and plums from the trees beside the river. Behind them was the dark forest they had passed safely through, although they had suffered many discouragements; but before them was a lovely, sunny country that seemed to beckon them on to the Emerald City.

To be sure, the broad river now cut them off from this beautiful land; but the raft was nearly done, and after the Tin Woodman had cut a few more logs and fastened them together with wooden pins, they were ready to start. Dorothy sat down in the middle of the raft and held Toto in her arms. When the Cowardly Lion stepped upon the raft it tipped badly, for he was big and heavy; but the Scarecrow and the Tin Woodman stood upon the other end to steady it, and they had long poles in their hands to push the raft through the water.

They got along quite well at first, but when they reached the middle of the river the swift current swept the raft downstream, farther and farther away from the road of yellow brick; and the water grew so deep that the long poles would not touch the bottom.

"This is bad," said the Tin Woodman, "for if we cannot get to the land we shall be carried into the country of the wicked Witch of the West, and she will enchant us and make us her slaves."

"And then I should get no brains," said the Scarecrow.

"And I should get no courage," said the Cowardly Lion.

"And I should get no heart," said the Tin Woodman.

"And I should never get back to Kansas," said Dorothy.

"We must certainly get to the Emerald City if we can," the Scarecrow continued, and he pushed so hard on his long pole that it stuck fast in the mud at the bottom of the river, and before he could pull it out again—or let go—the raft was swept away, and the poor Scarecrow left clinging to the pole in the middle of the river.

"Good-bye!" he called after them, and they were very sorry to leave him; indeed, the Tin Woodman began to cry, but fortunately remembered that he might rust, and so dried his tears on Dorothy's apron.

Of course this was a bad thing for the Scarecrow.

"I am now worse off than when I first met Dorothy," he thought. "Then, I was stuck on a pole in a cornfield, where I could make believe scare the crows, at any rate; but surely there is no use for a Scarecrow stuck on a pole in the middle of a river. I am afraid I shall never have any brains, after all!"

Down the stream the raft floated, and the poor Scarecrow was left far behind. Then the Lion said:

"Something must be done to save us. I think I can swim to the shore and pull the raft after me, if you will only hold fast to the tip of my tail."

So he sprang into the water, and the Tin Woodman caught fast hold of his tail, when the Lion began to swim with all his might toward the shore. It was hard work, although he was so big; but by and by they were drawn out of the current, and then Dorothy took the Tin Woodman's long pole and helped push the raft to the land.

They were all tired out when they reached the shore at last and stepped off upon the pretty green grass, and they also knew that the stream had carried them a long way past the road of yellow brick that led to the Emerald City.

"What shall we do now?" asked the Tin Woodman, as the Lion lay down on the grass to let the sun dry him.

"We must get back to the road, in some way," said Dorothy.

"The best plan will be to walk along the river bank until we come to the road again," remarked the Lion.

So, when they were rested, Dorothy picked up her basket and they started along the grassy bank, to the road from which the river had carried them. It was a lovely country, with plenty of flowers and fruit trees and sunshine to cheer them, and had they not felt so sorry for the poor Scarecrow, they could have been very happy.

They walked along as fast as they could, Dorothy only stopping once to pick a beautiful flower; and after a time the Tin Woodman cried out,

"Look!"

Then they all looked at the river and saw the Scarecrow perched upon his pole in the middle of the water, looking very lonely and sad.

"What can we do to save him?" asked Dorothy.

The Lion and the Woodman both shook their heads, for they did not know. So they sat down upon the bank and gazed wistfully at the Scarecrow until a Stork flew by, who, upon seeing them, stopped to rest at the water's edge.

"Who are you and where are you going?" asked the Stork.

"I am Dorothy," answered the girl, "and these are my friends, the Tin Woodman and the Cowardly Lion; and we are going to the Emerald City."

"This isn't the road," said the Stork, as she twisted her long neck and looked sharply at the queer party.

"I know it," returned Dorothy, "but we have lost the Scarecrow, and are wondering how we shall get him again."

"Where is he?" asked the Stork.

"Over there in the river," answered the little girl.

"If he wasn't so big and heavy I would get him for you," remarked the Stork.

"He isn't heavy a bit," said Dorothy, eagerly, "for he is stuffed with straw; and if you will bring him back to us, we shall thank you ever and ever so much."

"Well, I'll try," said the Stork; "but if I find he is too heavy to carry I shall have to drop him in the river again."

So the big bird flew into the air and over the water till she came to where the Scarecrow was perched upon his pole. Then the Stork with her great claws grabbed the Scarecrow by the arm and carried him up into the air and back to the bank, where Dorothy and the Lion and the Tin Woodman and Toto were sitting.

When the Scarecrow found himself among his friends again, he was so happy that he hugged them all, even the Lion and Toto; and as they walked along he sang "Tol-de-ri-de-oh!" at every step, he felt so gay.

"I was afraid I should have to stay in the river forever," he said, "but the kind Stork saved me, and if I ever get any brains I shall find the Stork again and do her some kindness in return."

"That's all right," said the Stork, who was flying along beside them. "I always like to help anyone in trouble. But I must go now, for my babies are waiting in the nest for me. I hope you will find the Emerald City and that Oz will help you."

"Thank you," replied Dorothy, and then the kind Stork flew into the air and was soon out of sight.[28]

They walked along listening to the singing of the bright-colored birds and looking at the lovely flowers which now became so thick that the ground was carpeted with them. There were big yellow and white and blue and purple blossoms, besides great clusters of scarlet poppies, which were so brilliant in color they almost dazzled Dorothy's eyes.

"Aren't they beautiful?" the girl asked, as she breathed in the spicy scent of the bright flowers.

"I suppose so," answered the Scarecrow. "When I have brains, I shall probably like them better."

"If I only had a heart I should love them," added the Tin Woodman.

"I always did like flowers," said the Lion; "they seem so helpless and frail. But there are none in the forest so bright as these."

They now came upon more and more of the big scarlet poppies, and fewer and fewer of the other flowers; and soon they found themselves in the midst of a great meadow of poppies. Now it is well known that when there are many of these flowers together their odor is so powerful that anyone who breathes it falls asleep, and if the sleeper is not carried away from the scent of the flowers he sleeps on and on forever.[29] But Dorothy did not know this, nor could she get away from the bright red flowers that were everywhere about; so presently her eyes grew heavy and she felt she must sit down to rest and to sleep.

But the Tin Woodman would not let her do this.

"We must hurry and get back to the road of yellow brick before dark," he said; and the Scarecrow agreed with him. So they kept walking until Dorothy could stand no longer. Her eyes closed in spite of herself and she forgot where she was and fell among the poppies, fast asleep.

---

28. In a Populist interpretation, the Stork, who is female, could represent the Populists' allies in the woman suffrage movement. A few prominent suffragists, such as Annie Diggs, were Populists; and the Populist Party's representatives in Congress in the 1890s took the lead in introducing bills to grant women the right to vote (Clanton 1991, p. 131).

29. By one interpretation, the poppies represent the issue of anti-imperialism, which many silverites in the late 1890s believed Bryan was starting to emphasize at the expense of the silver issue (Rockoff 1990, p. 749). The connection between poppies and anti-imperialism could be the Opium Wars that imperial Britain fought in China earlier in the nineteenth century, since poppies are the source of opium.

"What shall we do?" asked the Tin Woodman.

"If we leave her here she will die," said the Lion. "The smell of the flowers is killing us all. I myself can scarcely keep my eyes open, and the dog is asleep already."

It was true; Toto had fallen down beside his little mistress. But the Scarecrow and the Tin Woodman, not being made of flesh, were not troubled by the scent of the flowers.

"Run fast," said the Scarecrow to the Lion, "and get out of this deadly flower-bed as soon as you can. We will bring the little girl with us, but if you should fall asleep you are too big to be carried."

So the Lion aroused himself and bounded forward as fast as he could go. In a moment he was out of sight.

"Let us make a chair with our hands and carry her," said the Scarecrow. So they picked up Toto and put the dog in Dorothy's lap, and then they made a chair with their hands for the seat and their arms for the arms and carried the sleeping girl between them through the flowers.

On and on they walked, and it seemed that the great carpet of deadly flowers that surrounded them would never end. They followed the bend of the river, and at last came upon their friend the Lion, lying fast asleep among the poppies. The flowers had been too strong for the huge beast and he had given up at last, and fallen only a short distance from the end of the poppy-bed, where the sweet grass spread in beautiful green fields before them.

"We can do nothing for him," said the Tin Woodman, sadly; "for he is much too heavy to lift. We must leave him here to sleep on forever, and perhaps he will dream that he has found courage at last."

"I'm sorry," said the Scarecrow; "the Lion was a very good comrade for one so cowardly. But let us go on."

They carried the sleeping girl to a pretty spot beside the river, far enough from the poppy field to prevent her breathing any more of the poison of the flowers, and here they laid her gently on the soft grass and waited for the fresh breeze to waken her.

Chapter IX.
The Queen of the Field Mice.

"We cannot be far from the road of yellow brick, now," remarked the Scarecrow, as he stood beside the girl, "for we have come nearly as far as the river carried us away."

The Tin Woodman was about to reply when he heard a low growl, and turning his head (which worked beautifully on hinges) he saw a strange beast come bounding over the grass toward them. It was, indeed, a great yellow Wildcat, and the Woodman thought it must be chasing something, for its ears were lying close to its head and its mouth was wide open, showing two rows of ugly teeth, while its red eyes glowed like balls of fire. As it came nearer the Tin Woodman saw that running before the beast was a little gray field-mouse, and although he had no heart he knew it was wrong for the Wildcat to try to kill such a pretty, harmless creature.

So the Woodman raised his axe, and as the Wildcat ran by he gave it a quick blow that cut the beast's head clean off from its body, and it rolled over at his feet in two pieces.

The field-mouse, now that it was freed from its enemy, stopped short; and coming slowly up to the Woodman it said, in a squeaky little voice,

"Oh, thank you! Thank you ever so much for saving my life."

"Don't speak of it, I beg of you," replied the Woodman. "I have no heart, you know, so I am careful to help all those who may need a friend, even if it happens to be only a mouse."

"Only a mouse!" cried the little animal, indignantly; "why, I am a Queen—the Queen of all the field-mice!"

"Oh, indeed," said the Woodman, making a bow.

"Therefore you have done a great deed, as well as a brave one, in saving my life," added the Queen.

At that moment several mice were seen running up as fast as their little legs could carry them, and when they saw their Queen they exclaimed,

"Oh, your Majesty, we thought you would be killed! How did you manage to escape the great Wildcat?" and they all bowed so low to the little Queen that they almost stood upon their heads.

"This funny tin man," she answered, "killed the Wildcat and saved my life. So hereafter you must all serve him, and obey his slightest wish."

"We will!" cried all the mice, in a shrill chorus. And then they scampered in all directions, for Toto had awakened from his sleep, and seeing all these mice around him he gave one bark of delight and jumped right into the middle of the group. Toto had always loved to chase mice when he lived in Kansas, and he saw no harm in it.

But the Tin Woodman caught the dog in his arms and held him tight, while he called to the mice, "Come back! come back! Toto shall not hurt you."

At this the Queen of the Mice stuck her head out from underneath a clump of grass and asked, in a timid voice, "Are you sure he will not bite us?"

"I will not let him," said the Woodman; "so do not be afraid."

One by one the mice came creeping back, and Toto did not bark again, although he tried to get out of the Woodman's arms, and would have bitten him had he not known very well he was made of tin. Finally one of the biggest mice spoke.

"Is there anything we can do," it asked, "to repay you for saving the life of our Queen?"

"Nothing that I know of," answered the Woodman; but the Scarecrow, who had been trying to think, but could not because his head was stuffed with straw, said, quickly,

"Oh, yes; you can save our friend, the Cowardly Lion, who is asleep in the poppy bed."

"A Lion!" cried the little Queen; "why, he would eat us all up."

"Oh, no," declared the Scarecrow; "this Lion is a coward."

"Really?" asked the Mouse.

"He says so himself," answered the Scarecrow, "and he would never hurt any-one who is our friend. If you will help us to save him I promise that he shall treat you all with kindness."

"Very well," said the Queen, "we will trust you. But what shall we do?"

"Are there many of these mice which call you Queen and are willing to obey you?"

"Oh, yes; there are thousands," she replied.

"Then send for them all to come here as soon as possible, and let each one bring a long piece of string."

The Queen turned to the mice that attended her and told them to go at once and get all her people. As soon as they heard her orders they ran away in every direction as fast as possible.

"Now," said the Scarecrow to the Tin Woodman, "you must go to those trees by the river-side and make a truck that will carry the Lion."

So the Woodman went at once to the trees and began to work; and he soon made a truck out of the limbs of trees, from which he chopped away all the leaves and branches. He fastened it together with wooden pegs and made the four wheels out of short pieces of a big tree-trunk. So fast and so well did he work that by the time the mice began to arrive the truck was all ready for them.

They came from all directions, and there were thousands of them: big mice and little mice and middle-sized mice; and each one brought a piece of string in his mouth. It was about this time that Dorothy woke from her long sleep and opened her eyes. She was greatly astonished to find herself lying upon the grass, with thousands of mice standing around and looking at her timidly. But the Scarecrow told her about everything, and turning to the dignified little Mouse, he said,

"Permit me to introduce to you her Majesty, the Queen."

Dorothy nodded gravely and the Queen made a curtsy, after which she became quite friendly with the little girl.

The Scarecrow and the Woodman now began to fasten the mice to the truck, using the strings they had brought. One end of a string was tied around the neck of each mouse and the other end to the truck. Of course the truck was a thousand times bigger than any of the mice who were to draw it; but when all the mice had been harnessed, they were able to pull it quite easily. Even the Scarecrow and the Tin Woodman could sit on it, and were drawn swiftly by their queer little horses to the place where the Lion lay asleep.

After a great deal of hard work, for the Lion was heavy, they managed to get him up on the truck. Then the Queen hurriedly gave her people the order to start, for she feared if the mice stayed among the poppies too long they also would fall asleep.

At first the little creatures, many though they were, could hardly stir the heavily loaded truck; but the Woodman and the Scarecrow both pushed from behind, and they got along better. Soon they rolled the Lion out of the poppy bed to the green fields, where he could breathe the sweet, fresh air again, instead of the poisonous scent of the flowers.

Dorothy came to meet them and thanked the little mice warmly for saving her companion from death.[30] She had grown so fond of the big Lion she was glad he had been rescued.

Then the mice were unharnessed from the truck and scampered away through the grass to their homes. The Queen of the Mice was the last to leave.

"If ever you need us again," she said, "come out into the field and call, and we shall hear you and come to your assistance. Good bye!"

"Good bye!" they all answered, and away the Queen ran, while Dorothy held Toto tightly lest he should run after her and frighten her.

After this they sat down beside the Lion until he should awaken; and the Scarecrow brought Dorothy some fruit from a tree near by, which she ate for her dinner.

Chapter X.
The Guardian of the Gate.

It was some time before the Cowardly Lion awakened, for he had lain among the poppies a long while, breathing in their deadly fragrance; but when he did open his eyes and roll off the truck he was very glad to find himself still alive.

"I ran as fast as I could," he said, sitting down and yawning; "but the flowers were too strong for me. How did you get me out?"

Then they told him of the field-mice, and how they had generously saved him from death; and the Cowardly Lion laughed, and said,

"I have always thought myself very big and terrible; yet such little things as flowers came near to killing me, and such small animals as mice have saved my life. How strange it all is! But, comrades, what shall we do now?"

"We must journey on until we find the road of yellow brick again," said Dorothy; "and then we can keep on to the Emerald City."

So, the Lion being fully refreshed, and feeling quite himself again, they all started upon the journey, greatly enjoying the walk through the soft, fresh grass; and it was not long before they reached the road of yellow brick and turned again toward the Emerald City where the great Oz dwelt.

The road was smooth and well paved, now, and the country about was beautiful; so that the travelers rejoiced in leaving the forest far behind, and with it the many dangers they had met in its gloomy shades. Once more they could see fences built beside the road; but these were painted green, and when they came to a small house, in which a farmer evidently lived, that also was painted green. They passed by several of these houses during the afternoon, and sometimes people came to the doors and looked at them as if they would like to ask questions; but no one came

---

30. The field mice could symbolize the rank-and-file Populists—the "little people"—whose turnout and support were crucial to Bryan's presidential hopes. In keeping with his interpretation of the Deadly Poppy Field as anti-imperialism, Rockoff says it is appropriate that the mice, as "little folk concerned with everyday issues (such as the price of corn)," are the ones who pull the Lion to safety (1990, p. 749).

near them nor spoke to them because of the great Lion, of which they were very much afraid. The people were all dressed in clothing of a lovely emerald green color and wore peaked hats like those of the Munchkins.

"This must be the Land of Oz," said Dorothy, "and we are surely getting near the Emerald City."

"Yes," answered the Scarecrow; "everything is green here, while in the country of the Munchkins blue was the favorite color. But the people do not seem to be as friendly as the Munchkins, and I'm afraid we shall be unable to find a place to pass the night."

"I should like something to eat besides fruit," said the girl, "and I'm sure Toto is nearly starved. Let us stop at the next house and talk to the people."

So, when they came to a good sized farmhouse, Dorothy walked boldly up to the door and knocked. A woman opened it just far enough to look out, and said,

"What do you want, child, and why is that great Lion with you?"

"We wish to pass the night with you, if you will allow us," answered Dorothy; "and the Lion is my friend and comrade, and would not hurt you for the world."

"Is he tame?" asked the woman, opening the door a little wider.

"Oh, yes," said the girl; "and he is a great coward, too; so that he will be more afraid of you than you are of him."

"Well," said the woman, after thinking it over and taking another peep at the Lion, "if that is the case you may come in, and I will give you some supper and a place to sleep."

So they all entered the house, where there were, besides the woman, two children and a man. The man had hurt his leg, and was lying on the couch in a corner. They seemed greatly surprised to see so strange a company, and while the woman was busy laying the table the man asked,

"Where are you all going?"

"To the Emerald City," said Dorothy, "to see the Great Oz."

"Oh, indeed!" exclaimed the man. "Are you sure that Oz will see you?"

"Why not?" she replied.

"Why, it is said that he never lets anyone come into his presence. I have been to the Emerald City many times, and it is a beautiful and wonderful place; but I have never been permitted to see the Great Oz, nor do I know of any living person who has seen him."

"Does he never go out?" asked the Scarecrow.

"Never. He sits day after day in the great throne room of his palace, and even those who wait upon him do not see him face to face."

"What is he like?" asked the girl.

"That is hard to tell," said the man thoughtfully. "You see, Oz is a great Wizard, and can take on any form he wishes. So that some say he looks like a bird; and some say he looks like an elephant; and some say he looks like a cat. To others he appears as a beautiful fairy, or a brownie, or in any other form that pleases him.

But who the real Oz is, when he is in his own form, no living person can tell."[31]

"That is very strange," said Dorothy; "but we must try, in some way, to see him, or we shall have made our journey for nothing."

"Why do you wish to see the terrible Oz?" asked the man.

"I want him to give me some brains," said the Scarecrow, eagerly.

"Oh, Oz could do that easily enough," declared the man. "He has more brains than he needs."

"And I want him to give me a heart," said the Tin Woodman.

"That will not trouble him," continued the man, "for Oz has a large collection of hearts, of all sizes and shapes."

"And I want him to give me courage," said the Cowardly Lion.

"Oz keeps a great pot of courage in his Throne Room," said the man, "which he has covered with a golden plate, to keep it from running over.[32] He will be glad to give you some."

"And I want him to send me back to Kansas," said Dorothy.

"Where is Kansas?" asked the man, with surprise.

"I don't know," replied Dorothy, sorrowfully; "but it is my home, and I'm sure it's somewhere."

"Very likely. Well, Oz can do anything; so I suppose he will find Kansas for you. But first you must get to see him, and that will be a hard task; for the great Wizard does not like to see anyone, and he usually has his own way. But what do YOU want?" he continued, speaking to Toto. Toto only wagged his tail; for, strange to say, he could not speak.

The woman now called to them that supper was ready, so they gathered around the table and Dorothy ate some delicious porridge and a dish of scrambled eggs and a plate of nice white bread, and enjoyed her meal. The Lion ate some of the porridge, but did not care for it, saying it was made from oats and oats were food for horses, not for lions. The Scarecrow and the Tin Woodman ate nothing at all. Toto ate a little of everything, and was glad to get a good supper again.

The woman now gave Dorothy a bed to sleep in, and Toto lay down beside her, while the Lion guarded the door of her room so she might not be disturbed. The Scarecrow and the Tin Woodman stood up in a corner and kept quiet all night,

---

31. We learn for the first time that Oz, as a great wizard, "can take on any form he wishes." In this sense the Wizard is like a master politician who manages to be all things to all people (Littlefield 1964, p. 54). And, like many a politician, nobody knows precisely what he stands for: "who the real Oz is, when he is in his own form, no living person can tell." The political overtones of the Wizard become more apparent as the story unfolds.

32. The golden plate that covers Oz's great pot of courage "to keep it from running over" is symbolic of the gold standard and the restraint that it exercises on the economy and the price level (Rockoff 1990, p. 749).

One could also view the pot and plate as symbolizing the tremendous courage that would be required for any president to reject the gold standard in the face of pressure from bankers, bondholders, and other wealthy interests. Courageous action to combat the depression of the mid-1890s was impossible, many Populists believed, as long as the gold standard remained in place.

although of course they could not sleep.

The next morning, as soon as the sun was up, they started on their way, and soon saw a beautiful green glow in the sky just before them.

"That must be the Emerald City," said Dorothy.

As they walked on, the green glow became brighter and brighter, and it seemed that at last they were nearing the end of their travels. Yet it was afternoon before they came to the great wall that surrounded the City. It was high, and thick, and of a bright green color.

In front of them, and at the end of the road of yellow brick, was a big gate, all studded with emeralds that glittered so in the sun that even the painted eyes of the Scarecrow were dazzled by their brilliancy.

There was a bell beside the gate, and Dorothy pushed the button and heard a silvery tinkle sound within. Then the big gate swung slowly open, and they all passed through and found themselves in a high arched room, the walls of which glistened with countless emeralds.

Before them stood a little man about the same size as the Munchkins. He was clothed all in green, from his head to his feet, and even his skin was of a greenish tint. At his side was a large green box.

When he saw Dorothy and her companions the man asked,

"What do you wish in the Emerald City?"

"We came here to see the Great Oz," said Dorothy.

The man was so surprised at this answer that he sat down to think it over.

"It has been many years since anyone asked me to see Oz," he said, shaking his head in perplexity. "He is powerful and terrible, and if you come on an idle or foolish errand to bother the wise reflections of the Great Wizard, he might be angry and destroy you all in an instant."

"But it is not a foolish errand, nor an idle one," replied the Scarecrow; "it is important. And we have been told that Oz is a good Wizard."

"So he is," said the green man; "and he rules the Emerald City wisely and well. But to those who are not honest, or who approach him from curiosity, he is most terrible, and few have ever dared ask to see his face. I am the Guardian of the Gates, and since you demand to see the Great Oz I must take you to his palace. But first you must put on the spectacles."

"Why?" asked Dorothy.

"Because if you did not wear spectacles the brightness and glory of the Emerald City would blind you. Even those who live in the City must wear spectacles night and day. They are all locked on, for Oz so ordered it when the City was first built, and I have the only key that will unlock them."

He opened the big box, and Dorothy saw that it was filled with spectacles of every size and shape. All of them had green glasses in them. The Guardian of the gates found a pair that would just fit Dorothy and put them over her eyes. There were two golden bands fastened to them that passed around the back of her head, where they were locked together by a little key that was at the end of a chain the Guardian of the Gates wore around his neck. When they were on, Dorothy could not take them off had she wished, but of course she did not wish to be blinded by the glare of the Emerald City, so she said nothing.

Then the green man fitted spectacles for the Scarecrow and the Tin Woodman and the Lion, and even on little Toto; and all were locked fast with the key.[33]

Then the Guardian of the Gates put on his own glasses and told them he was ready to show them to the Palace. Taking a big golden key from a peg on the wall he opened another gate, and they all followed him through the portal into the streets of the Emerald City.

Chapter XI.
The Wonderful Emerald City of Oz.

Even with eyes protected by the green spectacles, Dorothy and her friends were at first dazzled by the brilliancy of the wonderful City. The streets were lined with beautiful houses all built of green marble and studded everywhere with sparkling emeralds. They walked over a pavement of the same green marble, and where the blocks were joined together were rows of emeralds, set closely, and glittering in the brightness of the sun. The window panes were of green glass; even the sky above the City had a green tint, and the rays of the sun were green.

There were many people, men, women, and children, walking about, and these were all dressed in green clothes and had greenish skins. They looked at Dorothy and her strangely assorted company with wondering eyes, and the children all ran away and hid behind their mothers when they saw the Lion; but no one spoke to them. Many shops stood in the street, and Dorothy saw that everything in them was green. Green candy and green pop-corn were offered for sale, as well as green shoes, green hats, and green clothes of all sorts. At one place a man was selling green lemonade, and when the children bought it Dorothy could see that they paid for it with green pennies.[34]

---

33. The green spectacles, which are locked on with golden bands and which everyone in the Emerald City must wear, force everyone in the city "to look at the world through money-colored glasses" (Rockoff 1990, p. 750). In Chapter XV we discover that the real reason for the spectacles is different from the one given by the Guardian, but the monetary symbolism remains.

34. In the standard political interpretation the Emerald City is Washington, D.C., but it is widely believed that Baum drew much of the inspiration for the Emerald City from the grandiose "White City" that was specially created for the 1893 Columbian Exposition, better known as the World's Fair, in Chicago (Riley 1998). The White City occupied 633 acres and included 200 buildings, done up in spectacular architectural styles.

The commercial aspects of the Emerald City are in keeping with the commercial nature of the Exposition. The fair's 65,000 exhibits displayed an endless array of consumer goods. The fair marked the introduction of such venerable brand-name products as Cracker Jacks, Aunt Jemima Syrup, Cream of Wheat, Juicy Fruit Gum, and Pabst Beer, as well as carbonated soda and hamburgers. William Leach (1991, 1993) has offered an extensive interpretation of the Emerald City as a consumer paradise.

Among the many luminaries on the program at the World's Fair was historian Frederick Jackson Turner, who presented his famous paper on the closing of the Western frontier. The frontier, long regarded as a land of opportunity and a safety valve for working-class discontent, had effectively disappeared as more and more Americans moved West. As many

There seemed to be no horses nor animals of any kind; the men carried things around in little green carts, which they pushed before them. Everyone seemed happy and contented and prosperous.

The Guardian of the Gates led them through the streets until they came to a big building, exactly in the middle of the City, which was the Palace of Oz, the Great Wizard. There was a soldier before the door, dressed in a green uniform and wearing a long green beard.

"Here are strangers," said the Guardian of the Gates to him, "and they demand to see the Great Oz."

"Step inside," answered the soldier, "and I will carry your message to him."

So they passed through the Palace gates and were led into a big room with a green carpet and lovely green furniture set with emeralds. The soldier made them all wipe their feet upon a green mat before entering this room, and when they were seated he said, politely:

"Please make yourselves comfortable while I go to the door of the Throne Room and tell Oz you are here."

They had to wait a long time before the soldier returned. When, at last, he came back, Dorothy asked,

"Have you seen Oz?"

"Oh, no," returned the soldier; "I have never seen him. But I spoke to him as he sat behind his screen and gave him your message. He said he will grant you an audience, if you so desire; but each one of you must enter his presence alone, and he will admit but one each day. Therefore, as you must remain in the Palace for several days, I will have you shown to rooms where you may rest in comfort after your journey."

"Thank you," replied the girl; "that is very kind of Oz."

The soldier now blew upon a green whistle, and at once a young girl, dressed in a pretty green silk gown, entered the room. She had lovely green hair and green eyes, and she bowed low before Dorothy as she said, "Follow me and I will show you your room."

So Dorothy said good-bye to all her friends except Toto, and taking the dog in her arms followed the green girl through seven passages and up three flights of stairs until they came to a room at the front of the Palace.[35] It was the sweetest little room in the world, with a soft comfortable bed that had sheets of green silk and a green velvet counterpane. There was a tiny fountain in the middle of the room, that

---

historians see it, the closing of that frontier precipitated violent conflicts with the Western Indians (culminating in their massacre at Wounded Knee in 1890) and ushered in an age of American overseas expansionism, since there was no longer any "virgin territory" in the American West.

35. " through seven passages and up three flights of stairs": Put those two numbers side by side and you get seventy-three, which corresponds to the so-called Crime of '73—that is, the Coinage Act of 1873, which discontinued federal minting of the silver dollar. To the free-silver Populists, the Crime of '73 was the government's Original Sin, "the source of all future difficulties" (Rockoff 1990, p. 750).

shot a spray of green perfume into the air, to fall back into a beautifully carved green marble basin. Beautiful green flowers stood in the windows, and there was a shelf with a row of little green books. When Dorothy had time to open these books she found them full of queer green pictures that made her laugh, they were so funny.

In a wardrobe were many green dresses, made of silk and satin and velvet; and all of them fitted Dorothy exactly.

"Make yourself perfectly at home," said the green girl, "and if you wish for anything ring the bell. Oz will send for you to-morrow morning."

She left Dorothy alone and went back to the others. These she also led to rooms, and each one of them found himself lodged in a very pleasant part of the Palace. Of course this politeness was wasted on the Scarecrow; for when he found himself alone in his room he stood stupidly in one spot, just within the doorway, to wait till morning. It would not rest him to lie down, and he could not close his eyes; so he remained all night staring at a little spider which was weaving its web in a corner of the room, just as if it were not one of the most wonderful rooms in the world. The Tin Woodman lay down on his bed from force of habit, for he remembered when he was made of flesh; but not being able to sleep, he passed the night moving his joints up and down to make sure they kept in good working order. The Lion would have preferred a bed of dried leaves in the forest, and did not like being shut up in a room; but he had too much sense to let this worry him, so he sprang upon the bed and rolled himself up like a cat and purred himself asleep in a minute.

The next morning, after breakfast, the green maiden came to fetch Dorothy, and she dressed her in one of the prettiest gowns—made of green brocaded satin. Dorothy put on a green silk apron and tied a green ribbon around Toto's neck, and they started for the Throne Room of the Great Oz.

First they came to a great hall in which were many ladies and gentlemen of the court, all dressed in rich costumes. These people had nothing to do but talk to each other, but they always came to wait outside the Throne Room every morning, although they were never permitted to see Oz. As Dorothy entered they looked at her curiously, and one of them whispered,

"Are you really going to look upon the face of Oz the Terrible?"

"Of course," answered the girl, "if he will see me."

"Oh, he will see you," said the soldier who had taken her message to the Wizard, "although he does not like to have people ask to see him. Indeed, at first he was angry and said I should send you back where you came from. Then he asked me what you looked like, and when I mentioned your silver shoes he was very much interested. At last I told him about the mark upon your forehead, and he decided he would admit you to his presence."

Just then a bell rang, and the green girl said to Dorothy,

"That is the signal. You must go into the Throne Room alone."

She opened a little door and Dorothy walked boldly through and found herself in a wonderful place. It was a big, round room with a high arched roof, and the walls and ceiling and floor were covered with large emeralds set closely together.[36] In the center of the roof was a great light, as bright as the sun, which made the emeralds sparkle in a wonderful manner.

But what interested Dorothy most was the big throne of green marble that stood in the middle of the room. It was shaped like a chair and sparkled with gems, as did everything else. In the center of the chair was an enormous Head, without a body to support it or any arms or legs whatever. There was no hair upon this head, but it had eyes and a nose and mouth, and was much bigger than the head of the biggest giant.

As Dorothy gazed upon this in wonder and fear, the eyes turned slowly and looked at her sharply and steadily. Then the mouth moved, and Dorothy heard a voice say:

"I am Oz, the Great and Terrible. Who are you, and why do you seek me?"

It was not such an awful voice as she had expected to come from the big Head; so she took courage and answered:

"I am Dorothy, the Small and Meek. I have come to you for help."

The eyes looked at her thoughtfully for a full minute. Then said the voice:

"Where did you get the silver shoes?"

"I got them from the wicked Witch of the East, when my house fell on her and killed her," she replied.

"Where did you get the mark upon your forehead?" continued the voice.

"That is where the good Witch of the North kissed me when she bade me good-bye and sent me to you," said the girl.

Again the eyes looked at her sharply, and they saw she was telling the truth. Then Oz asked,

"What do you wish me to do?"

"Send me back to Kansas, where my Aunt Em and Uncle Henry are," she answered, earnestly. "I don't like your country, although it is so beautiful. And I am sure Aunt Em will be dreadfully worried over my being away so long."

The eyes winked three times, and then they turned up to the ceiling and down to the floor and rolled around so queerly that they seemed to see every part of the room. And at last they looked at Dorothy again.

"Why should I do this for you?" asked Oz.

"Because you are strong and I am weak; because you are a Great Wizard and I am only a little girl."

"But you were strong enough to kill the wicked Witch of the East," said Oz.

"That just happened," returned Dorothy simply; "I could not help it."

"Well," said the Head, "I will give you my answer. You have no right to expect me to send you back to Kansas unless you do something for me in return. In this country everyone must pay for everything he gets. If you wish me to use my

---

36. Just as the Palace of Oz seems symbolic of the White House, so does the big, round Throne Room suggest the Oval Office. This particular correspondence could not possibly have been intentional, however, since the Oval Office was not built until 1909.

magic power to send you home again you must do something for me first. Help me
and I will help you."

"What must I do?" asked the girl.

"Kill the wicked Witch of the West," answered Oz.[37]

"But I cannot!" exclaimed Dorothy, greatly surprised.

"You killed the Witch of the East and you wear the silver shoes, which bear
a powerful charm. There is now but one Wicked Witch left in all this land, and
when you can tell me she is dead I will send you back to Kansas—but not before."

The little girl began to weep, she was so much disappointed; and the eyes
winked again and looked upon her anxiously, as if the Great Oz felt that she could
help him if she would.

"I never killed anything, willingly," she sobbed. "Even if I wanted to, how
could I kill the Wicked Witch? If you, who are Great and Terrible, cannot kill her
yourself, how do you expect me to do it?"

"I do not know," said the Head; "but that is my answer, and until the Wicked
Witch dies you will not see your uncle and aunt again. Remember that the Witch
is Wicked—tremendously Wicked—and ought to be killed. Now go, and do not
ask to see me again until you have done your task."

Sorrowfully Dorothy left the Throne Room and went back where the Lion and
the Scarecrow and the Tin Woodman were waiting to hear what Oz had said to her.

"There is no hope for me," she said sadly, "for Oz will not send me home until
I have killed the Wicked Witch of the West; and that I can never do."

Her friends were sorry, but could do nothing to help her; so Dorothy went to
her own room and lay down on the bed and cried herself to sleep.

The next morning the soldier with the green whiskers came to the Scarecrow
and said,

"Come with me, for Oz has sent for you."

So the Scarecrow followed him and was admitted into the great Throne Room,

---

37. Oz's instruction to "kill the wicked Witch of the West" recalls a line in an
inflammatory letter by then-disaffected Kansas Populist Mary Elizabeth Lease, alleging a
Populist plot against her: "It is necessary to 'kill me politically' ere they can succeed" (letter
in the *Pleasanton Herald*, January 26, 1894; quoted in Clanton 1968, p. 197). By that time,
Lease was seen by Annie Diggs and others as an enemy of the Populists. Always a lightning
rod for controversy, Lease became an increasingly easy figure for Populists and progressives
to detest (see notes to Baum, Chapter I).

While the more abstract interpretation of the Western Witch as malign nature seems
more promising, one can make a case for Lease as a partial inspiration for the Witch. Lease
"surely provided more raw material for zany caricature than any public figure of her
generation." She stood nearly six feet tall, with "what William Allen White described as the
'most ungodly hats I ever saw a women wear' and features that moved one Kansas editor
to describe her (somewhat unfairly) as a 'lantern-jawed, goggle-eyed nightmare.' " A
newspaper cartoon in 1896 depicted her as "a broom-toting prune-faced harridan" (Fischer
1996, p. 66). White's "What's the Matter with Kansas?" called her a "harpy." The severe-
visaged Lease even bears a passing resemblance to Margaret Hamilton's wicked Witch of
the West in the 1939 MGM film.

where he saw, sitting in the emerald throne, a most lovely lady. She was dressed in green silk gauze and wore upon her flowing green locks a crown of jewels. Growing from her shoulders were wings, gorgeous in color and so light that they fluttered if the slightest breath of air reached them.

When the Scarecrow had bowed, as prettily as his straw stuffing would let him, before this beautiful creature, she looked upon him sweetly, and said:

"I am Oz, the Great and Terrible. Who are you, and why do you seek me?"

Now the Scarecrow, who had expected to see the great Head Dorothy had told him of, was much astonished; but he answered her bravely.

"I am only a Scarecrow, stuffed with straw. Therefore I have no brains, and I come to you praying that you will put brains in my head instead of straw, so that I may become as much a man as any other in your dominions."

"Why should I do this for you?" asked the lady.

"Because you are wise and powerful, and no one else can help me," answered the Scarecrow.

"I never grant favors without some return," said Oz; "but this much I will promise. If you will kill for me the Wicked Witch of the West, I will bestow upon you a great many brains, and such good brains that you will be the wisest man in all the Land of Oz."

"I thought you asked Dorothy to kill the Witch," said the Scarecrow, in surprise.

"So I did. I don't care who kills her. But until she is dead I will not grant your wish. Now go, and do not seek me again until you have earned the brains you so greatly desire."

The Scarecrow went sorrowfully back to his friends and told them what Oz had said; and Dorothy was surprised to find that the Great Wizard was not a Head, as she had seen him, but a lovely lady.

"All the same," said the Scarecrow, "she needs a heart as much as the Tin Woodman."

On the next morning the soldier with the green whiskers came to the Tin Woodman and said,

"Oz has sent for you. Follow me."

So the Tin Woodman followed him and came to the great Throne Room. He did not know whether he would find Oz a lovely lady or a Head, but he hoped it would be the lovely lady. "For," he said to himself, "if it is the Head, I am sure I shall not be given a heart, since a head has no heart of its own and therefore cannot feel for me. But if it is the lovely lady I shall beg hard for a heart, for all ladies are themselves said to be kindly hearted.

But when the Woodman entered the great Throne Room he saw neither the Head nor the Lady, for Oz had taken the shape of a most terrible Beast. It was nearly as big as an elephant, and the green throne seemed hardly strong enough to hold its weight. The Beast had a head like that of a rhinoceros, only there were five eyes in its face. There were five long arms growing out of its body, and it also had five long, slim legs. Thick, woolly hair covered every part of it, and a more dreadful looking monster could not be imagined. It was fortunate the Tin Woodman had no heart at that moment, for it would have beat loud and fast from terror. But being only tin, the Woodman was not at all afraid, although he was much disappointed.

"I am Oz, the Great and Terrible," spake the Beast, in a voice that was one great roar. "Who are you, and why do you seek me?"

"I am a Woodman, and made of tin. Therefore I have no heart, and cannot love. I pray you to give me a heart that I may be as other men are."

"Why should I do this?" demanded the Beast.

"Because I ask it, and you alone can grant my request," answered the Woodman.

Oz gave a low growl at this, but said, gruffly,

"If you indeed desire a heart, you must earn it."

"How?" asked the Woodman.

"Help Dorothy to kill the Wicked Witch of the West," replied the Beast. "When the Witch is dead, come to me, and I will then give you the biggest and kindest and most loving heart in all the Land of Oz."

So the Tin Woodman was forced to return sorrowfully to his friends and tell them of the terrible Beast he had seen. They all wondered greatly at the many forms the Great Wizard could take upon himself, and the Lion said,

"If he is a Beast when I go to see him, I shall roar my loudest, and so frighten him that he will grant all I ask. And if he is the lovely lady, I shall pretend to spring upon her, and so compel her to do my bidding. And if he is the great Head, he will be at my mercy; for I will roll this head all about the room until he promises to give us what we desire. So be of good cheer, my friends, for all will yet be well."

The next morning the soldier with the green whiskers led the Lion to the great Throne Room and bade him enter the presence of Oz.

The Lion at once passed through the door, and glancing around saw, to his surprise, that before the throne was a Ball of Fire, so fierce and glowing he could scarcely bear to gaze upon it.[38] His first thought was that Oz had by accident caught on fire and was burning up; but when he tried to go nearer, the heat was so intense that it singed his whiskers, and he crept back tremblingly to a spot nearer the door.

Then a low, quiet voice came from the Ball of Fire, and these were the words it spoke:

"I am Oz, the Great and Terrible. Who are you, and why do you seek me?"

And the Lion answered, "I am a Cowardly Lion, afraid of everything. I came

---

38. The Wizard takes on an entirely different form for each of the four travelers, just as the man in the farm house had said he could. Again, this is in keeping with the notion of the Wizard as a politician who can be all things to all people.

In one of the later Oz books (*Dorothy and the Wizard of Oz*, 1908), in fact, the Wizard turns out to be the son of a politician (Hearn 1973, p. 266). In the same book, the Wizard reveals that his given last name was Diggs, recalling one of the great Kansas Populists, Annie Diggs. The Wizard also reveals that his given name was Oscar Zoroaster Phadrig Isaac Norman Henkle Emmanuel Ambroise Diggs, which he shortened to OZ, after the first two initials. He notes that the rest of his initials spell PINHEAD (and that he obviously didn't want people to associate him with that word), which could be yet another of Baum's playful swipes at politicians in general and, just maybe, Populists in particular.

to you to beg that you give me courage, so that in reality I may become the King of Beasts, as men call me."

"Why should I give you courage?" demanded Oz.

"Because of all Wizards you are the greatest, and alone have power to grant my request," answered the Lion.

The Ball of Fire burned fiercely for a time, and the voice said,

"Bring me proof that the Wicked Witch is dead, and that moment I will give you courage. But as long as the Witch lives, you must remain a coward."

The Lion was angry at this speech, but could say nothing in reply, and while he stood silently gazing at the Ball of Fire it became so furiously hot that he turned tail and rushed from the room. He was glad to find his friends waiting for him, and told them of his terrible interview with the Wizard.

"What shall we do now?" asked Dorothy, sadly.

"There is only one thing we can do," returned the Lion, "and that is to go to the land of the Winkies, seek out the Wicked Witch, and destroy her."

"But suppose we cannot?" said the girl.

"Then I shall never have courage," declared the Lion.

"And I shall never have brains," added the Scarecrow.

"And I shall never have a heart," spoke the Tin Woodman.

"And I shall never see Aunt Em and Uncle Henry," said Dorothy, beginning to cry.

"Be careful!" cried the green girl. "The tears will fall on your green silk gown, and spot it."

So Dorothy dried her eyes and said,

"I suppose we must try it; but I am sure I do not want to kill anybody, even to see Aunt Em again."

"I will go with you; but I'm too much of a coward to kill the Witch," said the Lion.

"I will go too," declared the Scarecrow; "but I shall not be of much help to you, I am such a fool."

"I haven't the heart to harm even a Witch," remarked the Tin Woodman; "but if you go I certainly shall go with you."

Therefore it was decided to start upon their journey the next morning, and the Woodman sharpened his axe on a green grindstone and had all his joints properly oiled. The Scarecrow stuffed himself with fresh straw and Dorothy put new paint on his eyes that he might see better. The green girl, who was very kind to them, filled Dorothy's basket with good things to eat, and fastened a little bell around Toto's neck with a green ribbon.

They went to bed quite early and slept soundly until daylight, when they were awakened by the crowing of a green cock that lived in the back yard of the Palace, and the cackling of a hen that had laid a green egg.

Chapter XII.
The Search for the Wicked Witch.

The soldier with the green whiskers led them through the streets of the Emerald City until they reached the room where the Guardian of the Gates lived. This officer unlocked their spectacles to put them back in his great box, and then he politely opened the gate for our friends.

"Which road leads to the Wicked Witch of the West?" asked Dorothy.

"There is no road," answered the Guardian of the Gates; "no one ever wishes to go that way."

"How, then, are we to find her?" enquired the girl.

"That will be easy," replied the man, "for when she knows you are in the Country of the Winkies she will find you, and make you all her slaves."

"Perhaps not," said the Scarecrow, "for we mean to destroy her."

"Oh, that is different," said the Guardian of the Gates. "No one has ever destroyed her before, so I naturally thought she would make slaves of you, as she has of the rest. But take care; for she is wicked and fierce, and may not allow you to destroy her. Keep to the West, where the sun sets, and you cannot fail to find her."

They thanked him and bade him good-bye, and turned toward the West, walking over fields of soft grass dotted here and there with daisies and buttercups. Dorothy still wore the pretty silk dress she had put on in the palace, but now, to her surprise, she found it was no longer green, but pure white. The ribbon around Toto's neck had also lost its green color and was as white as Dorothy's dress.

The Emerald City was soon left far behind. As they advanced the ground became rougher and hillier, for there were no farms nor houses in this country of the West, and the ground was untilled.

In the afternoon the sun shone hot in their faces, for there were no trees to offer them shade; so that before night Dorothy and Toto and the Lion were tired, and lay down upon the grass and fell asleep, with the Woodman and the Scarecrow keeping watch.

Now the Wicked Witch of the West had but one eye, yet that was as powerful as a telescope, and could see everywhere. So, as she sat in the door of her castle, she happened to look around and saw Dorothy lying asleep, with her friends all about her. They were a long distance off, but the Wicked Witch was angry to find them in her country; so she blew upon a silver whistle that hung around her neck.[39]

---

39. "The Witch of the West uses natural forces to achieve her ends," writes Littlefield; "she is Baum's version of sentient and malign nature." The harshness of the land in the Western Witch's kingdom is evident from Baum's descriptions: "there were no farms nor houses in this country of the West, and the ground was untilled. In the afternoon the sun shone hot in their faces, for there were no trees to offer them shade." Littlefield sees the Witch as a composite of both the malign forces of Western nature and also the same sort of evil financial-industrial interests that the Eastern Witch represents. "The Witch assumes the proportions of a kind of Western Mark Hanna or Banker Boss, who, through natural malevolence, manipulates the people and holds them prisoner by cynically taking advantage of their innate innocence" (1964, p. 55). Thus her enslavement of the Winkies could be seen

At once there came running to her from all directions a pack of great wolves. They had long legs and fierce eyes and sharp teeth.

"Go to those people," said the Witch, "and tear them to pieces."

"Are you not going to make them your slaves?" asked the leader of the wolves.

"No," she answered, "one is of tin, and one of straw; one is a girl and another a Lion. None of them is fit to work, so you may tear them into small pieces."

"Very well," said the wolf, and he dashed away at full speed, followed by the others.

It was lucky the Scarecrow and the Woodman were wide awake and heard the wolves coming.

"This is my fight," said the Woodman, "so get behind me and I will meet them as they come."

He seized his axe, which he had made very sharp, and as the leader of the wolves came on the Tin Woodman swung his arm and chopped the wolf's head from its body, so that it immediately died. As soon as he could raise his axe another wolf came up, and he also fell under the sharp edge of the Tin Woodman's weapon. There were forty wolves, and forty times a wolf was killed, so that at last they all lay dead in a heap before the Woodman.

Then he put down his axe and sat beside the Scarecrow, who said,

"It was a good fight, friend."

They waited until Dorothy awoke the next morning. The little girl was quite frightened when she saw the great pile of shaggy wolves, but the Tin Woodman told her all. She thanked him for saving them and sat down to breakfast, after which they started again upon their journey.

Now this same morning the Wicked Witch came to the door of her castle and looked out with her one eye that could see far off. She saw all her wolves lying dead, and the strangers still travelling through her country. This made her angrier than before, and she blew her silver whistle twice.

---

as akin to wage slavery, just like the Eastern Witch's enslavement of the Munchkins.

Rockoff, as noted previously, sees the Witch as symbolizing President McKinley of Ohio, another backer of the gold standard.

In a polar-opposite interpretation that nevertheless works, the Western Witch represents the Populists themselves, or "agrarian radicalism, socialism, or those on the left wing of the political spectrum generally," and the book can be read as an *anti*-Populist parable. In this reading, the Witch's obsession with the silver shoes, as well as the silver whistle she wears around her neck, assumes central importance. Viewed this way, the direct inspiration for the Western Witch could be Mary Lease or the one-eyed Senator Benjamin R. Tillman of South Carolina, known as the "One-Eyed Plowboy" or "Pitchfork Ben" Tillman. Though Tillman never actually was a member of the Populist Party, his roots as an upland farmer and in the Farmers' Alliance, together with his "reactionary agrarianism," caused Tillman and the Populists to be lumped together in many people's minds. The racist, demagogic Tillman "symbolized in the minds of establishment types the worst side of the agrarian revolt" (Clanton 1991, p. 150). Also, some anti-Populist cartoons of the time deployed images of witchcraft, such as Bryan as a would-be sorcerer wearing a witch's hat, or a coven of male witches stirring a Populist "Hell Broth."

Straightway a great flock of wild crows came flying toward her, enough to darken the sky.

And the Wicked Witch said to the King Crow,

"Fly at once to the strangers; peck out their eyes and tear them to pieces."

The wild crows flew in one great flock toward Dorothy and her companions. When the little girl saw them coming she was afraid. But the Scarecrow said,

"This is my battle; so lie down beside me and you will not be harmed."

So they all lay upon the ground except the Scarecrow, and he stood up and stretched out his arms. And when the crows saw him they were frightened, as these birds always are by scarecrows, and did not dare to come any nearer. But the King Crow said,

"It is only a stuffed man. I will peck his eyes out."

The King Crow flew at the Scarecrow, who caught it by the head and twisted its neck until it died. And then another crow flew at him, and the Scarecrow twisted its neck also. There were forty crows, and forty times the Scarecrow twisted a neck, until at last all were lying dead beside him. Then he called to his companions to rise, and again they went upon their journey.

When the Wicked Witch looked out again and saw all her crows lying in a heap, she got into a terrible rage, and blew three times upon her silver whistle.[40]

Forthwith there was heard a great buzzing in the air, and a swarm of black bees came flying toward her.[41]

"Go to the strangers and sting them to death!" commanded the Witch, and the bees turned and flew rapidly until they came to where Dorothy and her friends were walking. But the Woodman had seen them coming, and the Scarecrow had decided what to do.

"Take out my straw and scatter it over the little girl and the dog and the Lion," he said to the Woodman, "and the bees cannot sting them." This the Woodman did, and as Dorothy lay close beside the Lion and held Toto in her arms, the straw covered them entirely.

The bees came and found no one but the Woodman to sting, so they flew at him and broke off all their stings against the tin, without hurting the Woodman at all. And as bees cannot live when their stings are broken that was the end of the black bees, and they lay scattered thick about the Woodman, like little heaps of fine coal.

---

40. The Western Witch, with her ability to summon menacing wild animals by blowing on her silver whistle, also knows the magical powers of silver.

If one chooses to view the story as an anti-Populist parable, then the Witch's blowing of the silver whistle could symbolize the Populists' and Bryan's shrillness on the silver issue. Clanton (1998, p. 186 n.8) says it symbolizes the beguiling nature of the free-silver issue to Western farmers and the way the Populists (and perhaps Bryan) used it to enthrall them.

41. The "swarm of black bees" parallels the so-called Plague of Grasshoppers that devastated Western farmlands beginning in 1873, the same year as the Crime of '73.

The swarm of bees and the other quasi-biblical plagues the Western Witch summons are in keeping with the notion of that Witch as a symbol of the malign forces of nature, including wild animals, birds, and crop-eating insects (Lurie 1990, p. 12).

Then Dorothy and the Lion got up, and the girl helped the Tin Woodman put the straw back into the Scarecrow again, until he was as good as ever. So they started upon their journey once more.

The Wicked Witch was so angry when she saw her black bees in little heaps like fine coal that she stamped her foot and tore her hair and gnashed her teeth. And then she called a dozen of her slaves, who were the Winkies, and gave them sharp spears, telling them to go to the strangers and destroy them.[42]

The Winkies were not a brave people, but they had to do as they were told. So they marched away until they came near to Dorothy. Then the Lion gave a great roar and sprang towards them, and the poor Winkies were so frightened that they ran back as fast as they could.

When they returned to the castle the Wicked Witch beat them well with a strap, and sent them back to their work, after which she sat down to think what she should do next. She could not understand how all her plans to destroy these strangers had failed; but she was a powerful Witch, as well as a wicked one, and she soon made up her mind how to act.

There was, in her cupboard, a Golden Cap, with a circle of diamonds and rubies running round it. This Golden Cap had a charm. Whoever owned it could call three times upon the Winged Monkeys, who would obey any order they were given. But no person could command these strange creatures more than three times. Twice already the Wicked Witch had used the charm of the Cap. Once was when she had made the Winkies her slaves, and set herself to rule over their country. The Winged Monkeys had helped her do this. The second time was when she had fought against the Great Oz himself, and driven him out of the land of the West. The Winged Monkeys had also helped her in doing this. Only once more could she

---

42. Logical Populist counterparts to the Winkies are the besieged Western farmers (also symbolized by the Scarecrow), as well as the Midwestern industrial workers, whose struggles with employers in the Pullman railroad strike of 1894 and other major work stoppages became landmark events.

The Winkies are later referred to as the "yellow Winkies," since they inhabit the yellow Land of the West. Consistent with an interpretation of the Western Witch as President McKinley, the Winkies could symbolize the people of the Philippines, since McKinley had refused to grant their independence after gaining control of the Philippines in the Spanish-American War of 1898. At the time of *Wizard*'s publication, the United States was in the midst of a three-year military campaign, involving 70,000 American troops, to put down an insurrection by Filipinos seeking self-rule. "To a modern ear there is a condescending tone to 'yellow Winkies,' but clearly Baum was sympathetic to the plight of the Philippines," suggests Rockoff (1990, p. 751). In Baum's original script for the stage musical version of *Wizard,* the Scarecrow wryly tells Dorothy: "It isn't the people who live in a country who know the most about it. . . . Look at the Filipinos. Everybody knows more about their country than they do" (1902, p. 353).

The yellow Winkies could also represent Asian laborers in California, whose harsh employment conditions in the mines, railroads, and elsewhere constituted exploitation by almost any definition, thus the Winkies' enslavement by the Western Witch. Yellow is an appropriate color for the Land of the West, which back then was closely associated with the California gold rush of the mid-nineteenth century—yellow gold once again.

use this Golden Cap, for which reason she did not like to do so until all her other powers were exhausted.[43] But now that her fierce wolves and her wild crows and her stinging bees were gone, and her slaves had been scared away by the Cowardly Lion, she saw there was only one way left to destroy Dorothy and her friends.

So the Wicked Witch took the Golden Cap from her cupboard and placed it upon her head. Then she stood upon her left foot and said, slowly,

"Ep-pe, pep-pe, kak-ke!"

Next she stood upon her right foot and said,

"Hil-lo, hol-lo, hel-lo!"

After this she stood upon both feet and cried in a loud voice,

"Ziz-zy, zuz-zy, zik!"

Now the charm began to work. The sky was darkened, and a low rumbling sound was heard in the air. There was a rushing of many wings, a great chattering and laughing, and the sun came out of the dark sky to show the Wicked Witch surrounded by a crowd of monkeys, each with a pair of immense and powerful wings on his shoulders.

One, much bigger than the others, seemed to be their leader. He flew close to the Witch and said,

"You have called us for the third and last time. What do you command?"

"Go to the strangers who are within my land and destroy them all except the Lion," said the Wicked Witch. "Bring that beast to me, for I have a mind to harness him like a horse, and make him work."

"Your commands shall be obeyed," said the leader; and then, with a great deal of chattering and noise, the Winged Monkeys flew away to the place where Dorothy and her friends were walking.

Some of the Monkeys seized the Tin Woodman and carried him through the air until they were over a country thickly covered with sharp rocks. Here they dropped the poor Woodman, who fell a great distance to the rocks, where he lay so battered and dented that he could neither move nor groan.

Others of the Monkeys caught the Scarecrow, and with their long fingers pulled all of the straw out of his clothes and head. They made his hat and boots and clothes into a small bundle and threw it into the top branches of a tall tree.

The remaining Monkeys threw pieces of stout rope around the Lion and wound many coils about his body and head and legs, until he was unable to bite or scratch or struggle in any way. Then they lifted him up and flew away with him to the Witch's castle, where he was placed in a small yard with a high iron fence around it, so that he could not escape.

But Dorothy they did not harm at all. She stood, with Toto in her arms, watching the sad fate of her comrades and thinking it would soon be her turn. The leader of the Winged Monkeys flew up to her, his long, hairy arms stretched out and his ugly face grinning terribly; but he saw the mark of the Good Witch's kiss upon her

---

43. Like the silver shoes, the Golden Cap conveys a charm. The free silver Populists likewise envisioned coinage of both silver *and* gold as essential to prosperity. Notably, however, the Golden Cap's charm is finite, exhausting itself after three uses.

forehead and stopped short, motioning the others not to touch her.

"We dare not harm this little girl," he said to them, "for she is protected by the Power of Good, and that is greater than the Power of Evil. All we can do is to carry her to the castle of the Wicked Witch and leave her there."

So, carefully and gently, they lifted Dorothy in their arms and carried her swiftly through the air until they came to the castle, where they set her down upon the front doorstep. Then the leader said to the Witch:

"We have obeyed you as far as we were able. The Tin Woodman and the Scarecrow are destroyed, and the Lion is tied up in your yard. The little girl we dare not harm, nor the dog she carries in her arms. Your power over our band is now ended, and you will never see us again."

Then all the Winged Monkeys, with much laughing and chattering and noise, flew into the air and were soon out of sight.

The Wicked Witch was both surprised and worried when she saw the mark on Dorothy's forehead, for she knew well that neither the Winged Monkeys nor she, herself, dare hurt the girl in any way. She looked down at Dorothy's feet, and seeing the Silver Shoes, began to tremble with fear, for she knew what a powerful charm belonged to them. At first the Witch was tempted to run away from Dorothy; but she happened to look into the child's eyes and saw how simple the soul behind them was, and that the little girl did not know of the wonderful power the Silver Shoes gave her. So the Wicked Witch laughed to herself, and thought, "I can still make her my slave, for she does not know how to use her power." Then she said to Dorothy, harshly and severely,

"Come with me; and see that you mind everything I tell you, for if you do not I will make an end of you, as I did of the Tin Woodman and the Scarecrow."

Dorothy followed her through many of the beautiful rooms in her castle until they came to the kitchen, where the Witch bade her clean the pots and kettles and sweep the floor and keep the fire fed with wood.

Dorothy went to work meekly, with her mind made up to work as hard as she could; for she was glad the Wicked Witch had decided not to kill her.

With Dorothy hard at work, the Witch thought she would go into the court-yard and harness the Cowardly Lion like a horse; it would amuse her, she was sure, to make him draw her chariot whenever she wished to go to drive. But as she opened the gate the Lion gave a loud roar and bounded at her so fiercely that the Witch was afraid, and ran out and shut the gate again.

"If I cannot harness you," said the Witch to the Lion, speaking through the bars of the gate, "I can starve you. You shall have nothing to eat until you do as I wish."

So after that she took no food to the imprisoned Lion; but every day she came to the gate at noon and asked, "Are you ready to be harnessed like a horse?"

And the Lion would answer,

"No. If you come in this yard, I will bite you."

The reason the Lion did not have to do as the Witch wished was that every night, while the woman was asleep, Dorothy carried him food from the cupboard. After he had eaten he would lie down on his bed of straw, and Dorothy would lie beside him and put her head on his soft, shaggy mane, while they talked of their troubles and tried to plan some way to escape. But they could find no way to get out of the castle, for it was constantly guarded by the yellow Winkies, who were the slaves of the Wicked Witch and too afraid of her not to do as she told them.

The girl had to work hard during the day, and often the Witch threatened to beat her with the same old umbrella she always carried in her hand. But, in truth, she did not dare to strike Dorothy, because of the mark upon her forehead. The child did not know this, and was full of fear for herself and Toto. Once the Witch struck Toto a blow with her umbrella and the brave little dog flew at her and bit her leg in return. The Witch did not bleed where she was bitten, for she was so wicked that the blood in her had dried up many years before.

Dorothy's life became very sad as she grew to understand that it would be harder than ever to get back to Kansas and Aunt Em again. Sometimes she would cry bitterly for hours, with Toto sitting at her feet and looking into her face, whining dismally to show how sorry he was for his little mistress. Toto did not really care whether he was in Kansas or the Land of Oz so long as Dorothy was with him; but he knew the little girl was unhappy, and that made him unhappy too.

Now the Wicked Witch had a great longing to have for her own the Silver Shoes which the girl always wore. Her bees and her crows and her wolves were lying in heaps and drying up, and she had used up all the power of the Golden Cap; but if she could only get hold of the Silver Shoes, they would give her more power than all the other things she had lost. She watched Dorothy carefully, to see if she ever took off her shoes, thinking she might steal them. But the child was so proud of her pretty shoes that she never took them off except at night and when she took her bath. The Witch was too much afraid of the dark to dare go in Dorothy's room at night to take the shoes, and her dread of water was greater than her fear of the dark, so she never came near when Dorothy was bathing. Indeed, the old Witch never touched water, nor ever let water touch her in any way.

But the wicked creature was very cunning, and she finally thought of a trick that would give her what she wanted. She placed a bar of iron in the middle of the kitchen floor, and then by her magic arts made the iron invisible to human eyes. So that when Dorothy walked across the floor she stumbled over the bar, not being able to see it, and fell at full length. She was not much hurt, but in her fall one of the Silver Shoes came off; and before she could reach it, the Witch had snatched it away and put it on her own skinny foot.

The wicked woman was greatly pleased with the success of her trick, for as long as she had one of the shoes she owned half the power of their charm, and Dorothy could not use it against her, even had she known how to do so.

The little girl, seeing she had lost one of her pretty shoes, grew angry, and said to the Witch,

"Give me back my shoe!"

"I will not," retorted the Witch, "for it is now my shoe, and not yours."

"You are a wicked creature!" cried Dorothy. "You have no right to take my shoe from me."

"I shall keep it, just the same," said the Witch, laughing at her, "and someday I shall get the other one from you, too."

This made Dorothy so very angry that she picked up the bucket of water that stood near and dashed it over the Witch, wetting her from head to foot.

Instantly the wicked woman gave a loud cry of fear, and then, as Dorothy looked at her in wonder, the Witch began to shrink and fall away.

"See what you have done!" she screamed. "In a minute I shall melt away."

"I'm very sorry, indeed," said Dorothy, who was truly frightened to see the Witch actually melting away like brown sugar before her very eyes.

"Didn't you know water would be the end of me?" asked the Witch, in a wailing, despairing voice.

"Of course not," answered Dorothy. "How should I?"

"Well, in a few minutes I shall be all melted, and you will have the castle to yourself. I have been wicked in my day, but I never thought a little girl like you would ever be able to melt me and end my wicked deeds. Look out—here I go!"

With these words the Witch fell down in a brown, melted, shapeless mass and began to spread over the clean boards of the kitchen floor. Seeing that she had really melted away to nothing, Dorothy drew another bucket of water and threw it over the mess. She then swept it all out the door.[44] After picking out the silver shoe, which was all that was left of the old woman, she cleaned and dried it with a cloth, and put it on her foot again. Then, being at last free to do as she chose, she ran out to the court-yard to tell the Lion that the Wicked Witch of the West had come to an end, and that they were no longer prisoners in a strange land.

Chapter XIII.
The Rescue.

The Cowardly Lion was much pleased to hear that the Wicked Witch had been melted by a bucket of water, and Dorothy at once unlocked the gate of his prison and set him free. They went in together to the castle, where Dorothy's first act was

---

44. The Witch's dissolution by water is the basis of Littlefield's interpretation of the Western Witch as the heat and drought that plagued the Western farmer. More than anything else, the farmers needed rain to end their years of misery at the hands of nature (Littlefield 1964, p. 56). The Witch melts away into a "brown . . . shapeless mass," just as a desperately needed heavy rainfall on the desolate Midwestern prairie would create a lot of mud.

This scene is also consistent with Clanton's (1991, 1998) interpretation of the Western Witch as symbolizing the worst of agrarian radicalism, since heavy rains could potentially bring about a return to farm prosperity that would effectively silence the farmers' complaints.

Baum's South Dakota newspaper editorials from 1890–91 suggest a preoccupation with water—irrigation in particular—as the solution to the farmers' woes. Nancy Tystad Koupal writes: "A cursory perusal of the *[Aberdeen Saturday] Pioneer* leaves no doubt that Baum believed strongly, almost mystically, in irrigation as the salvation of Dakota farmers." Baum even penned the following tidbit, which is consistent with either Littlefield's or Clanton's interpretation, in 1890: "The farmer who, with a rainy season before him, wont [*sic*] subscribe for the *Pioneer*, must be wetted down until, like the ducked witches of years ago, he cries for mercy" (Koupal 1989, p. 212). Equally striking is a poem Baum wrote for the *Pioneer*, which began: "Oh the rain, beautiful rain . . . / Bringing a thousand joys in your train / And knowledge that drought at last is slain" (quoted by Gage 1966, p. 12).

to call all the Winkies together and tell them that they were no longer slaves.

There was great rejoicing among the yellow Winkies, for they had been made to work hard during many years for the Wicked Witch, who had always treated them with great cruelty. They kept this day as a holiday, then and ever after, and spent the time in feasting and dancing.

"If our friends, the Scarecrow and the Tin Woodman, were only with us," said the Lion, "I should be quite happy."

"Don't you suppose we could rescue them?" asked the girl, anxiously.

"We can try," answered the Lion.

So they called the yellow Winkies and asked them if they would help to rescue their friends, and the Winkies said that they would be delighted to do all in their power for Dorothy, who had set them free from bondage. So she chose a number of the Winkies who looked as if they knew the most, and they all started away. They travelled that day and part of the next until they came to the rocky plain where the Tin Woodman lay, all battered and bent. His axe was near him, but the blade was rusted and the handle broken off short.

The Winkies lifted him tenderly in their arms, and carried him back to the Yellow Castle again, Dorothy shedding a few tears by the way at the sad plight of her old friend, and the Lion looking sober and sorry. When they reached the castle Dorothy said to the Winkies,

"Are any of your people tinsmiths?"

"Oh, yes; some of us are very good tinsmiths," they told her.

"Then bring them to me," she said. And when the tinsmiths came, bringing with them all their tools in baskets, she enquired,

"Can you straighten out those dents in the Tin Woodman, and bend him back into shape again, and solder him together where he is broken?"

The tinsmiths looked the Woodman over carefully and then answered that they thought they could mend him so he would be as good as ever. So they set to work in one of the big yellow rooms of the castle and worked for three days and four nights, hammering and twisting and bending and soldering and polishing and pounding at the legs and body and head of the Tin Woodman, until at last he was straightened out into his old form, and his joints worked as well as ever. To be sure, there were several patches on him, but the tinsmiths did a good job, and as the Woodman was not a vain man he did not mind the patches at all.

When, at last, he walked into Dorothy's room and thanked her for rescuing him, he was so pleased that he wept tears of joy, and Dorothy had to wipe every tear carefully from his face with her apron, so his joints would not be rusted. At the same time her own tears fell thick and fast at the joy of meeting her old friend again, and these tears did not need to be wiped away. As for the Lion, he wiped his eyes so often with the tip of his tail that it became quite wet, and he was obliged to go out into the court-yard and hold it in the sun till it dried.

"If we only had the Scarecrow with us again," said the Tin Woodman, when Dorothy had finished telling him everything that had happened, "I should be quite happy."

"We must try to find him," said the girl.

So she called the Winkies to help her, and they walked all that day and part of the next until they came to the tall tree in the branches of which the Winged Monkeys had tossed the Scarecrow's clothes.

It was a very tall tree, and the trunk was so smooth that no one could climb it; but the Woodman said at once,

"I'll chop it down, and then we can get the Scarecrow's clothes."

Now while the tinsmiths had been at work mending the Woodman himself, another of the Winkies, who was a goldsmith, had made an axe-handle of solid gold and fitted it to the Woodman's axe, instead of the old broken handle. Others polished the blade until all the rust was removed and it glistened like burnished silver.[45]

As soon as he had spoken, the Tin Woodman began to chop, and in a short time the tree fell over with a crash, when the Scarecrow's clothes fell out of the branches and rolled off on the ground.

Dorothy picked them up and had the Winkies carry them back to the castle, where they were stuffed with nice, clean straw; and behold! here was the Scarecrow, as good as ever, thanking them over and over again for saving him.

Now that they were reunited, Dorothy and her friends spent a few happy days at the Yellow Castle, where they found everything they needed to make them comfortable.

But one day the girl thought of Aunt Em, and said,

"We must go back to Oz, and claim his promise."

"Yes," said the Woodman, "at last I shall get my heart."

"And I shall get my brains," added the Scarecrow, joyfully.

"And I shall get my courage," said the Lion, thoughtfully.

"And I shall get back to Kansas," cried Dorothy, clapping her hands. "Oh, let us start for the Emerald City to-morrow!"

This they decided to do. The next day they called the Winkies together and bade them good-bye. The Winkies were sorry to have them go, and they had grown so fond of the Tin Woodman that they begged him to stay and rule over them and the Yellow Land of the West. Finding they were determined to go, the Winkies gave Toto and the Lion each a golden collar; and to Dorothy they presented a beautiful bracelet studded with diamonds; and to the Scarecrow they gave a gold-headed walking stick, to keep him from stumbling; and to the Tin Woodman they offered a silver oil-can, inlaid with gold and set with precious jewels.[46]

Every one of the travellers made the Winkies a pretty speech in return, and all shook hands with them until their arms ached.

---

45. The tin man's new axe, with its gold handle and blade "like burnished silver," works as a symbol of the Populists' demands for bimetallism.

46. Here we see still more gold and silver imagery. The tin man's new oil can, like his new axe, is a tidy symbol of bimetallism, since it contains both metals and its purpose is to keep him from rusting (becoming unemployed) again. "Bryan frequently received gifts of this sort to portray the battle of the standards. There was an ink bottle made of gold and silver, a gold pen with a silver holder, gold-headed canes like the one given to the Scarecrow, and so forth" (Rockoff 1990, p. 753).

Dorothy went to the Witch's cupboard to fill her basket with food for the journey, and there she saw the Golden Cap. She tried it on her own head and found that it fitted her exactly. She did not know anything about the charm of the Golden Cap, but she saw that it was pretty, so she made up her mind to wear it and carry her sunbonnet in the basket.

Then, being prepared for the journey, they all started for the Emerald City; and the Winkies gave them three cheers and many good wishes to carry with them.

Chapter XIV.
The Winged Monkeys.

You will remember there was no road—not even a pathway—between the castle of the Wicked Witch and the Emerald City. When the four travellers went in search of the Witch she had seen them coming, and so sent the Winged Monkeys to bring them to her. It was much harder to find their way back through the big fields of buttercups and yellow daisies than it was being carried. They knew, of course, they must go straight east, toward the rising sun; and they started off in the right way. But at noon, when the sun was over their heads, they did not know which was east and which was west, and that was the reason they were lost in the great fields. They kept on walking, however, and at night the moon came out and shone brightly. So they lay down among the sweet smelling yellow flowers and slept soundly until morning—all but the Scarecrow and the Tin Woodman.

The next morning the sun was behind a cloud, but they started on, as if they were quite sure which way they were going.

"If we walk far enough," said Dorothy, "we shall sometime come to some place, I am sure."

But day by day passed away, and they still saw nothing before them but the yellow fields. The Scarecrow began to grumble a bit.

"We have surely lost our way," he said, "and unless we find it again in time to reach the Emerald City, I shall never get my brains."

"Nor I my heart," declared the Tin Woodman. "It seems to me I can scarcely wait till I get to Oz, and you must admit this is a very long journey."

"You see," said the Cowardly Lion, with a whimper, "I haven't the courage to keep tramping forever, without getting anywhere at all."

Then Dorothy lost heart. She sat down on the grass and looked at her companions, and they sat down and looked at her, and Toto found that for the first time in his life he was too tired to chase a butterfly that flew past his head; so he put out his tongue and panted and looked at Dorothy as if to ask what they should do next.

"Suppose we call the Field Mice," she suggested. "They could probably tell us the way to the Emerald City."

"To be sure they could," cried the Scarecrow. "Why didn't we think of that before?"

Dorothy blew the little whistle she had always carried about her neck since the Queen of the Mice had given it to her. In a few minutes they heard the pattering of tiny feet, and many of the small gray mice came running up to her. Among them was the Queen herself, who asked, in her squeaky little voice,

"What can I do for my friends?"

"We have lost our way," said Dorothy. "Can you tell us where the Emerald City is?"

"Certainly," answered the Queen; "but it is a great way off, for you have had it at your backs all this time." Then she noticed Dorothy's Golden Cap, and said, "Why don't you use the charm of the Cap, and call the Winged Monkeys to you? They will carry you to the City of Oz in less than an hour."

"I didn't know there was a charm," answered Dorothy, in surprise. "What is it?"

"It is written inside the Golden Cap," replied the Queen of the Mice; "but if you are going to call the Winged Monkeys we must run away, for they are full of mischief and think it great fun to plague us."

"Won't they hurt me?" asked the girl anxiously.

"Oh, no; they must obey the wearer of the Cap. Good-bye!" And she scampered out of sight, with all the mice hurrying after her.

Dorothy looked inside the Golden Cap and saw some words written upon the lining. These, she thought, must be the charm, so she read the directions carefully and put the Cap upon her head.

"Ep-pe, pep-pe, kak-ke!" she said, standing on her left foot.

"What did you say?" asked the Scarecrow, who did not know what she was doing.

"Hil-lo, hol-lo, hel-lo!" Dorothy went on, standing this time on her right foot.

"Hello!" replied the Tin Woodman, calmly.

"Ziz-zy, zuz-zy, zik!" said Dorothy, who was now standing on both feet. This ended the saying of the charm, and they heard a great chattering and flapping of wings, as the band of Winged Monkeys flew up to them.

The King bowed low before Dorothy, and asked,

"What is your command?"

"We wish to go to the Emerald City," said the child, "and we have lost our way."

"We will carry you," replied the King, and no sooner had he spoken than two of the Monkeys caught Dorothy in their arms and flew away with her. Others took the Scarecrow and the Woodman and the Lion, and one little Monkey seized Toto and flew after them, although the dog tried hard to bite him.

The Scarecrow and the Tin Woodman were rather frightened at first, for they remembered how badly the Winged Monkeys had treated them before; but they saw that no harm was intended, so they rode through the air quite cheerfully, and had a fine time looking at the pretty gardens and woods far below them.

Dorothy found herself riding easily between two of the biggest Monkeys, one of them the King himself. They had made a chair of their hands and were careful not to hurt her.

"Why do you have to obey the charm of the Golden Cap?" she asked.

"That is a long story," answered the King, with a Winged laugh; "but as we have a long journey before us, I will pass the time by telling you about it, if you wish."

"I shall be glad to hear it," she replied.

"Once," began the leader, "we were a free people, living happily in the great forest, flying from tree to tree, eating nuts and fruit, and doing just as we pleased without calling anybody master. Perhaps some of us were rather too full of mischief at times, flying down to pull the tails of the animals that had no wings, chasing birds, and throwing nuts at the people who walked in the forest. But we were careless and happy and full of fun, and enjoyed every minute of the day. This was many years ago, long before Oz came out of the clouds to rule over this land.[47]

"There lived here then, away at the North, a beautiful princess, who was also a powerful sorceress. All her magic was used to help the people, and she was never known to hurt anyone who was good. Her name was Gayelette, and she lived in a handsome palace built from great blocks of ruby. Everyone loved her, but her greatest sorrow was that she could find no one to love in return, since all the men were much too stupid and ugly to mate with one so beautiful and wise. At last, however, she found a boy who was handsome and manly and wise beyond his years. Gayelette made up her mind that when he grew to be a man she would make him her husband, so she took him to her ruby palace and used all her magic powers to make him as strong and good and lovely as any woman could wish. When he grew to manhood, Quelala, as he was called, was said to be the best and wisest man in all the land, while his manly beauty was so great that Gayelette loved him

---

47. The Winged Monkeys could represent the Plains Indians, especially in the personi-fication, "Once we were a free people, living happily in the great forest" (Littlefield 1964, p. 55). Baum had some familiarity with the Plains Indians, having lived among them in South Dakota. (In fact, the Wounded Knee massacre, in which federal agents took the Sioux Indians' "Ghost Dance" as a provocation and proceeded to kill about 200 Indians, including Sitting Bull, occurred in South Dakota in 1890, at the same time that Baum was living there. Baum, like many other Western settlers, was easily led to feel hostility toward the Sioux, and, sadly, penned some truly genocidal editorials for the *Aberdeen Saturday Pioneer*, in which he called for the Sioux's "annihilation" and called them "untamed and untamable creatures" who should be wiped "from the face of the earth" [*Pioneer*, December 20, 1890; Clanton 1998, p. 185 n.3]. As monstrous and inexcusable as those editorials were, however, there is little in Baum's life and writing to suggest that they were typical of his thinking [Hearn 2000, p. xxiv]. Baum's mother-in-law, the prominent feminist Matilda Joslyn Gage, who is believed to have strongly influenced Baum's political thinking, championed Indian causes and was even adopted into the wolf clan of the Mohawk nation in 1893 [Hearn 1973, pp. 14, 19; Wagner 1998, pp. 34–38, 62–63].)

Along similar lines, as drawn by Denslow the Winged Monkeys bear a strong facial resemblance to cartoonist Frederick Burr Opper's depictions of Irish immigrants as monkeys, which regularly ran in the magazine *Puck* in the late nineteenth century. Such racist caricatures of "shanty Irish" were common in the political cartoons of the time (see Fischer 1996, pp. 70–93, for information and examples).

Still another alternative interpretation is that Winged Monkeys symbolize their initial-sake William McKinley. Just as the Winged Monkeys are controlled by the Western Witch, so did his detractors paint McKinley as a puppet whose every move was directed by Mark Hanna (the Western Witch, in Littlefield's interpretation). And just as the Winged Monkeys will take orders from different masters (namely, whoever has the Golden Cap), McKinley the politician was a classic straddler of issues, most notably the silver issue, on which he took different, seemingly opposite, positions at various times.

dearly, and hastened to make everything ready for the wedding.

"My grandfather was at that time the King of the Winged Monkeys which lived in the forest near Gayelette's palace, and the old fellow loved a joke better than a good dinner. One day, just before the wedding, my grandfather was flying out with his band when he saw Quelala walking beside the river. He was dressed in a rich costume of pink silk and purple velvet, and my grandfather thought he would see what he could do. At his word the band flew down and seized Quelala, carried him in their arms until they were over the middle of the river, and then dropped him into the water.

" 'Swim out, my fine fellow,' cried my grandfather, 'and see if the water has spotted your clothes.' Quelala was much too wise not to swim, and he was not in the least spoiled by all his good fortune. He laughed, when he came to the top of the water, and swam in to shore. But when Gayelette came running out to him she found his silks and velvet all ruined by the river.

"The princess was angry, and she knew, of course, who did it. She had all the Winged Monkeys brought before her, and she said at first that their wings should be tied and they should be treated as they had treated Quelala, and dropped in the river. But my grandfather pleaded hard, for he knew the Monkeys would drown in the river with their wings tied, and Quelala said a kind word for them also; so that Gayelette finally spared them, on condition that the Winged Monkeys should ever after do three times the bidding of the owner of the Golden Cap. This Cap had been made for a wedding present to Quelala, and it is said to have cost the princess half her kingdom. Of course my grandfather and all the other Monkeys at once agreed to the condition, and that is how it happens that we are three times the slaves of the owner of the Golden Cap, whomsoever he may be."

"And what became of them?" asked Dorothy, who had been greatly interested in the story.

"Quelala being the first owner of the Golden Cap," replied the Monkey, "he was the first to lay his wishes upon us. As his bride could not bear the sight of us, he called us all to him in the forest after he had married her and ordered us always to keep where she could never again set eyes on a Winged Monkey, which we were glad to do, for we were all afraid of her.

"This was all we ever had to do until the Golden Cap fell into the hands of the Wicked Witch of the West, who made us enslave the Winkies, and afterward drive Oz himself out of the Land of the West. Now the Golden Cap is yours, and three times you have the right to lay your wishes upon us."

As the Monkey King finished his story Dorothy looked down and saw the green, shining walls of the Emerald City before them. She wondered at the rapid flight of the Monkeys, but was glad the journey was over. The strange creatures set the travellers down carefully before the gate of the City, the King bowed low to Dorothy, and then flew swiftly away, followed by all his band.

"That was a good ride," said the little girl.

"Yes, and a quick way out of our troubles," replied the Lion. "How lucky it was you brought away that wonderful Cap!"

Chapter XV.
The Discovery of Oz, the Terrible.

The four travellers walked up to the great gate of Emerald City and rang the bell. After ringing several times, it was opened by the same Guardian of the Gate they had met before.

"What! are you back again?" he asked, in surprise.

"Do you not see us?" answered the Scarecrow.

"But I thought you had gone to visit the Wicked Witch of the West."

"We did visit her," said the Scarecrow.

"And she let you go again?" asked the man, in wonder.

"She could not help it, for she is melted," explained the Scarecrow.

"Melted! Well, that is good news, indeed," said the man. "Who melted her?"

"It was Dorothy," said the Lion, gravely.

"Good gracious!" exclaimed the man, and he bowed very low indeed before her.

Then he led them into his little room and locked the spectacles from the great box on all their eyes, just as he had done before. Afterward they passed on through the gate into the Emerald City. When the people heard from the Guardian of the Gate that Dorothy had melted the Wicked Witch of the West, they all gathered around the travellers and followed them in a great crowd to the Palace of Oz.

The soldier with the green whiskers was still on guard before the door, but he let them in at once, and they were again met by the beautiful green girl, who showed each of them to their old rooms at once, so they might rest until the Great Oz was ready to receive them.

The soldier had the news carried straight to Oz that Dorothy and the other travellers had come back again, after destroying the Wicked Witch; but Oz made no reply. They thought the Great Wizard would send for them at once, but he did not. They had no word from him the next day, nor the next, nor the next. The waiting was tiresome and wearing, and at last they grew vexed that Oz should treat them in so poor a fashion, after sending them to undergo hardships and slavery. So the Scarecrow at last asked the green girl to take another message to Oz, saying if he did not let them in to see him at once they would call the Winged Monkeys to help them, and find out whether he kept his promises or not. When the Wizard was given this message he was so frightened that he sent word for them to come to the Throne Room at four minutes after nine o'clock the next morning.[48] He had once met the Winged Monkeys in the Land of the West, and he did not wish to meet them again.

---

48. "Four minutes after nine o'clock": The Wizard makes an odd choice of meeting times. "Four . . . after nine" conjures up '94—that is, 1894—the same year that Coxey's Army made its famous march from Ohio to Washington. The similarity between Dorothy's party and Coxey's Army has already been noted.

Eighteen-ninety-four is also the year in which the leading Populist monetary tract, a short book called *Coin's Financial School*, by William H. Harvey of Chicago, was published. The book was one of the most widely read of the 1890s.

The four travellers passed a sleepless night, each thinking of the gift Oz had promised to bestow on him.[49] Dorothy fell asleep only once, and then she dreamed she was in Kansas, where Aunt Em was telling her how glad she was to have her little girl at home again.

Promptly at nine o'clock the next morning the green whiskered soldier came to them, and four minutes later they all went into the Throne Room of the Great Oz.

Of course each one of them expected to see the Wizard in the shape he had taken before, and all were greatly surprised when they looked about and saw no one at all in the room. They kept close to the door and closer to one another, for the stillness of the empty room was more dreadful than any of the forms they had seen Oz take.

Presently they heard a Voice, seeming to come from somewhere near the top of the great dome, and it said, solemnly:

"I am Oz, the Great and Terrible. Why do you seek me?"

They looked again in every part of the room, and then, seeing no one, Dorothy asked, "Where are you?"

"I am everywhere," answered the Voice, "but to the eyes of common mortals I am invisible. I will now seat myself upon my throne, that you may converse with me." Indeed, the Voice seemed just then to come straight from the throne itself; so they walked toward it and stood in a row while Dorothy said:

"We have come to claim our promise, O Oz."

"What promise?" asked Oz.

"You promised to send me back to Kansas when the Wicked Witch was destroyed," said the girl.

"And you promised to give me brains," said the Scarecrow.

"And you promised to give me a heart," said the Tin Woodman.

"And you promised to give me courage," said the Cowardly Lion.

"Is the Wicked Witch really destroyed?" asked the Voice, and Dorothy thought it trembled a little.

"Yes," she answered, "I melted her with a bucket of water."

"Dear me," said the Voice, "how sudden! Well, come to me to-morrow, for I must have time to think it over."

"You've had plenty of time already," said the Tin Woodman angrily.

"We shan't wait a day longer," said the Scarecrow.

"You must keep your promises to us!" exclaimed Dorothy.

The Lion thought it might be as well to frighten the Wizard, so he gave a large, loud roar, which was so fierce and dreadful that Toto jumped away from him in alarm and tipped over the screen that stood in a corner. As it fell with a crash they looked that way, and the next moment all of them were filled with wonder. For they saw, standing in just the spot the screen had hidden, a little old man, with a bald head and a wrinkled face, who seemed to be as much surprised as they were.

---

49. Like any successful politician, the Wizard has made numerous promises, not all of which he will be able to keep.

The Tin Woodman, raising his axe, rushed toward the little man and cried out, "Who are you?"

"I am Oz, the Great and Terrible," said the little man, in a trembling voice, "but don't strike me—please don't!—and I'll do anything you want me to."

Our friends looked at him in surprise and dismay.

"I thought Oz was a great Head," said Dorothy.

"And I thought Oz was a lovely Lady," said the Scarecrow.

"And I thought Oz was a terrible Beast," said the Tin Woodman.

"And I thought Oz was a Ball of Fire," exclaimed the Lion.

"No, you are all wrong," said the little man meekly. "I have been making believe."

"Making believe!" cried Dorothy. "Are you not a great Wizard?"

"Hush, my dear," he said; "don't speak so loud, or you will be overheard—and I should be ruined. I'm supposed to be a Great Wizard."

"And aren't you?" she asked.

"Not a bit of it, my dear; I'm just a common man."[50]

---

50. "The Wizard, a little bumbling old man, hiding behind a facade of papier mâché and noise, might be any President from Grant to McKinley" (Littlefield 1964, p. 54). This interpretation is highly apt, since the decades between the administrations of Abraham Lincoln (1861–65) and Theodore Roosevelt (1901–9) were times of extremely weak presidents whose power and influence were far less than the average American probably realized. Littlefield later noted that when he taught high school history in 1963, "our textbook political cartoons of a tiny President Benjamin Harrison [1889–93] in a large oval office chair bore a striking resemblance to Denslow's Wizard!" (1992b, p. 24).

The Wizard also recalls Republican kingmaker Mark Hanna, McKinley's campaign manager and chairman of the Republican National Committee. Hanna was commonly viewed and depicted as the man who pulled the strings behind McKinley, a perception in keeping with the Wizard's speaking "through various figureheads." Rockoff says the Wizard displays "a purely Republican world view" in telling Dorothy and her comrades that he will help them only if they can do something for him first (1990, p. 750). The Wizard, after all, told Dorothy, "In this country everyone must pay for everything he gets." Rockoff also notes that Hanna repackaged himself as a "common man" when he ran for the Senate after the 1896 election.

Littlefield's interpretation strikes me as the better fit here. The Wizard had asked Dorothy and her comrades to destroy the Western Witch, whom Rockoff identifies with McKinley. While the Wizard did not expect them to succeed, it is hard to see why Hanna would have told anyone to go out and destroy his charge McKinley. Although Rockoff says, "The Wizard does not always tell the truth" (1990, p. 751), at no point is it revealed that the Wizard and the Witch are in league with each other. Also, to the Populists Hanna was something of an evil genius, just the opposite of the "very good man . . . but . . . very bad wizard" that the Wizard later reveals himself to be.

Perhaps an even better fit is to view the Wizard as Bryan (Earle 1993, p. 10). After all, we later learn that the Wizard is from Omaha, the largest city in Bryan's home state of Nebraska. The Wizard's line "I'm just a common man" is reminiscent of Bryan's famous nickname, The Great Commoner, which he picked up during the 1896 campaign (Coletta 1964, p. 152). The Wizard also recalls South Dakota's Henry Loucks, president of the National Farmers' Alliance and Industrial Union and an early leader of South Dakota's

"You're more than that," said the Scarecrow, in a grieved tone; "you're a humbug."

"Exactly so!" declared the little man, rubbing his hands together as if it pleased him; "I am a humbug."[51]

"But this is terrible," said the Tin Woodman; "how shall I ever get my heart?"

"Or I my courage?" asked the Lion.

"Or I my brains?" wailed the Scarecrow, wiping the tears from his eyes with his coat-sleeve.

"My dear friends," said Oz, "I pray you not to speak of these little things. Think of me, and the terrible trouble I'm in at being found out."

"Doesn't anyone else know you're a humbug?" asked Dorothy.

"No one knows it but you four—and myself," replied Oz. "I have fooled everyone so long that I thought I should never be found out. It was a great mistake my ever letting you into the Throne Room. Usually I will not see even my subjects, and so they believe I am something terrible."

"But, I don't understand," said Dorothy, in bewilderment. "How was it that you appeared to me as a great Head?"

"That was one of my tricks," answered Oz. "Step this way, please, and I will tell you all about it."

He led the way to a small chamber in the rear of the Throne Room, and they all followed him. He pointed to one corner, in which lay the Great Head, made out of many thicknesses of paper, and with a carefully painted face.

"This I hung from the ceiling by a wire," said Oz. "I stood behind the screen and pulled a thread, to make the eyes move and the mouth open."

"But how about the voice?" she enquired.

"Oh, I am a ventriloquist," said the little man. "I can throw the sound of my voice wherever I wish; so that you thought it was coming out of the Head. Here are

---

(proto-Populist) Independent Party (Koupal 2001, pp. 158–59). Loucks was active in South Dakota politics, and was even the Independents' candidate for governor in 1890, during Baum's editorship of the *Aberdeen Saturday Pioneer*. Baum viewed Loucks as well intentioned and having "a sort of magnetism about him which attracts his farmer friends," but complained that Loucks "loads his remarks with misstatements, with wilfully or ignorantly preverted [*sic*] statistics, with misleading and absurd arguments, well knowing that . . . his friends are not well enough posted to know that he is deceiving them" (*Pioneer*, July 26, 1890).

51. The term *humbug*, meaning "deceiver" or "fake," is rarely used today but was fairly common in the late nineteenth century. Consider, for example, the *Brooklyn Citizen*'s dismissal of the delegates to the American Bimetallic League's sessions in Chicago in 1893 as "a pack of brainless dupes and impudent humbugs" (quoted in Glad 1964, p. 116).

In the context of presidential politics, "humbug" recalls both "silver bug," perhaps the most commonly employed symbol of Bryan's 1896 campaign, and "gold bug," a popular term in the 1890s to describe adherents of the gold standard and a symbol employed by the Republicans (Shields-West 1992, p. 126). Gold-bug pins and figurines were used by the Republicans in both the 1896 and 1900 elections. The Wizard's unmasking as a humbug implies that there are gold bugs and silver bugs, but ultimately these politicians are really just humbugs.

the other things I used to deceive you." He showed the Scarecrow the dress and the mask he had worn when he seemed to be the lovely Lady; and the Tin Woodman saw that his Terrible Beast was nothing but a lot of skins, sewn together, with slats to keep their sides out. As for the Ball of Fire, the false Wizard had hung that also from the ceiling. It was really a ball of cotton, but when oil was poured upon it the ball burned fiercely.

"Really," said the Scarecrow, "you ought to be ashamed of yourself for being such a humbug."

"I am—I certainly am," answered the little man sorrowfully; "but it was the only thing I could do. Sit down, please, there are plenty of chairs; and I will tell you my story."

So they sat down and listened while he told the following tale.

"I was born in Omaha—"[52]

"Why, that isn't very far from Kansas!" cried Dorothy.

"No; but it's farther from here," he said, shaking his head at her, sadly. "When I grew up I became a ventriloquist, and at that I was very well trained by a great master. I can imitate any kind of a bird or beast." Here he mewed so like a kitten that Toto pricked up his ears and looked everywhere to see where she was. "After a time," continued Oz, "I tired of that, and became a balloonist."

"What is that?" asked Dorothy.

"A man who goes up in a balloon on circus day, so all to draw a crowd of people together and get them to pay to see the circus," he explained.

"Oh," she said; "I know."

"Well, one day I went up in a balloon and the ropes got twisted, so that I couldn't come down again. It went way up above the clouds, so far that a current of air struck it and carried it many, many miles away. For a day and a night I travelled through the air, and on the morning of the second day I awoke and found the balloon floating over a strange and beautiful country.

"It came down gradually, and I was not hurt a bit. But I found myself in the midst of a strange people, who, seeing me come from the clouds, thought I was a great Wizard. Of course I let them think so, because they were afraid of me, and promised to do anything I wished them to.

"Just to amuse myself, and keep the good people busy, I ordered them to build this City, and my palace; and they did it all willingly and well. Then I thought, as the country was so green and beautiful, I would call it the Emerald City; and to make the name fit better I put green spectacles on all the people, so that everything they saw was green."

"But isn't everything here green?" asked Dorothy.

"No more than in any other city," replied Oz; "but when you wear green

---

52. Aside from its association with Bryan, Omaha was notable as the site of the People's Party's 1892 convention. The "Omaha platform" that the party ratified on July 4 was hailed as a "second Declaration of Independence" and came to take on even greater significance. "This Omaha platform became the bible of the movement" (Clanton 1991, pp. 81–82).

spectacles, why of course everything you see looks green to you. The Emerald City was built a great many years ago, for I was a young man when the balloon brought me here, and I am a very old man now. But my people have worn green glasses on their eyes so long that most of them think it really is an Emerald City,[53] and it certainly is a beautiful place, abounding in jewels and precious metals, and every good thing that is needed to make one happy. I have been good to the people, and they like me; but ever since this Palace was built, I have shut myself up and would not see any of them.

"One of my greatest fears was the Witches, for while I had no magical powers at all I soon found out that the Witches were really able to do wonderful things. There were four of them in this country, and they ruled the people who live in the North and South and East and West. Fortunately, the Witches of the North and South were good, and I knew they would do me no harm; but the Witches of the East and West were terribly wicked, and had they not thought I was more powerful than they themselves, they would surely have destroyed me. As it was, I lived in deadly fear of them for many years; so you can imagine how pleased I was when I heard your house had fallen on the Wicked Witch of the East. When you came to me, I was willing to promise anything if you would only do away with the other Witch; but, now that you have melted her, I am ashamed to say that I cannot keep my promises."

"I think you are a very bad man," said Dorothy.

"Oh, no, my dear; I'm really a very good man; but I'm a very bad Wizard, I must admit."

"Can't you give me brains?" asked the Scarecrow.

"You don't need them. You are learning something every day. A baby has brains, but it doesn't know much. Experience is the only thing that brings knowledge, and the longer you are on earth the more experience you are sure to get."

"That may all be true," said the Scarecrow, "but I shall be very unhappy unless you give me brains."

The false wizard looked at him carefully.

---

53. The Guardian of the Gates had told Dorothy that the green spectacles were necessary to protect everyone's eyes from the brilliance of the Emerald City, but now we learn that they are in fact part of the Wizard's trickery. The Emerald City is in fact no greener than any other city, but the spectacles make everything appear green, and the people who live there have been wearing them for so long that they believe it really is an Emerald City.

Here Baum has created, albeit probably unintentionally, a glorious metaphor of how a fiat-money system works. Fiat money is money that has no intrinsic value. Unlike gold or silver, it is valuable simply because people accept it. When the United States was on the gold standard (and before that, a gold-and-silver standard), dollar bills could be redeemed for a fixed amount of gold or silver. Since the abandonment of the gold standard in 1933, dollar bills are no longer backed by gold. The government is no longer obligated to exchange gold or silver for dollars, so dollar bills today are only valuable because they are generally accepted as payment. If people suddenly decided that dollar bills were worthless pieces of paper, the dollar's value would evaporate, just as people in the Emerald City, if they removed their green glasses, would see that the City is not so green after all.

"Well," he said with a sigh, "I'm not much of a magician, as I said; but if you will come to me to-morrow morning, I will stuff your head with brains. I cannot tell you how to use them, however; you must find that out for yourself."

"Oh, thank you—thank you!" cried the Scarecrow. "I'll find a way to use them, never fear!"

"But how about my courage?" asked the Lion anxiously.

"You have plenty of courage, I am sure," answered Oz. "All you need is confidence in yourself. There is no living thing that is not afraid when it faces danger. True courage is in facing danger when you are afraid, and that kind of courage you have in plenty."

"Perhaps I have, but I'm scared just the same," said the Lion. "I shall really be very unhappy unless you give me the sort of courage that makes one forget he is afraid."

"Very well; I will give you that sort of courage to-morrow," replied Oz.

"How about my heart?" asked the Tin Woodman.

"Why, as for that," answered Oz, "I think you are wrong to want a heart. It makes most people unhappy. If you only knew it, you are in luck not to have a heart."

"That must be a matter of opinion," said the Tin Woodman. "For my part, I will bear all the unhappiness without a murmur, if you will give me the heart."

"Very well," answered Oz meekly. "Come to me to-morrow and you shall have a heart. I have played Wizard for so many years that I may as well continue the part a little longer."

"And now," said Dorothy, "how am I to get back to Kansas?"

"We shall have to think about that," replied the little man. "Give me two or three days to consider the matter and I'll try to find a way to carry you over the desert. In the meantime you shall all be treated as my guests, and while you live in the Palace my people will wait upon you and obey your slightest wish. There is only one thing I ask in return for my help—such as it is. You must keep my secret and tell no one I am a humbug."

They agreed to say nothing of what they had learned, and went back to their rooms in high spirits. Even Dorothy had hope that "The Great and Terrible Humbug," as she called him, would find a way to send her back to Kansas, and if he did that she was willing to forgive him everything.

Chapter XVI.
The Magic Art of the Great Humbug.

Next morning the Scarecrow said to his friends:

"Congratulate me. I am going to Oz to get my brains at last. When I return I shall be as other men are."

"I have always liked you as you were," said Dorothy, simply.

"It is kind of you to like a Scarecrow," he replied. "But surely you will think more of me when you hear the splendid thoughts my new brain is going to turn out." Then he said good-bye to them all in a cheerful voice and went to the Throne Room, where he rapped upon the door.

"Come in," said Oz.

The Scarecrow went in and found the little man sitting down by the window, engaged in deep thought.

"I have come for my brains," remarked the Scarecrow, a little uneasily.

"Oh, yes; sit down in that chair, please," replied Oz. "You must excuse me for taking your head off, but I shall have to do it in order to put your brains in their proper place."

"That's all right," said the Scarecrow. "You are quite welcome to take my head off, as long as it will be a better one when you put it on again."

So the Wizard unfastened his head and emptied out the straw. Then he entered the back room and took up a measure of bran, which he mixed with a great many pins and needles. Having shaken them together thoroughly, he filled the top of the Scarecrow's head with the mixture and stuffed the rest of the space with straw, to hold it in place. When he had fastened the Scarecrow's head on his body again he said to him,

"Hereafter you will be a great man, for I have given you a lot of bran-new brains."

The Scarecrow was both pleased and proud at the fulfillment of his greatest wish, and having thanked Oz warmly he went back to his friends.

Dorothy looked at him curiously. His head was quite bulged out at the top with brains.

"How do you feel?" she asked.

"I feel wise indeed," he answered earnestly. "When I get used to my brains I shall know everything."

"Why are those needles and pins sticking out of your head?" asked the Tin Woodman.

"That is proof that he is sharp," remarked the Lion.

"Well, I must go to Oz and get my heart," said the Woodman. So he walked to the Throne Room and knocked at the door.

"Come in," called Oz, and the Woodman entered and said, "I have come for my heart."

"Very well," answered the little man. "But I shall have to cut a hole in your breast, so I can put your heart in the right place. I hope it won't hurt you."

"Oh, no," answered the Woodman. "I shall not feel it at all."

So Oz brought a pair of tinsmith's shears and cut a small, square hole in the left side of the Tin Woodman's breast. Then, going to a chest of drawers, he took out a pretty heart, made entirely of silk and stuffed with sawdust.

"Isn't it a beauty?" he asked.

"It is, indeed!" replied the Woodman, who was greatly pleased. "But is it a kind heart?"

"Oh, very!" answered Oz. He put the heart in the Woodman's breast and then replaced the square of tin, soldering it neatly together where it had been cut.

"There," said he; "now you have a heart that any man might be proud of. I'm sorry I had to put a patch on your breast, but it really couldn't be helped."

"Never mind the patch," exclaimed the happy Woodman. "I am very grateful to you, and shall never forget your kindness."

"Don't speak of it," replied Oz.

Then the Tin Woodman went back to his friends, who wished him every joy on account of his good fortune.

The Lion now walked to the Throne Room and knocked at the door.

"Come in," said Oz.

"I have come for my courage," announced the Lion, entering the room.

"Very well," answered the little man; "I will get it for you."

He went to a cupboard and reaching up to a high shelf took down a square green bottle, the contents of which he poured into a green-gold dish, beautifully carved. Placing this before the Cowardly Lion, who sniffed at it as if he did not like it, the Wizard said,

"Drink."

"What is it?" asked the Lion.

"Well," answered Oz, "if it were inside of you, it would be courage. You know, of course, that courage is always inside one; so that this really cannot be called courage until you have swallowed it. Therefore I advise you to drink it as soon as possible."

The Lion hesitated no longer, but drank till the dish was empty.

"How do you feel now?" asked Oz.

"Full of courage," replied the Lion, who went joyfully back to his friends to tell them of his good fortune.[54]

Oz, left to himself, smiled to think of his success in giving the Scarecrow and the Tin Woodman and the Lion exactly what they thought they wanted. "How can I help being a humbug," he said, "when all these people make me do things that everybody knows can't be done? It was easy to make the Scarecrow and the Lion and the Woodman happy, because they imagined I could do anything.[55] But it will

---

54. The Lion receives his courage from a liquid poured out of a green bottle into a green-gold dish. The colors-of-money imagery here is more evocative of the Greenbackers than the free-silverites, but, with the benefit of a century of economic hindsight, it appears appropriate because the Greenbackers' position was arguably more courageous and far-sighted than the free-silver position. The fiat-money system advocated by the Greenbackers is much closer to the monetary system we have today.

With the founding of the Federal Reserve System in 1913 and the abandonment of the gold standard in 1933, the United States moved to a pure fiat-money system, whereby the Treasury prints money, the Federal Reserve regulates its supply, and neither has any legal obligation to redeem it for gold. While some monetary conservatives yearn for a return to the gold standard, the dominant view among economists today is that the current system serves the economy well. The Fed earned particularly high marks from economists for its stewardship of the economy in the 1980s and 1990s, under chairmen Paul Volcker and Alan Greenspan.

55. The Wizard's hokey solutions to the problems of the Scarecrow, the Tin Woodman, and the Lion are at the heart of the political parable that Littlefield sees in the story. Littlefield says this aspect of the book offers

a gentle and friendly Midwestern critique of the Populist rationale . . . Led by naive innocence and protected by good will, the farmer, the laborer and the politician approach the mystic holder of national

take more than imagination to carry Dorothy back to Kansas, and I'm sure I don't know how it can be done."

Chapter XVII.
How the Balloon Was Launched.

For three days Dorothy heard nothing from Oz. These were sad days for the little girl, although her friends were all quite happy and contented. The Scarecrow told them there were wonderful thoughts in his head; but he would not say what they were because he knew no one could understand them but himself. When the Tin Woodman walked about he felt his heart rattling around in his breast; and he told Dorothy he had discovered it to be a kinder and more tender heart than the one he had owned when he was made of flesh. The Lion declared he was afraid of nothing on earth, and would gladly face an army or a dozen of the fierce Kalidahs.

Thus each of the little party was satisfied except Dorothy, who longed more than ever to get back to Kansas.

On the fourth day, to her great joy, Oz sent for her, and when she entered the Throne Room he said, pleasantly:

"Sit down, my dear; I think I have found the way to get you out of this country."

"And back to Kansas?" she asked, eagerly.

"Well, I'm not sure about Kansas," said Oz, "for I haven't the faintest notion which way it lies. But the first thing to do is to cross the desert, and then it should be easy to find your way home."

"How can I cross the desert?" she inquired.

"Well, I'll tell you what I think," said the little man. "You see, when I came to this country it was in a balloon. You also came through the air, being carried by a cyclone. So I believe the best way to get across the desert will be through the air. Now, it is quite beyond my powers to make a cyclone; but I've been thinking the matter over, and I believe I can make a balloon."

"How?" asked Dorothy.

"A balloon," said Oz, "is made of silk, which is coated with glue to keep the gas in it. I have plenty of silk in the Palace, so it will be no trouble to make the balloon. But in all this country there is no gas to fill the balloon with, to make it float."

"If it won't float," remarked Dorothy, "it will be of no use to us."

"True," answered Oz. "But there is another way to make it float, which is to fill it with hot air. Hot air isn't as good as gas, for if the air should get cold the balloon would come down in the desert, and we should be lost."

"We!" exclaimed the girl. "Are you going with me?"

---

power to ask for personal fulfillment. Their desires, as well as the Wizard's cleverness in answering them, are all self-delusion. Each of these characters carries within him the solution to his own problems, were he only to view himself objectively. The fearsome Wizard turns out to be nothing more than a common man, capable of shrewd but mundane answers to these self-induced needs. Like any good politician he gives the people what they want. (1964, p. 57)

"Yes, of course," replied Oz. "I am tired of being such a humbug. If I should go out of this Palace my people would soon discover I am not a Wizard, and then they would be vexed with me for having deceived them. So I have to stay shut up in these rooms all day, and it gets tiresome. I'd much rather go back to Kansas with you and be in a circus again."

"I shall be glad to have your company," said Dorothy.

"Thank you," he answered. "Now, if you will help me sew the silk together, we will begin to work on our balloon."

So Dorothy took a needle and thread, and as fast as Oz cut the strips of silk into proper shape the girl sewed them neatly together. First there was a strip of light green silk, then a strip of dark green and then a strip of emerald green; for Oz had a fancy to make the balloon in different shades of the color about them. It took three days to sew all the strips together, but when it was finished they had a big bag of green silk more than twenty feet long.

Then Oz painted it on the inside with a coat of thin glue, to make it air-tight, after which he announced that the balloon was ready.

"But we must have a basket to ride in," he said. So he sent the soldier with the green whiskers for a big clothes basket, which he fastened with many ropes to the bottom of the balloon.

When it was all ready, Oz sent word to his people that he was going to make a visit to a great brother Wizard who lived in the clouds. The news spread rapidly throughout the city and everyone came to see the wonderful sight.

Oz ordered the balloon carried out in front of the Palace, and the people gazed upon it with much curiosity. The Tin Woodman had chopped a big pile of wood, and now he made a fire of it, and Oz held the bottom of the balloon over the fire so that the hot air that arose from it would be caught in the silken bag. Gradually the balloon swelled out and rose into the air, until finally the basket just touched the ground.

Then Oz got into the basket and said to all the people in a loud voice:

"I am now going away to make a visit. While I am gone the Scarecrow will rule over you. I command you to obey him as you would me."

The balloon was by this time tugging hard at the rope that held it to the ground, for the air within it was hot, and this made it so much lighter in weight than the air without that it pulled hard to rise into the sky.

"Come, Dorothy!" cried the Wizard. "Hurry up, or the balloon will fly away."

"I can't find Toto anywhere," replied Dorothy, who did not wish to leave her little dog behind. Toto had run into the crowd to bark at a kitten, and Dorothy at last found him. She picked him up and ran towards the balloon.

She was within a few steps of it, and Oz was holding out his hands to help her into the basket, when, crack! went the ropes, and the balloon rose into the air without her.

"Come back!" she screamed. "I want to go, too!"

"I can't come back, my dear," called Oz from the basket. "Good-bye!"

"Good-bye!" shouted everyone, and all eyes were turned upward to where the Wizard was riding in the basket, rising every moment farther and farther into the sky.

And that was the last any of them ever saw of Oz, the Wonderful Wizard, though he may have reached Omaha safely, and be there now, for all we know. But the people remembered him lovingly, and said to one another,

"Oz was always our friend. When he was here he built for us this beautiful Emerald City, and now he is gone he has left the Wise Scarecrow to rule over us."

Still, for many days they grieved over the loss of the Wonderful Wizard, and would not be comforted.

Chapter XVIII.
Away to the South.

Dorothy wept bitterly at the passing of her hope to get home to Kansas again; but when she thought it all over she was glad she had not gone up in a balloon. And she also felt sorry at losing Oz, and so did her companions.

The Tin Woodman came to her and said:

"Truly I should be ungrateful if I failed to mourn for the man who gave me my lovely heart. I should like to cry a little because Oz is gone, if you will kindly wipe away my tears, so that I shall not rust."

"With pleasure," she answered, and brought a towel at once. Then the Tin Woodman wept for several minutes, and she watched the tears carefully and wiped them away with the towel. When he had finished, he thanked her kindly and oiled himself thoroughly with his jeweled oil-can, to guard against mishap.

The Scarecrow was now the ruler of the Emerald City, and although he was not a Wizard the people were proud of him. "For," they said, "there is not another city in all the world that is ruled by a stuffed man." And, so far as they knew, they were quite right.

The morning after the balloon had gone up with Oz, the four travellers met in the Throne Room and talked matters over. The Scarecrow sat in the big throne and the others stood respectfully before him.

"We are not so unlucky," said the new ruler, "for this Palace and the Emerald City belong to us, and we can do just as we please. When I remember that a short time ago I was up on a pole in a farmer's cornfield, and that now I am the ruler of this beautiful City, I am quite satisfied with my lot."

"I also," said the Tin Woodman, "am well pleased with my new heart; and, really, that was the only thing I wished in all the world."

"For my part, I am content in knowing I am as brave as any beast that ever lived, if not braver," said the Lion, modestly.

"If Dorothy would only be contented to live in the Emerald City," continued the Scarecrow, "we might all be happy together."

"But I don't want to live here," cried Dorothy. "I want to go to Kansas, and live with Aunt Em and Uncle Henry."

"Well, then, what can be done?" enquired the Woodman.

The Scarecrow decided to think, and he thought so hard that the pins and needles began to stick out of his brains. Finally he said:

"Why not call the Winged Monkeys, and ask them to carry you over the desert?"

"I never thought of that!" said Dorothy joyfully. "It's just the thing. I'll go at once for the Golden Cap."

When she brought it into the Throne Room she spoke the magic words, and soon the band of Winged Monkeys flew in through the open window and stood beside her.

"This is the second time you have called us," said the Monkey King, bowing before the little girl. "What do you wish?"

"I want you to fly with me to Kansas," said Dorothy.

But the Monkey King shook his head.

"That cannot be done," he said. "We belong to this country alone, and cannot leave it. There has never been a Winged Monkey in Kansas yet, and I suppose there never will be, for they don't belong there. We shall be glad to serve you in any way in our power, but we cannot cross the desert. Good-bye."

And with another bow, the Monkey King spread his wings and flew away through the window, followed by all his band.

Dorothy was almost ready to cry with disappointment.

"I have wasted the charm of the Golden Cap to no purpose," she said, "for the Winged Monkeys cannot help me."

"It is certainly too bad!" said the tender hearted Woodman.

The Scarecrow was thinking again, and his head bulged out so horribly that Dorothy feared it would burst.

"Let us call in the soldier with the green whiskers," he said, "and ask his advice."

So the soldier was summoned and entered the Throne Room timidly, for while Oz was alive he never was allowed to come farther than the door.

"This little girl," said the Scarecrow to the soldier, "wishes to cross the desert. How can she do so?"

"I cannot tell," answered the soldier; "for nobody has ever crossed the desert, unless it is Oz himself."

"Is there no one who can help me?" asked Dorothy, earnestly.

"Glinda might," he suggested.

"Who is Glinda?" enquired the Scarecrow.

"The Witch of the South. She is the most powerful of all the Witches, and rules over the Quadlings. Besides, her castle stands on the edge of the desert, so she may know a way to cross it."

"Glinda is a good Witch, isn't she?" asked the child.[56]

---

56. Bryan's Democratic-Populist ticket swept the South in the 1896 election, so it is appropriate that Glinda would be a good Witch. Also, some of the most ardent silverites in Congress—notably Senator James K. Jones of Arkansas and the infamous Senator "Pitchfork Ben" Tillman of South Carolina, both of whom played prominent roles at the 1896 Democratic Convention—were from the South.

Later we discover that Glinda, unlike the Wizard or the good Witch of the North, understands the power of Dorothy's silver shoes. That the Southern Witch understands the

"The Quadlings think she is good," said the soldier, "and she is kind to everyone. I have heard that Glinda is a beautiful woman, who knows how to keep young in spite of the many years she has lived."

"How can I get to her castle?" asked Dorothy.

"The road is straight to the South," he answered, "but it is said to be full of dangers to travellers. There are wild beasts in the woods, and a race of queer men who do not like strangers to cross their country. For this reason none of the Quadlings ever come to the Emerald City."[57]

The soldier then left them and the Scarecrow said,

"It seems, in spite of dangers, that the best thing Dorothy can do is to travel to the Land of the South and ask Glinda to help her. For, of course, if Dorothy stays here she will never get back to Kansas."

"You must have been thinking again," remarked the Tin Woodman.

"I have," said the Scarecrow.

"I shall go with Dorothy," declared the Lion, "for I am tired of your city and long for the woods and the country again. I am really a wild beast, you know. Besides, Dorothy will need someone to protect her."

"That is true," agreed the Woodman. "My axe may be of service to her; so I also will go with her to the Land of the South."

"When shall we start?" asked the Scarecrow.

"Are you going?" they asked, in surprise.

"Certainly. If it wasn't for Dorothy I should never have had brains. She lifted me from the pole in the cornfield and brought me to the Emerald City. So my good luck is all due to her, and I shall never leave her until she starts back to Kansas for good and all."

"Thank you," said Dorothy, gratefully. "You are all very kind to me. But I should like to start as soon as possible."

----

silver shoes' power while the Northern Witch does not is also in keeping with the electoral geography of 1896. Bryan and the Populists carried some Northern states but had their greatest success in the South.

Note how "Glinda" is very close to "glint," a verb that is often used to describe shiny metals like silver (and closer still to *glinta*, a Swedish word that is part of the etymology of *glint*).

57. In keeping with the political symbolism, it is fitting that the Quadlings (people of the South) never come to the Emerald City, just as no Southerner had served as president in the three decades since the 1860s.

The South's isolation is economically symbolic as well. For roughly half a century after the Civil War, the South was somewhat isolated from the rest of the country economically, largely because of the antipathy of Southern economic and political elites to new investment inflows, which they felt would jeopardize their continued supply of cheap labor on the farms. Hence the "race of queer men who do not like strangers to cross their country." Likewise, it is fitting that the road to the South is "full of dangers to travellers," just as immigrants generally shunned the South in favor of the cities of the North. (For more information on these aspects of Southern economic history, a good source is Gavin Wright's *Old South, New South: Revolutions in the Southern Economy* [1986].)

"We shall go to-morrow morning," returned the Scarecrow. "So now let us all get ready, for it will be a long journey."

Chapter XIX.
Attacked by the Fighting Trees.

The next morning Dorothy kissed the pretty green girl good-bye, and they all shook hands with the soldier with the green whiskers, who had walked with them as far as the gate. When the Guardian of the Gate saw them again he wondered greatly that they could leave the beautiful City to get into new trouble. But he at once unlocked their spectacles, which he put back into the green box, and gave them many good wishes to carry with them.

"You are now our ruler," he said to the Scarecrow; "so you must come back to us as soon as possible."

"I certainly shall if I am able," the Scarecrow replied; "but I must help Dorothy to get home, first."

As Dorothy bade the good-natured Guardian a last farewell she said,

"I have been very kindly treated in your lovely City, and everyone has been good to me. I cannot tell you how grateful I am."

"Don't try, my dear," he answered. "We should like to keep you with us, but if it is your wish to return to Kansas, I hope you will find a way." He then opened the gate of the outer wall and they walked forth and started upon their journey.

The sun shone brightly as our friends turned their faces toward the Land of the South. They were all in the best of spirits, and laughed and chatted together. Dorothy was once more filled with the hope of getting home, and the Scarecrow and the Tin Woodman were glad to be of use to her. As for the Lion, he sniffed the fresh air with delight and whisked his tail from side to side in pure joy at being in the country again, while Toto ran around them and chased the moths and butter-flies, barking merrily all the time.

"City life does not agree with me at all," remarked the Lion, as they walked along at a brisk pace. "I have lost much flesh since I lived there, and now I am anxious for a chance to show the other beasts how courageous I have grown."

They now turned and took a last look at the Emerald City. All they could see was a mass of towers and steeples behind the green walls, and high up above everything the spires and dome of the Palace of Oz.

"Oz was not such a bad Wizard, after all," said the Tin Woodman, as he felt his heart rattling around in his breast.

"He knew how to give me brains, and very good brains, too," said the Scare-crow.

"If Oz had taken a dose of the same courage he gave me," added the Lion, "he would have been a brave man."

Dorothy said nothing. Oz had not kept the promise he made her, but he had done his best, so she forgave him. As he said, he was a good man, even if he was a bad Wizard.

The first day's journey was through the green fields and bright flowers that stretched about the Emerald City on every side. They slept that night on the grass, with nothing but the stars over them; and they rested very well indeed.

In the morning they travelled on until they came to a thick wood. There was no way of going around it, for it seemed to extend to the right and left as far as they could see; and, besides, they did not dare change the direction of their journey for fear of getting lost. So they looked for the place where it would be easiest to get into the forest.

The Scarecrow, who was in the lead, finally discovered a big tree with such wide spreading branches that there was room for the party to pass underneath. So he walked forward to the tree, but just as he came under the first branches they bent down and twined around him, and the next minute he was raised from the ground and flung headlong among his fellow travellers.

This did not hurt the Scarecrow, but it surprised him, and he looked rather dizzy when Dorothy picked him up.

"Here is another space between the trees," called the Lion.

"Let me try it first," said the Scarecrow, "for it doesn't hurt me to get thrown about." He walked up to another tree, as he spoke, but its branches immediately seized him and tossed him back again.

"This is strange," exclaimed Dorothy. "What shall we do?"

"The trees seem to have made up their minds to fight us, and stop our journey," remarked the Lion.

"I believe I will try it myself," said the Woodman, and shouldering his axe, he marched up to the first tree that had handled the Scarecrow so roughly. When a big branch bent down to seize him the Woodman chopped at it so fiercely that he cut it in two. At once the tree began shaking all its branches as if in pain, and the Tin Woodman passed safely under it.

"Come on!" he shouted to the others. "Be quick!"

They all ran forward and passed under the tree without injury, except Toto, who was caught by a small branch and shaken until he howled. But the Woodman promptly chopped off the branch and set the little dog free.

The other trees of the forest did nothing to keep them back, so they made up their minds that only the first row of trees could bend down their branches, and that probably these were the policemen of the forest, and given this wonderful power in order to keep strangers out of it.

The four travellers walked with ease through the trees until they came to the further edge of the wood. Then, to their surprise, they found before them a high wall which seemed to be made of white china. It was smooth, like the surface of a dish, and higher than their heads.

"What shall we do now?" asked Dorothy.

"I will make a ladder," said the Tin Woodman, "for we certainly must climb over the wall."

Chapter XX.
The Dainty China Country.

While the Woodman was making a ladder from wood which he found in the forest Dorothy lay down and slept, for she was tired by the long walk. The Lion also curled himself up to sleep and Toto lay beside him.

The Scarecrow watched the Woodman while he worked, and said to him:

"I cannot think why this wall is here, nor what it is made of."

"Rest your brains and do not worry about the wall," replied the Woodman; "when we have climbed over it, we shall know what is on the other side."

After a time the ladder was finished. It looked clumsy, but the Tin Woodman was sure it was strong and would answer their purpose. The Scarecrow waked Dorothy and the Lion and Toto, and told them that the ladder was ready. The Scarecrow climbed up the ladder first, but he was so awkward that Dorothy had to follow close behind and keep him from falling off. When he got his head over the top of the wall the Scarecrow said,

"Oh, my!"

"Go on," exclaimed Dorothy.

So the Scarecrow climbed farther up and sat down on the top of the wall, and Dorothy put her head over and cried,

"Oh, my!" just as the Scarecrow had done.

Then Toto came up, and immediately began to bark, but Dorothy made him be still.

The Lion climbed the ladder next, and the Tin Woodman came last; but both of them cried, "Oh, my!" as soon as they looked over the wall. When they were all sitting in a row on the top of the wall, they looked down and saw a strange sight.

Before them was a great stretch of country having a floor as smooth and shining and white as the bottom of a big platter.[58] Scattered around were many houses made entirely of china and painted in the brightest colors. These houses were quite small, the biggest of them reaching only as high as Dorothy's waist. There were also pretty little barns, with china fences around them; and many cows and sheep and horses and pigs and chickens, all made of china, were standing about in groups.

But the strangest of all were the people who lived in this queer country. There were milkmaids and shepherdesses, with bright-colored bodices and golden spots all over their gowns; and princesses with most gorgeous frocks of silver and gold and purple; and shepherds dressed in knee-breeches with pink and yellow and blue stripes down them, and golden buckles on their shoes; and princes with jeweled crowns upon their heads, wearing ermine robes and satin doublets; and funny clowns in ruffled gowns, with round red spots upon their cheeks and tall, pointed caps. And, strangest of all, these people were all made of china, even to their clothes, and were so small that the tallest of them was no higher than Dorothy's knee.

---

58. The most obvious interpretation of the Dainty China Country, with its high surrounding wall, is as the country of China and its Great Wall. (The chapter also surely draws on Baum's experience as a traveling china salesman.) That the surrounding wall and the "floor" of the Dainty China Country are both white fits with the colors-of-money imagery, since silver has long been "the white metal" and China was the only major country in the late nineteenth century that was still on a silver monetary standard.

No one did so much as look at the travellers at first, except one little purple china dog with an extra-large head, which came to the wall and barked at them in a tiny voice, afterwards running away again.

"How shall we get down?" asked Dorothy.

They found the ladder so heavy they could not pull it up, so the Scarecrow fell off the wall and the others jumped down upon him so that the hard floor would not hurt their feet. Of course they took pains not to light on his head and get the pins in their feet. When all were safely down they picked up the Scarecrow, whose body was quite flattened out, and patted his straw into shape again.

"We must cross this strange place in order to get to the other side," said Dorothy; "for it would be unwise for us to go any other way except due South."

They began walking through the country of the china people, and the first thing they came to was a china milk-maid milking a china cow. As they drew near, the cow suddenly gave a kick and kicked over the stool, the pail, and even the milk-maid herself, and all fell on the china ground with a great clatter.

Dorothy was shocked to see that the cow had broken her leg off, and that the pail was lying in several small pieces, while the poor milk-maid had a nick in her left elbow.

"There!" cried the milk-maid angrily; "see what you have done! My cow has broken her leg, and I must take her to the mender's shop and have it glued on again. What do you mean by coming here and frightening my cow?"

"I'm very sorry," returned Dorothy; "please forgive us."

But the pretty milk-maid was much too vexed to make any answer. She picked up the leg sulkily and led her cow away, the poor animal limping on three legs. As she left them the milk-maid cast many reproachful glances over her shoulder at the clumsy strangers, holding her nicked elbow close to her side.

Dorothy was quite grieved at this mishap.

"We must be very careful here," said the kind-hearted Woodman, "or we may hurt these pretty little people so they will never get over it."

A little farther on Dorothy met a most beautifully dressed young Princess, who stopped short as she saw the strangers and started to run away.

Dorothy wanted to see more of the Princess, so she ran after her; but the china girl cried out,

"Don't chase me! don't chase me!"

She had such a frightened little voice that Dorothy stopped and said,

"Why not?"

"Because," answered the Princess, also stopping, a safe distance away, "if I run I may fall down and break myself."

"But could you not be mended?" asked the girl.

"Oh, yes; but one is never so pretty after being mended, you know," replied the Princess.

"I suppose not," said Dorothy.

"Now there is Mr. Joker, one of our clowns," continued the china lady, "who is always trying to stand upon his head. He has broken himself so often that he is mended in a hundred places, and doesn't look at all pretty. Here he comes now, so you can see for yourself."

Indeed, a jolly little Clown came walking toward them, and Dorothy could see that in spite of his pretty clothes of red and yellow and green he was completely covered with cracks, running every which way and showing plainly that he had been mended in many places.

The Clown put his hands in his pockets, and after puffing out his cheeks and nodding his head at them saucily, he said:

> "My lady fair,
> Why do you stare
> At poor old Mr. Joker?
> You're quite as stiff
> And prim as if
> You'd eaten up a poker!"

"Be quiet, sir!" said the princess; "can't you see these are strangers, and should be treated with respect?"

"Well, that's respect, I expect," declared the Clown, and immediately stood upon his head.

"Don't mind Mr. Joker," said the Princess to Dorothy. "He is considerably cracked in his head, and that makes him foolish."

"Oh, I don't mind him a bit," said Dorothy. "But you are so beautiful," she continued, "that I am sure I could love you dearly. Won't you let me carry you back to Kansas, and stand you on Aunt Em's mantel-shelf? I could carry you in my basket."

"That would make me very unhappy," answered the china Princess. "You see, here in our country we live contentedly, and can talk and move around as we please. But whenever any of us are taken away our joints at once stiffen, and we can only stand straight and look pretty. Of course that is all that is expected of us when we are on mantel-shelves and cabinets and drawing-room tables, but our lives are much pleasanter here in our own country."

"I would not make you unhappy for all the world!" exclaimed Dorothy; "so I'll just say good-bye."

"Good-bye," replied the princess.

They walked carefully through the china country. The little animals and all the people scampered out of their way, fearing the strangers would break them, and after an hour or so the travellers reached the other side of the country and came to another china wall.

It was not so high as the first, however, and by standing upon the Lion's back they all managed to scramble to the top. Then the Lion gathered his legs under him and jumped on the wall; but just as he jumped, he upset a china church with his tail and smashed it all to pieces.[59]

---

59. Hearn sees a possible anti-imperialist theme in this chapter. He notes that Baum "does not indicate violence on the part of the natives; the only destruction results from the carelessness of the invaders" (1973, p. 311). The china Princess recalls the Dowager

"That was too bad," said Dorothy, "but really I think we were lucky in not doing these little people more harm than breaking a cow's leg and a church. They are all so brittle!"

"They are, indeed," said the Scarecrow, "and I am thankful I am made of straw and cannot be easily damaged. There are worse things in the world than being a Scarecrow."

Chapter XXI.
The Lion Becomes the King of Beasts.

After climbing down from the china wall the travellers found themselves in a disagreeable country, full of bogs and marshes and covered with tall, rank grass. It was difficult to walk without falling into muddy holes, for the grass was so thick that it hid them from sight. However, by carefully picking their way, they got safely along until they reached solid ground. But here the country seemed wilder than ever, and after a long and tiresome walk through the underbrush they entered another forest, where the trees were bigger and older than any they had ever seen.

"This forest is perfectly delightful," declared the Lion, looking around him with joy; "never have I seen a more beautiful place."

"It seems gloomy," said the Scarecrow.

"Not a bit of it," answered the Lion; "I should like to live here all my life. See how soft the dried leaves are under your feet and how rich and green the moss is that clings to these old trees. Surely no wild beast could wish a pleasanter home."

"Perhaps there are wild beasts in the forest now," said Dorothy.

"I suppose there are," returned the Lion, "but I do not see any of them about."

They walked through the forest until it became too dark to go any farther. Dorothy and Toto and the Lion lay down to sleep, while the Woodman and the Scarecrow kept watch over them as usual.

When morning came, they started again. Before they had gone far they heard a low rumble, as of the growling of many wild animals. Toto whimpered a little but none of the others was frightened, and they kept along the well-trodden path until they came to an opening in the wood, in which were gathered hundreds of beasts of every variety. There were tigers and elephants and bears and wolves and foxes and all the others in the natural history, and for a moment Dorothy was afraid. But the Lion explained that the animals were holding a meeting, and he judged by their snarling and growling that they were in great trouble.

Empress of China, Tzu Hsi, whose strong stand against "foreign barbarians" helped fuel the Boxer Rebellion of 1900, in which 231 foreigners were killed.

An anti-imperialist theme would have been timely even before that incident, for in the late nineteenth century the Chinese dynasty was weak and Japan and the imperial powers of Europe seemed well on their way to carving up China among themselves. The expansion of foreign influence in China was a prominent issue in the late 1890s. American exporters feared that a European and Japanese partition of China would jeopardize their business; anti-imperialists lamented the assault on Chinese self-determination.

As he spoke several of the beasts caught sight of him, and at once the great assemblage hushed as if by magic. The biggest of the tigers came up to the Lion and bowed, saying,

"Welcome, O King of Beasts! You have come in good time to fight our enemy and bring peace to all the animals of the forest once more."

"What is your trouble?" asked the Lion, quietly.

"We are all threatened," answered the tiger, "by a fierce enemy which has lately come into this forest. It is a most tremendous monster, like a great spider, with a body as big as an elephant and legs as long as a tree trunk. It has eight of these long legs, and as the monster crawls through the forest he seizes an animal with a leg and drags it to his mouth, where he eats it as a spider does a fly. Not one of us is safe while this fierce creature is alive, and we had called a meeting to decide how to take care of ourselves when you came among us."[60]

The Lion thought for a moment.

"Are there any other lions in this forest?" he asked.

"No; there were some, but the monster has eaten them all. And, besides, they were none of them nearly so large and brave as you."

"If I put an end to your enemy, will you bow down to me and obey me as King of the Forest?" enquired the Lion.

"We will do that gladly," returned the tiger; and all the other beasts roared with a mighty roar: "We will!"

"Where is this great spider of yours now?" asked the Lion.

"Yonder, among the oak trees," said the tiger, pointing with his fore-foot.

"Take good care of these friends of mine," said the Lion, "and I will go at once to fight the monster."

He bade his comrades good-bye and marched proudly away to do battle with the enemy.

The great spider was lying asleep when the Lion found him, and it looked so ugly that its foe turned up his nose in disgust. Its legs were quite as long as the tiger had said, and its body covered with coarse black hair. It had a great mouth, with a row of sharp teeth a foot long; but its head was joined to the pudgy body by a neck as slender as a wasp's waist. This gave the Lion a hint of the best way to attack the

---

60. The spiderlike monster recalls the monopolies and trusts, which were also viewed by many as threats to the public safety. The Lion's slaying of the beast is in keeping with the Populist dream of breaking up the monopolies.

Such metaphors were common in the 1890s. "Sockless" Jerry Simpson of Kansas, one of the leading Populists in Congress, spoke of the railroads as "the giant spider which controls our commerce and transportation" (quoted in Clanton 1991, p. 51). A cartoon in the free-silver manifesto *Coin's Financial School* (1894) used another eight-legged beast, an octopus, to represent the London-based Rothschild money trust, labeled "The Great English Devil Fish." Baum employed a similar metaphor in a comic opera he worked in 1901 called *The Octopus* or *The Title Trust*, and he even lampooned the monopoly-as-octopus metaphor in his script for the stage musical version of *The Wizard of Oz*. Likewise, in his later book *Sea Fairies* (1911), "an octopus expresses great indignation at having been likened to the Standard Oil monopoly" (Gardner and Nye, p. 29).

creature, and as he knew it was easier to fight it asleep than awake, he gave a great spring and landed directly upon the monster's back. Then, with one blow of his heavy paw, all armed with sharp claws, he knocked the spider's head from its body. Jumping down, he watched it until the long legs stopped wiggling, when he knew it was quite dead.

The Lion went back to the opening where the beasts of the forest were waiting for him and said proudly:

"You need fear your enemy no longer."

Then the beasts bowed down to the Lion as their King, and he promised to come back and rule over them as soon as Dorothy was safely on her way to Kansas.

Chapter XXII.
The Country of the Quadlings.

The four travellers passed through the rest of the forest in safety, and when they came out from its gloom saw before them a steep hill, covered from top to bottom with great pieces of rock.

"That will be a hard climb," said the Scarecrow, "but we must get over the hill, nevertheless."

So he led the way and the others followed. They had nearly reached the first rock when they heard a rough voice cry out,

"Keep back!"

"Who are you?" asked the Scarecrow. Then a head showed itself over the rock and the same voice said,

"This hill belongs to us, and we don't allow anyone to cross it."

"But we must cross it," said the Scarecrow. "We're going to the country of the Quadlings."

"But you shall not!" replied the voice, and there stepped from behind the rock the strangest man the travellers had ever seen.

He was quite short and stout and had a big head, which was flat at the top and supported by a thick neck full of wrinkles. But he had no arms at all, and, seeing this, the Scarecrow did not fear that so helpless a creature could prevent them from climbing the hill. So he said,

"I'm sorry not to do as you wish, but we must pass over your hill whether you like it or not," and he walked boldly forward.

As quick as lightning the man's head shot forward and his neck stretched out until the top of the head, where it was flat, struck the Scarecrow in the middle and sent him tumbling, over and over, down the hill. Almost as quickly as it came the head went back to the body, and the man laughed harshly as he said,

"It isn't as easy as you think!"

A chorus of boisterous laughter came from the other rocks, and Dorothy saw hundreds of the armless Hammer-Heads upon the hillside, one behind every rock.

The Lion became quite angry at the laughter caused by the Scarecrow's mishap, and giving a loud roar that echoed like thunder he dashed up the hill.

Again a head shot swiftly out, and the great Lion went rolling down the hill as if he had been struck by a cannon ball.

Dorothy ran down and helped the Scarecrow to his feet, and the Lion came up to her, feeling rather bruised and sore, and said,

"It is useless to fight people with shooting heads; no one can withstand them."[61]

"What can we do, then?" she asked.

"Call the Winged Monkeys," suggested the Tin Woodman; "you have still the right to command them once more."

"Very well," she answered, and putting on the Golden Cap she uttered the magic words. The Monkeys were as prompt as ever, and in a few moments the entire band stood before her.

"What are your commands?" inquired the King of the Monkeys, bowing low.

"Carry us over the hill to the country of the Quadlings," answered the girl.

"It shall be done," said the King, and at once the Winged Monkeys caught the four travellers and Toto up in their arms and flew away with them. As they passed over the hill the Hammer-Heads yelled with vexation, and shot their heads high in the air; but they could not reach the Winged Monkeys, which carried Dorothy and her comrades safely over the hill and set them down in the beautiful country of the Quadlings.

"This is the last time you can summon us," said the leader to Dorothy; "so good-bye and good luck to you."

"Good-bye, and thank you very much," returned the girl; and the Monkeys rose into the air and were out of sight in a twinkling.

The country of the Quadlings seemed rich and happy. There was field upon field of ripening grain, with well-paved roads running between, and pretty rippling brooks with strong bridges across them. The fences and houses and bridges were all painted bright red, just as they had been painted yellow in the country of the Winkies and blue in the country of the Munchkins.[62] The Quadlings themselves, who were short and fat and looked chubby and good-natured, were dressed all in red, which showed bright against the green grass and the yellowing grain.

The Monkeys had set them down near a farmhouse, and the four travellers

---

61. The Hammer-Heads, who are physically unimposing but pack a wallop with their heads, recall the Populists' numerous critics in the intellectual community. The Populists' economic platform was typically ignored or ridiculed by 1890s intellectuals and establishment thinkers, notably the critics who answered W.H. Harvey's classic monetary-populist tract *Coin's Financial School* with books of their own bearing titles like *Coin's Financial Fool, or the Artful Dodger Exposed*; *Coin's Financial Folly*; *A Freak in Finance*; and *Farmer Hayseed in Town*.

62. In the Land of Oz, the country of the South is red, just as the country of the East is blue, the country of the West is yellow, and the Emerald City is green. Viewing Oz as a fantasy counterpart to America, that color scheme seems appropriate. The industrial East was a blue-collar region, the first great waves of settlement of the far West were due to the California gold rush, and the South was well known for its red earth (and, of course, "rednecks"). The associations between the Emerald City, Washington, D.C., greenbacks, and money in general have already been noted.

walked up to it and knocked at the door. It was opened by the farmer's wife, and when Dorothy asked for something to eat the woman gave them all a good dinner, with three kinds of cake and four kinds of cookies, and a bowl of milk for Toto.

"How far is it to the Castle of Glinda?" asked the child.

"It is not a great way," answered the farmer's wife. "Take the road to the South and you will soon reach it.

Thanking the good woman, they started afresh and walked by the fields and across the pretty bridges until they saw before them a very beautiful Castle. Before the gates were three young girls, dressed in handsome red uniforms trimmed with gold braid; and as Dorothy approached one of them said to her:

"Why have you come to the South Country?"

"To see the Good Witch who rules here," she answered. "Will you take me to her?"

"Let me have your name, and I will ask Glinda if she will receive you." They told who they were, and the girl soldier went into the Castle. After a few moments she came back to say that Dorothy and the others were to be admitted at once.

Chapter XXIII.
The Good Witch Grants Dorothy's Wish.

Before they went to see Glinda, however, they were taken to a room of the Castle, where Dorothy washed her face and combed her hair, and the Lion shook the dust out of his mane, and the Scarecrow patted himself into his best shape, and the Woodman polished his tin and oiled his joints.

When they were all quite presentable they followed the soldier girl into a big room where the Witch Glinda sat upon a throne of rubies.

She was both beautiful and young to their eyes. Her hair was a rich red in color and fell in flowing ringlets over her shoulders. Her dress was pure white; but her eyes were blue, and they looked kindly upon the little girl.

"What can I do for you, my child?" she asked.

Dorothy told the Witch all her story; how the cyclone had brought her to the Land of Oz, how she had found her companions, and of the wonderful adventures they had met with.

"My greatest wish now," she added, "is to get back to Kansas, for Aunt Em will surely think something dreadful has happened to me, and that will make her put on mourning; and unless the crops are better this year than they were last, I am sure Uncle Henry cannot afford it."

Glinda leaned forward and kissed the sweet, upturned face of the loving little girl.

"Bless your dear heart," she said, "I am sure I can tell you of a way to get back to Kansas." Then she added:

"But, if I do, you must give me the Golden Cap."

"Willingly!" exclaimed Dorothy; "indeed, it is of no use to me now, and when you have it you can command the Winged Monkeys three times."

"And I think I shall need their service just those three times," answered Glinda, smiling.

Dorothy then gave her the Golden Cap, and the Witch said to the Scarecrow, "What will you do when Dorothy has left us?"

"I will return to the Emerald City," he replied, "for Oz has made me its ruler and the people like me. The only thing that worries me is how to cross the hill of the Hammer-Heads."

"By means of the Golden Cap I shall command the Winged Monkeys to carry you to the gates of the Emerald City," said Glinda, "for it would be a shame to deprive the people of so wonderful a ruler."

"Am I really wonderful?" asked the Scarecrow.

"You are unusual," replied Glinda.

Turning to the Tin Woodman, she asked:

"What will become of you when Dorothy leaves this country?"

He leaned on his axe and thought a moment. Then he said, "The Winkies were very kind to me, and wanted me to rule over them after the Wicked Witch died. I am fond of the Winkies, and if I could get back again to the Country of the West, I should like nothing better than to rule over them forever."

"My second command to the Winged Monkeys," said Glinda, "will be that they carry you safely to the land of the Winkies. Your brains may not be so large to look at as those of the Scarecrow, but you are really brighter than he is—when you are well polished—and I am sure you will rule the Winkies wisely and well."

Then the Witch looked at the big, shaggy Lion and asked,

"When Dorothy has returned to her own home, what will become of you?"

"Over the hill of the Hammer-Heads," he answered, "lies a grand old forest, and all the beasts that live there have made me their King. If I could only get back to this forest, I would pass my life very happily there."

"My third command to the Winged Monkeys," said Glinda, "shall be to carry you to your forest.[63] Then, having used up the powers of the Golden Cap, I shall

---

63. The Scarecrow comes to rule the Emerald City, the Tin Woodman the Western land of the Winkies, and the Lion the smaller beasts of the forest. As Rockoff puts it, "The populist dream of achieving political power with the help of the South is realized" (1990, p. 756). Littlefield finds the placement of leadership highly significant: "farm interests achieve national importance, industrialism moves West and Bryan commands only a forest full of lesser politicians" (1964, p. 58).

The Lion's dubious accomplishment might be seen as a playful swipe at the Democrats, in view of Baum's apparent Republicanism (first noted by Erisman 1968, p. 617 n.). If Baum was alluding to the Democrats, his symbolism here was prophetic, since Bryan would be the Democratic nominee in 1900, the year of *Wizard*'s publication, and also in 1908. He would later serve as secretary of state during the first administration of Woodrow Wilson, the first Democrat to win a presidential election since 1892. Bryan might not have been the standard-bearer for all Democrats in the early years of the twentieth century, but he was the closest thing the party had to a king in that time.

Then again, the Lion refers to his forest as a "grand old forest," evoking "Grand Old

give it to the King of the Monkeys, that he and his band may thereafter be free for evermore."

The Scarecrow and the Tin Woodman and the Lion now thanked the Good Witch earnestly for her kindness; and Dorothy exclaimed,

"You are certainly as good as you are beautiful! But you have not yet told me how to get back to Kansas."

"Your Silver Shoes will carry you over the desert," replied Glinda. "If you had known their power you could have gone back to your Aunt Em the very first day you came to this country."

"But then I should not have had my wonderful brains!" cried the Scarecrow. "I might have passed my whole life in the farmer's cornfield."

"And I should not have had my lovely heart," said the Tin Woodman. "I might have stood and rusted in the forest till the end of the world."

"And I should have lived a coward forever," declared the Lion, "and no beast in all the forest would have had a good word to say to me."

"This is all true," said Dorothy, "and I am glad I was of use to these good friends. But now that each of them has had what he most desired, and each is happy in having a kingdom to rule beside, I think I should like to go back to Kansas."

"The Silver Shoes," said the Good Witch, "have wonderful powers. And one of the most curious things about them is that they can carry you to any place in the world in three steps, and each step will be made in the wink of an eye. All you have to do is to knock the heels together three times and command the shoes to carry you wherever you wish to go."[64]

"If that is so," said the child joyfully, "I will ask them to carry me back to Kansas at once."

She threw her arms around the Lion's neck and kissed him, patting his big head tenderly. Then she kissed the Tin Woodman, who was weeping in a way most dangerous to his joints. But she hugged the soft, stuffed body of the Scarecrow in her arms instead of kissing his painted face, and found she was crying herself at this sorrowful parting from her loving comrades.

Glinda the Good stepped down from her ruby throne to give the little girl a good-bye kiss, and Dorothy thanked her for all the kindness she had shown to her friends and herself.

Dorothy now took Toto up solemnly in her arms, and having said one last good-bye she clapped the heels of her shoes together three times, saying:

Party," an epithet for the Republican Party since 1880. Perhaps the Lion's fate is best seen as symbolizing the notion of Bryan as just another politician, who would be at home in either party.

64. Glinda the good Witch of the South knows the power of the silver shoes, which Dorothy can command by clicking the heels three times. The "three times" is analogous to the fact that some silver was in the money supply already, but the Populists believed that more needed to be added to bring about reflation and recovery. "The power to solve her problems (by adding silver to the money stock) was there all the time" (Rockoff 1990, p. 756).

"Take me home to Aunt Em!"

*   *   *   *   *

Instantly she was whirling through the air, so swiftly that all she could see or feel was the wind whistling past her ears.

The Silver Shoes took but three steps, and then she stopped so suddenly that she rolled over upon the grass several times before she knew where she was.

At length, however, she sat up and looked about her.

"Good gracious!" she cried.

For she was sitting on the broad Kansas prairie, and just before her was the new farm-house Uncle Henry built after the cyclone had carried away the old one. Uncle Henry was milking the cows in the barnyard, and Toto had jumped out of her arms and was running toward the barn, barking furiously.

Dorothy stood up and found she was in her stocking-feet. For the Silver Shoes had fallen off in her flight through the air, and were lost forever in the desert.[65]

Chapter XXIV.
Home Again.

Aunt Em had just come out of the house to water the cabbages when she looked up and saw Dorothy running toward her.

"My darling child!" she cried, folding the little girl in her arms and covering her face with kisses. "Where in the world did you come from?"

"From the Land of Oz," said Dorothy gravely.[66] "And here is Toto, too. And oh, Aunt Em! I'm so glad to be at home again!"

---

65. The silver shoes' having fallen off in the desert is analogous to the disappearance of the free-silver issue shortly after the 1896 election (Littlefield 1964, p. 57). A rapid expansion of the money supply beginning in 1897, thanks to the discovery of new gold and the invention of the cyanide process for extracting gold more efficiently from ore, brought about an end to the depression of the 1890s.

66. Like the silver shoes' falling off in the desert, the word "gravely" could also symbolize the Populists and the free-silver issue, both of which were politically dead after the 1896 election and the inflation that began in 1897. McKinley's re-election in 1900, which was a foregone conclusion by the time *The Wonderful Wizard of Oz* was written, was the final nail in the Populist Party's coffin.

Appendix A

Another Fiat-Money Metaphor, from *The Marvelous Land of Oz*

In this passage from the second Oz book, published in 1904, Baum presents yet another episode that makes a tidy metaphor for the curative power of fiat money (i.e., of paper money that has value only by decree, as opposed to its being redeemable for gold or silver by the government). A character's idea to stuff the Scarecrow with dollar bills that had appeared to be "only worthless papers" ends up restoring the Scarecrow to good health. Afterwards, the Scarecrow reminds the group that his brains, not his paper-money stuffing, are what make him valuable, paralleling the economist's distinction between "real" economic inputs such as labor, land, and tools and "nominal" magnitudes such as the money supply. Real magnitudes are what determine a country's ultimate capacity to produce, and are what matter in the long run. In the short run, however, changes in the money supply—a nominal magnitude—can have very important effects, including ending economic recessions and depressions. This kind of monetary remedy is similar to what William Jennings Bryan and the Populists had in mind in the 1890s, and is virtually identical to the fiat-money proposals of the more radical Greenback populists.

This excerpt is from the nineteenth chapter, "Dr. Nikidik's Famous Wishing Pills." It follows the style conventions in Baum 1997 [1904], pp. 127–29.

"I am completely ruined!" declared the Scarecrow, as he noted their astonishment. "For where is the straw that stuffs my body?"

The awful question startled them all. They gazed around the nest with horror, for not a vestige of straw remained. The Jackdaws had stolen it to the last wisp and flung it all into the chasm that yawned for hundreds of feet beneath the nest.

"My poor, poor friend!" said the Tin Woodman, taking up the Scarecrow's head and caressing it tenderly; "whoever could imagine you would come to this untimely end?"

"I did it to save my friends," returned the head; "and I am glad that I perished in so noble and unselfish a manner."

But why are you all so despondent?" inquired the Woggle-Bug. "The Scarecrow's clothing is still safe."

"Yes," answered the Tin Woodman; "but our friend's clothes are useless without stuffing."

"Why not stuff him with money?" asked Tip.

"Money!" they all cried, in an amazed chorus.

"To be sure," said the boy. "In the bottom of the nest are thousands of dollar bills—and two-dollar bills—and five-dollar bills—and tens, and twenties, and fifties. There are enough of them to stuff a dozen Scarecrows. Why not use the money?"

The Tin Woodman began to turn over the rubbish with the handle of his axe; and, sure enough, what they had first thought only worthless papers were found to be all bills of various denominations, which the mischievous Jackdaws had for years been engaged in stealing from the villages and cities they visited.

There was an immense fortune lying in that inaccessible nest; and Tip's suggestion was, with the Scarecrow's consent, quickly acted upon.

They selected all the newest and cleanest bills and assorted them into various piles. The Scarecrow's left leg and boot were stuffed with five-dollar bills; his right leg was stuffed with ten-dollar bills, and his body so closely filled with fifties, one-hundreds and one-thousands that he could scarcely button his jacket with comfort.

"You are now," said the Woggle-Bug, impressively, when the task had been completed, "the most valuable member of our party; and as you are among faithful friends there is little danger of your being spent."

"Thank you," returned the Scarecrow, gratefully. "I feel like a new man; and although at first glance I might be mistaken for a Safety Deposit Vault, I beg you to remember that my Brains are still composed of the same old material. And these are the possessions that have always made me a person to be depended upon in an emergency."

Appendix B

William Jennings Bryan's "Cross of Gold" Speech

Bryan delivered this speech before the Democratic National Convention on July 9, 1896. The speech is widely credited with delivering the Democratic presidential nomination to Bryan, who up until then had been running something of a stealth campaign and had not been considered one of the front-runners. It remains a classic expression of masses-against-the-classes populism and perhaps the most stirring convention speech in American political history.

This transcript of the speech follows the style conventions in Bryan (1985 [1896]).

MR. CHAIRMAN AND GENTLEMEN OF THE CONVENTION:

I would be presumptuous, indeed, to present myself against the distinguished gentlemen to whom you have listened if this were mere measuring of abilities; but this is not a contest between persons. The humblest citizen in all the land, when clad in the armor of a righteous cause, is stronger than all the hosts of error. I come to speak to you in defense of a cause as holy as the cause of liberty—the cause of humanity.

When this debate is concluded, a motion will be made to lay upon the table the resolution offered in commendation of the [Cleveland] administration, and also the resolution offered in condemnation of the administration. We object to bringing this question down to the level of persons. The individual is but an atom; he is born, he acts, he dies; but principles are eternal; and this has been a contest over a principle.

Never before in the history of this country has there been witnessed such a contest as that through which we have just passed. Never before in the history of

American politics has a great issue been fought out as this issue has been, by the voters of a great party. On the fourth of March, 1895, a few Democrats, most of them members of Congress, issued an address to the Democrats of the nation, asserting that the money question was the paramount issue of the hour; declaring that a majority of the Democratic party had the right to control the action of the party on this paramount issue; and concluding with the request that the believers in the free coinage of silver in the Democratic party should organize, take charge of and control the policy of the Democratic party. Three months later, at Memphis, an organization was perfected, and the silver Democrats went forth openly and courageously proclaiming their belief, and declaring that, if successful, they would crystallize into a platform the declaration which they had made. Then began the conflict. With a zeal approaching the zeal which inspired the crusaders who follow-ed Peter the Hermit,[1] our silver Democrats went forth from victory unto victory, until they are now assembled, not to discuss, not to debate, but to enter up the judg-ment already rendered by the plain people of this country. In this contest brother has been arrayed against brother, father against son. The warmest ties of love, acquaintance and association have been disregarded; old leaders have been cast aside when they have refused to give expression to the sentiments of those whom they would lead, and new leaders have sprung up to give direction to this cause of truth. Thus has the contest been waged, and we have assembled here under as binding and solemn instructions as were ever imposed upon representatives of the people.

We do not come as individuals. As individuals we might have been glad to compliment the gentleman from New York [Senator David B. Hill, a gold-standard supporter], but we know that the people for whom we speak would never be willing to put him in a position where he could thwart the will of the Democratic party. I say it was not a question of persons; it was a question of principle, and it is not with gladness, my friends, that we find ourselves brought into conflict with those who are now arrayed on the other side.

The gentleman who preceded me [ex-Governor William E. Russell, another "gold Democrat"] spoke of the State of Massachusetts; let me assure him that not one present in all this convention entertains the least hostility to the people of the State of Massachusetts, but we stand here representing people who are the equals before the law, of the greatest citizens in the State of Massachusetts. When you [turning to the gold delegates] come before us and tell us that we are about to disturb your business interests, we reply that you have disturbed our business interests by your course.

We say to you that you have made the definition of a business man too limited in its application. The man who is employed for wages is as much a business man as his employer; the attorney in a country town is as much a business man as the corporation counsel in a great metropolis; the merchant at the cross-roads store is as much a business man as the merchant of New York; the farmer who goes forth

---

1. Here Bryan refers to the band of undisciplined Christian warriors who followed Peter the Hermit, a French preacher, to Constantinople during the First Crusade (1095–99).

in the morning and toils all day—who begins in the spring and toils all summer—and who by the application of brain and muscle to the natural resources of the country creates wealth, is as much a business man as the man who goes upon the board of trade and bets upon the price of grain; the miners who go down a thousand feet into the earth, or climb two thousand feet upon the cliffs, and bring forth from their hiding places the precious metals to be poured into the channels of trade are as much business men as the few financial magnates who, in a back room, corner the money of the world. We come to speak for this broader class of business men.

Ah, my friends, we say not one word against those who live upon the Atlantic coast, but the hardy pioneers who have braved all the dangers of the wilderness, who have made the desert to blossom as the rose—the pioneers away out there [pointing to the West], who rear their children near to Nature's heart, where they can mingle their voices with the voices of the birds—out there where they have erected schoolhouses for the education of their young, churches where they praise their Creator, and cemeteries where rest the ashes of their dead—these people, we say, are as deserving of the consideration of our party as any people in this country. It is for these that we speak. We do not come as aggressors. Our war is not a war of conquest; we are fighting in the defense of our homes, our families, and posterity. We have petitioned, and our petitions have been scorned; we have entreated, and our entreaties have been disregarded; we have begged, and they have mocked when our calamity came. We beg no longer; we entreat no more; we petition no more. We defy them.

The gentleman from Wisconsin has said that he fears a Robespierre.[2] My friends, in this land of the free you need not fear that a tyrant will spring up from among the people. What we need is an Andrew Jackson to stand, as Jackson stood, against the encroachments of organized wealth.[3]

They tell us that this platform was made to catch votes. We reply to them that changing conditions make new issues; that the principles upon which Democracy rests are as everlasting as the hills, but that they must be applied to new conditions as they arise. Conditions have arisen, and we are here to meet these conditions.

---

2. "The gentleman from Wisconsin" was Senator William F. Vilas, a supporter of President Cleveland and the gold standard. Robespierre was the French Revolutionary leader most closely associated with the "Reign of Terror" of 1793–94.

3. Part of the enduring (small-p) populist appeal of President Andrew Jackson (1829–37), the first popularly elected and the first Democratic president, was Jackson's war on the second Bank of the United States during the 1830s. Jackson viewed the bank, an early prototype of a Federal Reserve-like central bank, which had been chartered for 20 years in 1816, as a monopolistic threat to the American system and not only opposed its recharter but sought to sabotage it by removing the government's deposits from it in 1833. The resulting "bank war" between Jackson and Nicholas Biddle, the bank's president, is one of the most colorful episodes in American economic history. A classic account is Arthur M. Schlesinger, Jr.'s *The Age of Jackson* (1945); Peter Temin's *The Jacksonian Economy* (1969) uses sophisticated empirical analysis to topple the conventional wisdom that Jackson's bank policies caused the economic chaos of the 1830s.

They tell us that the income tax ought not to be brought in here; that it is a new idea. They criticize us for our criticism of the Supreme Court of the United States. My friends, we have not criticized; we have simply called attention to what you already know. If you want criticisms read the dissenting opinions of the court. There you will find criticism. They say that we passed an unconstitutional law; we deny it. The income tax law was not unconstitutional when it was passed; it was not unconstitutional when it went before the Supreme Court for the first time; it did not become unconstitutional until one of the judges changed his mind, and we cannot be expected to know when a judge will change his mind. The income tax is just. It simply intends to put the burdens of government justly upon the backs of the people. I am in favor of an income tax. When I find a man who is not willing to bear his share of the burdens of the government which protects him, I find a man who is unworthy to enjoy the blessings of a government like ours.

They say that we are opposing national bank currency; it is true. If you will read what Thomas Benton said, you will find he said that, in searching history, he would find but one parallel to Andrew Jackson; that was Cicero, who destroyed the conspiracy of Catiline and saved Rome. Benton said that Cicero only did for Rome what Jackson did for us when he destroyed the bank conspiracy and saved America.[4] We say in our platform that we believe that the right to coin and issue money is a function of government. We believe it. We believe that it is a part of sovereignty, and can no more with safety be delegated to private individuals than we could afford to delegate to private individuals the power to make penal statutes or levy taxes. Mr. Jefferson, who was once regarded as good Democratic authority, seems to have differed in opinion from the gentleman who has addressed us on the part of the minority. Those who are opposed to this proposition tell us that the issue of paper money is a function of the bank, and that the Government ought to go out of the banking business. I stand with Jefferson rather than with them, and tell them, as he did, that the issue of money is a function of government, and that the banks ought to go out of the governing business.

They complain about the plank which declares against life tenure in office. They have tried to strain it to mean that which it does not mean. What we oppose by that plank is the life tenure which is being built up in Washington, and which excludes from participation in official benefits the humbler members of society.

Let me call your attention to two or three important things. The gentleman from New York says that he will propose an amendment to the platform providing that the proposed change in our monetary system shall not affect contracts already made. Let me remind you that there is no intention of affecting those contracts which according to present laws are made payable in gold; but if he means to say that we cannot change our monetary system without protecting those who have loaned money before the change was made, I desire to ask him where, in law or in morals, he can find justification for not protecting the debtors when the act of 1873

---

4. Senator Thomas Hart Benton of Missouri, aside from being one of Jackson's strongest allies in the bank fight, was also the person responsible for establishing the 16-to-1 mint ratio of gold to silver.

was passed, if he now insists that we must protect the creditors.

He says he will also propose an amendment which will provide for the suspension of free coinage if we fail to maintain the parity within a year. We reply that when we advocate a policy which we believe will be successful, we are not compelled to raise a doubt as to our own sincerity by suggesting what we shall do if we fail. I ask him, if he would apply his logic to us, why he does not apply it to himself. He says he wants this country to try to secure an international agreement. Why does he not tell us what he is going to do if he fails to secure an international agreement? There is more reason for him to do that than there is for us to provide against the failure to maintain the parity. Our opponents have tried for twenty years to secure an international agreement, and those are waiting for it most patiently who do not want it at all.

And now, my friends, let me come to the paramount issue. If they ask us why it is that we say more on the money question than we say upon the tariff question, I reply that, if protection has slain its thousands, the gold standard has slain its tens of thousands. If they ask us why we do not embody in our platform all the things that we believe in, we reply that when we have restored the money of the Constitution all other necessary reform will be possible; but that until this is done there is no other reform that can be accomplished.

Why is it, that within three months, such a change has come over the country? Three months ago, when it was confidently asserted that those who believe in the gold standard would frame our platform and nominate our candidates, even the advocates to the gold standard did not think that we could elect a president. And they had good reason for their doubt, because there is scarcely a State here today asking for the gold standard which is not in the absolute control of the Republican party. But note the change. Mr. McKinley was nominated at St. Louis upon a platform which declared for the maintenance of the gold standard until it can be changed into bimetallism by international agreement. Mr. McKinley was the most popular man among the Republicans, and three months ago everybody in the Republican party prophesied his election. How is it today? Why, the man who was once pleased to think that he looked like Napoleon—that man shudders today when he remembers that he was nominated on the anniversary of the battle of Waterloo. Not only that, but as he listens he can hear with ever-increasing distinctness the sound of the waves as they beat upon the lonely shores of St. Helena.

Why this change? Ah, my friends, is not the reason for the change evident to any one who will look at the matter? No private character, however pure, no personal popularity, however great, can protect from the avenging wrath of an indignant people a man who will declare that he is in favor of fastening the gold standard upon this country, or who is willing to surrender the right of self-government and place the legislative control of our affairs in the hands of foreign potentates and powers.

We go forth confident that we shall win. Why? Because upon the paramount issue of this campaign there is not a spot of ground upon which the enemy will dare to challenge battle. If they tell us that the gold standard is a good thing, we shall point to their platform and tell them that their platform pledges the party to get rid of the gold standard and substitute bimetallism. If the gold standard is a good thing, why try to get rid of it? I call your attention to the fact that some of the very people who are in this convention today, and who tell us that we ought to declare in favor of international bimetallism—thereby declaring that the gold standard is wrong and that the principle of bimetallism is better—these very people four months ago were open and avowed advocates of the gold standard, and were then telling us that we could not legislate two metals together, even with the aid of all the world. If the gold standard is a good thing we ought to declare in favor of its retention, and not in favor of abandoning it, and if the gold standard is a bad thing, why should we wait until other nations are willing to help us to let go? Here is the line of battle, and we care not upon which issue they force the fight; we are prepared to meet them on either issue or on both. If they tell us that the gold standard is the standard of civilization, we reply to them that this, the most enlightened of all the nations of the earth, has never declared for a gold standard and that both the great parties this year are declaring against it. If the gold standard is the standard of civilization, why, my friends, should we not have it? If they come to meet us on that issue we can present the history of our nation. More than that; we can tell them that they will search the pages of history in vain to find a single instance where the common people of any land have ever declared themselves in favor of the gold standard. They can find where the holders of fixed investments have declared for a gold standard, but not where the masses have.

Mr. Carlisle said in 1878 that this was a struggle between "the idle holders of idle capital" and "the struggling masses, who produce the wealth and pay the taxes of the country"[5]; and, my friends, the question we are to decide is, upon which side will the Democratic party fight; upon the side of "the idle holders of idle capital," or upon the side of "the struggling masses"? That is the question which the party must answer first, and then it must be answered by each individual hereafter. The sympathies of the Democratic party, as shown by the platform, are on the side of the struggling masses who have ever been the foundation of the Democratic party. There are two ideas of government. There are those who believe that if you will only legislate to make the well-to-do prosperous their prosperity will leak through on those below. The Democratic idea, however, has been that if you legislate to make the masses prosperous their prosperity will find its way up through every class which rests upon them.

You come to us and tell us that the great cities are in favor of the gold standard; we reply that the great cities rest upon our broad and fertile prairies. Burn

---

5. As President Grover Cleveland's secretary of the Treasury, John G. Carlisle of Kentucky was one of the staunchest backers of the gold standard and a vigorous opponent of the free-silver movement. Yet, as pro-silver activists were eager to point out, Carlisle had taken exactly the opposite position in 1878, when he spoke out forcefully for bimetallism and against the demonetization of silver. In fact, other words of his were quoted on the front page of every issue of the *National Bimetallist* in 1895–96: "According to my view of the subject, the conspiracy which seems to have been formed here and in Europe to destroy by legislation and otherwise from three-sevenths to one-half the metallic money of the world is the most gigantic crime of this or any other age" (quoted in Jones 1964, p. 56).

down your cities and leave our farms, and your cities will spring up again as if by magic; but destroy our farms, and the grass will grow in the streets of every city in the country.

My friends, we declare that this nation is able to legislate for its own people on every question without waiting for the aid or consent of any other nation on earth; and upon that issue we expect to carry every State in the Union. I shall not slander the inhabitants of the fair State of Massachusetts nor the inhabitants of the State of New York by saying that, when they are confronted with the proposition, they will declare that this nation is not able to attend to its own business. It is the issue of 1776 over again. Our ancestors, when but three millions in number, had the courage to declare their political independence on every other nation; shall we, their descendants, when we have grown to seventy millions, declare that we are less independent than our forefathers? No, my friends, that will never be the verdict of our people. Therefore, we care not upon what lines the battle is fought. If they say bimetallism is good, but that we cannot have it until other nations help us, we reply that, instead of having a gold standard because England has, we will restore bimetallism, and then let England have bimetallism because the United States has it. If they dare to come out in the open field and defend the gold standard as a good thing we will fight them to the uttermost. Having behind us the producing masses of this nation and the world, supported by the commercial interests, the laboring interests, and the toilers everywhere, we will answer their demand for a gold standard by saying to them:

> You shall not press down upon the brow of labor this crown of thorns;
> you shall not crucify mankind upon a cross of gold.

Appendix C

The Quantity Theory of Money

While the word *theory* tends to make people's eyes glaze over, theory is indispensable to any understanding of cause and effect. The usual starting point for economists in discussing the relationship between the money supply, the price level, and real GDP or real output is the *quantity equation of money*, shown next. In this equation M stands for the money supply, P for the price level, Q for real GDP or real output, and V for *velocity*, defined as the ratio of the total dollar amount of transactions (P times Q, i.e., PQ) to the money supply[1]:

$$MV = PQ$$

With some mathematical manipulation, that equation becomes:

(percent change in M) + (percent change in V)
= (percent change in P) + (percent change in Q)

Since velocity is defined as PQ/M, those equations are always true (mathematically speaking, they are *identities*), so up to this point they would occasion no disagreements among economists.

1.As of the year 2000, the velocity of money—in particular, the ratio of GDP in current prices (PQ) to M1 (cash plus checking account deposits plus traveler's checks and money orders)—was about 10. That is, GDP was roughly $10 trillion and M1 was roughly $1 trillion. In other words, a trillion dollars of cash and checking deposits ("transactions money") was sufficient to finance about ten times that amount in purchases of goods and services over the course of the year. Velocity depends on factors affecting people's demand for money; as the United States has moved toward a "cashless society," with increased use of credit cards and debit cards and other innovations, the velocity of money has tended to rise in recent years.

One longstanding theory of the relationship between money and the economy is the *quantity theory of money*. Quantity theorists believe first and foremost that the changes in the money supply (and velocity) cause changes in output and prices, rather than the other way around. If that belief is correct (and a majority of economists appear to think so), an increase in the money supply will typically cause an increase in real output, the price level, or both. Quantity theorists further assume that velocity is fairly stable, with the result that an increase in the supply of money will cause a *proportional* combined increase in prices and real output. (For example, a 10 percent increase in the money supply could cause a 5 percent increase in prices and a 5 percent increase in real output.) That second assumption is more controversial, but it is widely accepted, based on empirical observation, that velocity does not automatically increase or decrease to offset changes in the money supply; thus, changes in money supply will tend to cause changes in prices and output, proportional or not.

A remarkable feature of the monetary populism of the late nineteenth century was the extent to which Bryan, William H. "Coin" Harvey, and other free-silver crusaders made use of abstract monetary theory. Harvey's *Coin's Financial School* and Bryan's memoirs both describe "the quantitative theory of money" and enlist it in support of their cause. For decades after the climactic silver battles of the 1890s, Bryan and the bimetallists were commonly dismissed as "monetary cranks"; see, for example, the entry on *bimetallism* in the 1993 *Columbia Encyclopedia*, which calls bimetallism "far too unstable a monetary system for most modern nations." But some current economic research, notably two 1990 articles in the prestigious *Journal of Political Economy*, goes a long way toward rehabilitating Bryan's monetary diagnosis and prescriptions.

The first of those articles, Hugh Rockoff's "The 'Wizard of Oz' as a Monetary Allegory," is best remembered for its reinterpretation of *The Wonderful Wizard of Oz*, but the evidence that Rockoff presents on the silver question is an equally important contribution. The second, Milton Friedman's "The Crime of 1873," concludes that the demonetization of silver in 1873 was indeed a bad policy that caused excessive deflation over the next quarter-century. While Friedman is less sympathetic than Rockoff to the notion that free coinage of silver would have been desirable in 1896, his reappraisal of Bryan is overall quite generous—appropriately so, considering that Friedman, who won the Nobel Prize for economics in 1976, was the twentieth century's most famous practitioner of the quantity theory of money. Friedman's *Money Mischief* (1994) contains three more essays on Bryan and bimetallism and describes Bryan as "one of the most colorful and least appreciated politicians of the past century" (p. x).

Bibliography

Attebery, Brian. 1980. *The Fantasy Tradition in American Literature*. Bloomington: Indiana University Press.

Baum, Frank Joslyn, and Russell P. MacFall. 1961. *To Please a Child: A Biography of L. Frank Baum*. Chicago: Reilly and Lee Company.

Baum, L. Frank. 1986 [originally published in 1897]. *Mother Goose in Prose*. New York: Bounty Books.

———. 1960 [1900]. *The Wonderful Wizard of Oz*. New York: Dover.

———. 1978 [1901]. *American Fairy Tales*. New York: Dover.

———. 1930 [1902]. *The Wizard of Oz* (typescript for stage version). New York: Witmark Music Library and Agency.

———. 1997 [1904]. *The Marvelous Land of Oz*. New York: Dover Children's Thrift Edition.

———. 1963 [1915]. *The Uplift of Lucifer: in which is included The corrugated giant, and some other Baumania mostly photographic*. Los Angeles: Manuel Weltman.

——— (as Edith Van Dyne). 1909. *Aunt Jane's Nieces at Work*. Chicago: Reilly and Britton.

Bellow, Saul. 2000. *Ravelstein*. New York: Viking Penguin.

Bernstein, Peter L. 2000. *The Power of Gold: The History of an Obsession*. New York: John Wiley and Sons.

Boorstin, Daniel J., ed. 1985 [1966]. *An American Primer*. New York: Meridian Classic.

Brands, H.W. 1995. *The Reckless Decade: America in the 1890s*. New York: St. Martin's Press.

Bryan, William Jennings. 1985 [1896]. "The 'Cross of Gold' Speech." Pp. 593–604 in *An American Primer*, ed. Daniel J. Boorstin. New York: Meridian Classic.

Bryan, William Jennings, and Mary Baird Bryan. 1925. *The Memoirs of William Jennings Bryan*. Chicago: The John C. Winston Company.

Bunyan, John. 1942 [1678]. *The Pilgrim's Progress*. New York: The Heritage Press.

Chernow, Barbara, and George A. Vallasi, eds. 1993. *The Columbia Encyclopedia*. Fifth edition. New York: Columbia University Press.

Clanton, O. Gene. 1968. "Intolerant Populist? The Disaffection of Mary Elizabeth Lease." *Kansas Historical Quarterly* 34 (Summer): 189–200.

Clanton, Gene. 1991. *Populism: The Humane Preference in America, 1890–1900*. Boston: Twayne Publishers.

———. 1998. *Congressional Populism and the Crisis of the 1890s*. Lawrence: University Press of Kansas.

———. 2000. "Origins of Populism." Manuscript. In possession of the author and available on the Internet.

Coletta, Paolo E. 1964. *William Jennings Bryan: I. Political Evangelist, 1860–1908*. Lincoln: University of Nebraska Press.

Durden, Robert F. 1965. *The Climax of Populism: The Election of 1896*. Lexington: University of Kentucky Press.

Earle, Neil. 1993. *The Wonderful Wizard of Oz in American Popular Culture: Uneasy in Eden*. Lewiston, NY: Edwin Miller Press.

Eichengreen, Barry. 1992. *Golden Fetters: The Gold Standard and the Great Depression, 1919–1939*. New York: Oxford University Press.

———. 1993. "As Good as Gold—by What Standard?" Pp. 79–87 in *Second Thoughts: Myths and Morals of U.S. Economic History*, ed. Donald McCloskey. New York: Oxford University Press.

Eichengreen, Barry, and Marc Flandreau, eds. 1997. *The Gold Standard in Theory and History*. Second edition. New York: Routledge.

Erisman, Fred. 1968. "L. Frank Baum and the Progressive Dilemma." *American Quarterly* 20: 616–23.

Fischer, Roger A. 1996. *Them Damned Pictures: Explorations in American Political Cartoon Art*. North Haven, CT: Archon Books.

Friedman, Milton. 1990. "The Crime of 1873." *Journal of Political Economy* 98: 1159–94. Also reprinted 1994 in *Money Mischief: Episodes in Monetary History*. New York: Harcourt Brace.

———. 1994. *Money Mischief: Episodes in Monetary History*. New York: Harcourt Brace.

Friedman, Milton, and Anna Jacobson Schwartz. 1990 [1963]. *A Monetary History of the United States, 1867–1960*. Princeton: Princeton University Press (for the National Bureau of Economic Research).

———. 1982. *Monetary Trends in the United States and the United Kingdom: Their Relationship to Income, Prices, and Interest Rates, 1867–1975*. Chicago: University of Chicago Press (for the National Bureau of Economic Research).

Gage, Matilda Jewell. 1966. "The Dakota Days of L. Frank Baum, Part II." *The Baum Bugle* (Autumn): 8–12.

Gardner, Martin and Russel B. Nye, eds. 1994 [1957]. *The Wizard of Oz and Who He Was*. East Lansing: Michigan State University Press.

Geer, John G., and Thomas R. Rochon. 1993. "William Jennings Bryan on the Yellow Brick Road." *Journal of American Culture* 16(4) (Winter): 59–63.

Gessel, Michael. 1992. "Tale of a Parable." *The Baum Bugle* (Spring): 19–23.

Glad, Paul W. 1964. *McKinley, Bryan, and the People*. Philadelphia: J.B. Lippincott.

Goodwyn, Lawrence. 1976. *Democratic Promise: The Populist Moment in America*. New York: Oxford University Press.

Harvey, William H. 1894. *Coin's Financial School*. Chicago: Coin Publishing Company.

Hearn, Michael Patrick. 1989. "Secret Heart of 'The Wizard of Oz' Unlocked; Kansas, Be Proud." Letter, *New York Times*, October 31.

———. 1991. "Baum Was a Skeptic." Letter, *New York Times*, December 20.

———. 1992. " 'Oz' Author Never Championed Populism." Letter, *New York Times*, January 10.

———, ed. 1973. *The Annotated Wizard of Oz*. New York: Clarkson N. Potter.

———, ed. 2000. *The Annotated Wizard of Oz*. Centennial edition. New York: W.W. Norton.

Hicks, John D. 1961 [1931]. *The Populist Revolt: A History of the Farmers' Alliance and the People's Party*. University of Nebraska Press.

Hofstadter, Richard, ed. 1963. *Coin's Financial School, by William H. Harvey*. Cambridge, MA: Belknap Press of Harvard University Press.

Jensen, Richard. 1971. *The Winning of the Midwest*. Chicago: University of Chicago Press.

Johnson, Walter. 1966. Comments on "What's the Matter with Kansas?" Pp. 605–12 in *An American Primer*, ed. Daniel J. Boorstin. New York: Meridian Classic.

Jones, Stanley L. 1964. *The Presidential Election of 1896*. Madison: University of Wisconsin Press.

Kelsay, Leslie J. 1987. "Oz Is Real." *The News Chronicle* (Thousand Oaks, CA), March 6.

Kolko, Gabriel. 1967 [1963]. *The Triumph of Conservatism: A Reinterpretation of American History, 1900–1916*. Chicago: Quadrangle Books.

Koupal, Nancy Tystad. 1989. "The Wonderful Wizard of the West: L. Frank Baum in South Dakota." *Great Plains Quarterly* 9 (Fall): 203–15.

———. 1996. Introduction, annotations, epilogue, notes, glossary, and bibliography to *Our Landlady*, by L. Frank Baum. Lincoln: University of Nebraska Press.

———. 2001. "Add a Pinch of Biography and Mix Well: Seasoning the Populist Allegory Theory with History." *South Dakota History* 31 (Summer): 153–62.

Leach, William. 1993. *Land of Desire: Merchants, Power and the Rise of a New American Culture*. New York: Vintage Books.

———, ed. 1991. *The Wonderful Wizard of Oz*. Belmont, CA: Wadsworth.

Lee, Susan, and Peter Passell. 1979. "The Puzzle of Farm Discontent." Pp. 292–301 in *A New Economic View of American History*. New York: W.W. Norton.

Littlefield, Henry M. 1964. "The Wizard of Oz: Parable on Populism." *American Quarterly* 16(1) (Spring): 47–58.

———. 1992a. " 'Oz' Author Kept Intentions to Himself." Letter, *New York Times*, February 7.

———. 1992b. "The Wizard of Allegory." *The Baum Bugle* (Spring): 24–25.

Lurie, Alison. 1990. *Don't Tell the Grown-ups: Subversive Children's Literature*. Boston: Little, Brown and Company.

Mantele, Ozma Baum. 2000. "Fairy Tales Can Come True If You're Young at Heart." *The Baum Bugle* (Spring): 12.

Mayer, Thomas, James S. Duesenberry, and Robert Z. Aliber. 1984. *Money, Banking, and the Economy*. Second edition. New York: W.W. Norton.

McCloskey, Donald N. 1993. *Second Thoughts: Myths and Morals of U.S. Economic History*, New York: Oxford University Press.

McMurry, Donald L. 1968 [1929]. *Coxey's Army: A Study of the Industrial Army Movement of 1894*. Seattle: University of Washington Press.

Moyer, David. 1998. "Oz in the News." *The Baum Bugle* (Winter): 46.

North, Douglass C., Terry L. Anderson, and Peter J. Hill. 1983 [1966]. "Economic Growth and Agrarian Discontent, 1865–1914." Pp. 123–33 in *Growth and Welfare in the American Past: A New Economic History*. Englewood Cliffs, NJ: Prentice Hall.

Nugent, Walter T.K. 1967. *The Money Question During Reconstruction*. New York: W.W. Norton.

Parker, David B. 1997. "The Rise and Fall of *The Wonderful Wizard of Oz* as a 'Parable on Populism.' " Manuscript. In possession of the author and available on the Internet. Originally published 1994 in *Journal of the Georgia Association of Historians* 15: 49–63.

Riley, Michael. 1998. "The Great City of Oz: L. Frank Baum at the 1893 World's Fair." *The Baum Bugle* (Winter): 32–38.

Ritter, Gretchen. 1997a. *Goldbugs and Greenbacks: The Antimonopoly Tradition and the Politics of Finance in America*. New York: Cambridge University Press.

———. 1997b. "Silver Slippers and a Golden Cap: L. Frank Baum's *The Wonderful Wizard of Oz* and Historical Memory in American Politics." *Journal of American Studies* 31: 171–202.

Rockoff, Hugh. 1990. "The 'Wizard of Oz' as a Monetary Allegory." *Journal of Political Economy* 98(4) (August): 739–60.

Shannon, Fred A. 1973 [1945]. *The Farmer's Last Frontier: Agriculture, 1860–1897*. White Plains, NY: M.E. Sharpe.

Shields-West, Eileen. 1992. *The World Almanac of Presidential Campaigns*. New York: World Almanac.

Stein, Herbert. 1994. *Presidential Economics: The Making of Economic Policy From Roosevelt to Clinton*. Third edition. Washington, DC: AEI Press.

Stern, C.A. 1970 [1964]. *Golden Republicanism*. Ann Arbor, MI: Edwards Brothers.

Sumner, Scott. 1997. "News, Financial Markets, and the Collapse of the Gold Standard: 1931–1932." *Research in Economic History* 17: 39–84.

Temin, Peter. 1990. *Lessons From the Great Depression*. Cambridge, MA: MIT Press.

Triffin, Robert. 1997 [1968]. "The Myth and Realities of the So-Called Gold Standard." Pp. 140–60 in *The Gold Standard in Theory and History*, second edition, ed. Barry Eichengreen and Marc Flandreau. New York: Routledge. Originally published 1968 in *Our International Monetary System: Yesterday, Today, and Tomorrow*. New York: Random House.

U.S. Department of Commerce, Bureau of the Census. 1975. *Historical Statistics of the United States*. Washington, DC: Government Printing Office.

Vidal, Gore. 1983 [1977]. "On Rereading the Oz Books." Pp. 256–70 in *The Wizard of Oz*, ed. Michael Patrick Hearn. New York: Schocken Books (Critical Heritage Series). Originally published 1977 in the *New York Review of Books*, October 13: 37–43.

Wagner, Sally Roesch. 1984. "Dorothy Gage and Dorothy Gale." *The Baum Bugle* (Autumn): 4–6.

———. 1998. *Matilda Joslyn Gage: She Who Holds the Sky*. Aberdeen, SD: Sky Carrier Press.

Walton, Gary M., and Hugh Rockoff. 1998. *History of the American Economy*. Eighth edition. Orlando, FL: Dryden Press.

"Warring Populisms." 2000. Editorial, *New York Times*, August 16.

Whaples, Robert. 1995. "Where Is There Consensus Among American Economic Historians? The Results of a Survey on Forty Propositions." *Journal of Economic History* 55: 139–54.

White, William Allen. 1985 [1896]. "What's the Matter with Kansas?" Pp. 605–12 in *An American Primer*, ed. Daniel J. Boorstin. New York: Meridian Classic.

Zinn, Howard. 1995. *A People's History of the United States: 1492–Present*. New York: Harper Perennial.

Index

Note: Many of the entries in this index refer to the annotations, rather than to Baum's text.

About the Editor

RANJIT S. DIGHE is Assistant Professor of Economics at the State University of New York at Oswego. His specialty is American macroeconomic history, and he has written extensively on American labor markets between the world wars.